THE ENGLISH GARDEN

THE ENGLISH GARDEN

EDWARD HYAMS

PHOTOGRAPHS BY

EDWIN SMITH

188 photogravure plates

17 in colour

THAMES AND HUDSON

LONDON

© THAMES AND HUDSON LTD LONDON 1964
TEXT PRINTED IN GREAT BRITAIN BY JARROLD AND SONS LTD
COLOUR PHOTOGRAVURE PLATES PRINTED IN WESTERN GERMANY BY CARL SCHÜNEMANN
MONOCHROME PHOTOGRAVURE PLATES PRINTED IN FRANCE BY ETS BRAUN ET CIE MULHOUSE
BOUND IN GREAT BRITAIN BY JARROLD AND SONS LTD

Contents

Acknowledgements

The author and publishers gratefully acknowledge the courtesy of the following who have granted permission for gardens to be photographed for this book:

His Grace the Duke of Marlborough, *Blenheim Palace*; Lord Aberconway and The National Trust, *Bodnant*; Julian Williams, Esq., *Caerhays Castle*; The Trustees of the Chatsworth Settlement; The Dartington Hall Trustees; The Regius Keeper, Royal Botanic Garden, Edinburgh; Mrs Nathaniel Lloyd, *Great Dixter*; The Ministry of Public Buildings and Works, *Hampton Court Palace*; The National Trust, *Hidcote Manor*; Sir Frederick Stern, *Highdown*; The Director, Royal Botanic Gardens, Kew; Sir John Heathcote-Amory, Bt, *Knightshayes Court*; The Marquess of Bath, *Longleat*; The Marquess of Lothian, *Melbourne Hall*; The Countess of Rosse and The National Trust, *Nymans*; T. Cottrell-Dormer, Esq., *Rousham Park*; The National Trust, *Sheffield Park*; Thomas Upcher, Esq., *Sheringham Hall*; Nigel Nicolson, Esq., *Sissinghurst Castle*; The Headmaster and Governors of Stowe School; Commander T. Dorrien Smith, *Tresco Abbey*; The Director, Royal Horticultural Society Gardens, Wisley.

FRONTISPIECE   *Stourhead, with the Pantheon. Of the English landscape gardens Stourhead, created by Henry Hoare in the first half of the eighteenth century, ranks as a major work of European art*

In the multiform and multicolour of the flowers and the trees,

he recognized the most direct and energetic efforts

of Nature at physical loveliness. And in the direction

or concentration of this effort — or more properly

in its adaptation to the eyes which were to behold it on earth,

he perceived that he should be employing the best means —

labouring to the greatest advantage — in the fulfilment not only

of his own destiny as a poet, but of the august purpose

for which the Deity had implanted the poetic sentiment in man.

EDGAR ALLAN POE
The Domain of Arnheim

Origins and Inspirations

IT IS PERHAPS RATHER FANCIFUL, but I believe that the two 'schools' of gardening, into one of which almost every garden since the memory of man runneth not to the contrary, until the ninteenth century, could be placed, can be traced back to the two distinct originals of our western Christian civilization. Until fairly recently most people in the western world were brought up if not on, at least more or less in touch with, the Bible; consequently, for most western men, Eden was *the* garden. Granted that no such place ever existed outside Jewish mythology, yet since a myth stands for something in the mind and soul of man, the nature of Eden is significant. And Eden was, clearly, an 'English' garden. This paradise was a natural garden of all manner of beautiful plants, a garden whose charm can only have depended on those plants, on the lie of the land, and the disposition of pleasant waters. Whoever conceived the myth conceived an ideal, something which nature unaided does not accomplish but which man perceives to be possible. God had scattered his best work about the world; he made a good effect here, contrived a lovely view there, so disposed land, water and trees in some corners that the mysterious demands of the aesthetic sense were satisfied; but what God had not done was to combine deliberately in a single masterwork all the triumphs of form and colour of which his art was capable. Eden was a vision of such a masterwork conceived by a people who did not imagine that anything surpassing it was to be done by the introduction of man's own arts.

The Hellenic concept of a garden seems to be very different. The description of Laertes' garden in the *Odyssey* at once suggests the neat order of a French fruit-and-vegetable garden. Here, if anywhere, is the origin of the regularity and rectangularity of the 'Latin' garden. Now it has been very widely remarked by authors in many fields of literature that the English, in the development of their native Church, have shown a remarkable and perhaps unique sensibility to the feeling and ideas of the Old Testament people. The ideas and feelings of the ancient Israelites were never much to the taste of the Italians and French; the Christianity which appealed to them was neo-platonic, and was the New Testament as rendered into a kind of Hellenism. In England, possibly because of the unique quality of the English Bible, a far less impressive book in other European languages, the Jewish, as opposed to the Greek, kind of Christianity had a far greater influence. It is not enough to explain this by reference to the quality of the English Bible. There is something in the English soul which rejoices in the works of nature, or as it would have been called until very recently, of God, more than in the works of man. Like W. S. Landor, Nature the English love, and after nature, Art. The Greeks, and their spiritual heirs, never had any doubt that the setting for the good life is what man makes it;

Paradise a garden

a house, a city, a garden which is itself a work of architecture. The English, like the Jews, have never been sure of this. For the English, the ideal remains to get back to the garden of Eden, to Paradise.

Since I shall refer from time to time to the 'paradise' garden, if only because the words 'English garden' still convey to so many people outside Britain a certain type of eighteenth-century landscape garden, but also because it is the name I should like to attach to the exotically romantic garden which succeeded pure landscape, it may be as well to say a little more about what we have in mind here.

Colour plate page 13

Plate II is one of Edwin Smith's Bodnant photographs; and plate IV he made in the Tresco Abbey gardens. The Bodnant picture was made in the part of that great garden which is called the Dell (see pp. 210–11); it is a small river valley with trees, shrubs and ground-plants such as are common enough in mountain and moorland country and such as nature-lovers rejoice in. But it is not 'natural', only 'after' nature, for it has been made over with exotic plant material, with trees and shrubs and ground-lings from the Himalaya, the Andes, the Alps, and I know not where else.

Colour plate page 17

The Tresco example is the extreme case: a lily pool with a view of more garden beyond is common; the material in which this view has been made is exotic. In both cases the result is the same: a dream realized. It is the practice of garden critics writing about the eighteenth-century landscape gardens to refer to them in terms of such landscape painters as Claude and Poussin: not their state of mind and spirit, but rather that of the Douanier Rousseau is evoked by the paradise garden; there are no tigers, but the scene suggests that at any moment one will appear and that when he does he will be tame and friendly, as is fitting in a paradise. The horticultural classicist will object that not even Rousseau should be mentioned; these gardens derive from a dream, no doubt, but a boyhood dream; they are out of *Coral Island,* or at best *Robinson Crusoe.* The fact is that the paradise-garden maker, and the critic with his aesthetic rules can each say to the other what the unhelpful local said to the stranger asking his way: 'By rights you oughtn't to be starting from here.'

As will appear, the romantic desire for a paradise garden is not the only influence at work: the English have always looked with half an eye towards the Mediterranean; and in some periods of their history, with both eyes. And it is out of the tension between the two principal influences already referred to, and from the traditions arising from them, that the design and detail of the best modern English gardens have come. The extreme case of the paradise garden should be Tresco Abbey, but excepting in certain of its points-of-view such as the one mentioned above, this is not the case. The vast range of exotic plants which flourish in the halcyon climate of that fortunate island have been used with imagination, but also with restraint, and what the Dorrien Smiths have planted is not an exotic wilderness. It is true that the romantic, the dream-like quality of that garden (see pp. 218–24) is remarkable: but it is owed to the detail of the picture, the exotic forms of the plants as illustrated in

Colour plates pages 19, 21

plate V, and much less to design of the gardens, as should be apparent from plate VI: for that design is in the formal tradition, or very nearly so.

The two traditions

We have a remarkable case of the two traditions at odds in Stourhead (see pp. 57–63). As its maker finished it, this masterpiece was all in greens, browns and the blues and greys of sky and water. The planting, by a later owner, of rhododendrons where Hoare had grass or laurels, has changed the picture entirely during the flowering season. (This is discussed at greater length in its place; here we are using it only as a demonstration of principle.) Now it is a fact that Stourhead as Hoare made it was one of the masterpieces of European art, and for many who realized this the introduction of flowering shrubs into the picture was an outrage. For horticultural aesthetes it was as if the owner of a Rembrandt who disliked the darkness of the picture, took a palette of bright colours and a brush and proceeded to brighten it up a bit. This kind of change is always liable to happen to English gardens simply because the inheritors or purchasers of old gardens are themselves gardeners and work in the fashion of their time. Fortunately, Stourhead can now be seen as two rather different gardens: out of the May to July flowering season it is very much what it was in 1760; in spring, on the other hand, it is halfway to being a paradise garden. The monochrome pictures of the garden (pp. 81–89) give an impression

Plates 26–36

I Bodnant in North Wales. A paradise garden in which both the formal and natural traditions are superbly represented and where the art of landscape gardening has been enriched by a great wealth of flowering species

Colour frontispiece
Colour plates pages 23, 25

of form and design; the frontispiece and plates VII and VIII tell the story of the nineteenth-century transformation, or, if you like, outrage.

There is no point in trying to arbitrate between the two opinions: the satisfactions sought by the paradise-gardener and the picture-gardener are not the same, they are hardly even of the same order, and by this I do not mean that for the first rare and strange plants are of interest in themselves whereas for the horticultural aesthete plants are materials of the art and it does not matter whether you obtain your effects with a common native or a rare alien. One can, perhaps, trace in the feeling which inspires the paradise-gardener an attitude to the visual and graphic arts with which Continental critics and their English allies long reproached English painting. The reproach was first clearly stated by the great French historian of English literature who was also a notable historian of painting, Hippolyte Taine: and simply stated it is that the English are incapable of not regarding painting as a branch of literature, even of moral or religious literature, and finally of ethics. I do not insist on the notion that the paradise garden is to some extent a by-product of a certain kind of romantic literature, and especially of the literature of travel and adventure; my opinion, for what it is worth, is that this is the case, but it may well be that the idea is far-fetched.

Scale and degree

Colour plate page 29

When it comes to compromise between schools of gardening, scale and degree become all-important to the final result. By the strict rules of picture gardening, as implied by garden-criticism rather than as written down by pundits, the boskage in the left middle-ground of plate X, a photograph made at Sheffield Park in a brave attempt by Edwin Smith to illustrate this point, should, I suppose, be composed of a flowerless evergreen or perhaps of a golden or silver-leaved bush. But the scale of this magnificent place is such that the use of a flowering shrub enhances the effect aimed at; it reinforces the seasonal change in the prospect by helping the spring sun to raise the whole scene in brightness and slightly sharpen the middle distances, throwing the foliage-haze into notice. Such a device completely divorces the art of the garden from the art of painting; and rightly so, for nothing can alter the fact that the changing light of the seasons alters what one is looking at in a garden from day to day, and the skilful use of flowering shrubs and trees recognizes what, it seems to me, the great picture-gardeners tried to ignore, that the material of which a garden is made is alive and growing. The regard, in the eighteenth century, for a seventeenth-century school of landscape painting, set gardeners trying to do something impossible, to make an unchanging picture with living material. Possibly that may explain the mania, among their extremists, for planting dead trees.

Colour plate page 31

At the other extreme is the Laburnum Arch at Bodnant in flowering time – plate XI; and, in the same category, there was the famous Punch Bowl in the Saville gardens at Windsor which many readers will recall with pleasure or revulsion. In these cases the temptation to push to the extreme the effects which our great wealth of plant material makes possible has been yielded to entirely. The result is overwhelming, very spectacular; it is, even, vulgar if you like. The merits of vulgarity in the garden are discussed in a later chapter. The tremendous impact of colours obtained at Bodnant has the merit of experiment from which may emerge rules, as ephemeral as those of the past but none the less useful for the present. One rule emerges at once: the Punch Bowl, and to some extent the crowding of intense colour in and about the Laburnum Arch at Bodnant, prove quickly fatiguing; which is never the case of a garden like Stourhead.

Scale and degree: and Bodnant in another aspect again serves as a demonstration, where the planting of flowering shrubs into open woodland of fine trees with broad grass spaces – parkland, in short, is a case not of altering an old picture-garden but of setting about the creation of a paradise-garden in the first place. But the garden which was and in some respects still is the supreme example in that class is Nymans: it was in the nature of the man who created it, Colonel Messel, to love the English scene but to express a romantic (which does not exclude scientific) yearning for the exotic. In that he followed William Robinson (see pp. 129–31). At Nymans the most generous, but never extravagant, use is made of exotics, but flamboyance is avoided. The garden early had one of the most remarkable collections

II   Bodnant. In the great English, as in the great Chinese gardens, water is of the first aesthetic importance. Here
the river Hiraethlyn has been planted along its banks with exotic shrubs

of plants from all over the world ever to be planted in one place, for it had the services of a very able, brave and successful plant-collector, Comber. As will appear in its place, the use of exotics there achieves an effect as powerful as romantic music. But it is not a garden in which one is overwhelmed, detail and scale are balanced, there are enough great trees, enough green, to absorb the colour; the point is well illustrated in plate XII.

Colour plate page 33

Alien origins

The two divergent tendencies in English gardening were as it happened strengthened by economic influences. Civilization, and therefore gardening, was born in parts of the world where physical difficulties offered such a challenge to man that he was forced to be inventive in order to survive. The earliest civilizations of which we have any knowledge are irrigation and terracing cultures; they arose not where conditions for food production were easy but where they were very difficult. In the course of struggling to survive, the men of the Near East, who taught arts and laws to the rest of the Old World, learnt of necessity to impose order on the natural scene, to change it, to make it into something different. If civilization did not arise in these lands where soil was fertile, water plentiful, game abundant, it was because man is not willingly civilized; he is probably as happy as he is capable of being as a hunter-artist. The nature of the civilization which spread westward by way of Greece into western Europe was, so to speak, not really suitable to the terrain it invaded. Still, such was its radiant energy that it imposed itself. Thus when the English had reached a stage of advancement such that they could begin gardening, the art of gardening which they received from the East had been contrived by men with no notion at all of a nature as gentle, as friendly to man, as generous in yielding sustenance, as that of north-west Europe. Nothing is more striking, in such early gardening books as those of Barnaby Googe for example, than the way in which instructions for doing things quite impossible in our climate, and other things quite unnecessary, were uncritically translated into the English language.

The Romans were the first people to make, or to have made, gardens in western Europe and therefore in Britain. But the Romans were not an inventive people; they had picked up their gardening, as they had picked up their other arts, from Greeks, Egyptians, Syrians. (The first good horticultural manual was, as a matter of fact, Carthaginian.) At least three other great schools of gardening developed in the world, but of them Europe knew nothing until the sixteenth or seventeenth centuries: gardening was a sophisticated art in China before, and probably very long before, the Roman empire came into existence. Japanese gardening, brilliant derivative of Chinese gardening, was likewise very ancient. On the other hand, the remarkable gardening arts of the Maya-Toltec-Aztec civilization, and of the pre-Inca and Inca peoples of the western Andes, were young when we came upon them, even by European standards.

Roman gardens

Rome, then, brought to Britain gardening of a kind devised in the Near East. There seems every reason to suppose that the gardens of Roman villas in Britain, far from making use of the nature of English soil, climate and flora, were simply aridland gardens of the south and east Mediterranean type as adapted to Italian conditions. There was, for example, a terrace by the villa, overlooking the garden, and designed as an open-air dining-room. It is true that such terraces were covered, yet this sort of thing is not really suitable to the English climate, though something of the kind has been repeated ever since, in diverse forms. Below the dining terrace or garden pavilion would be a lawn enclosed by a walk enclosed by a hedge of clipped box. That hedge, perhaps, represents the first adaptation to English conditions made by the clever Syrian slave gardeners imported by the Romans; for box is a native English plant. The clipped yew hedge which some think of as an ancient feature of the English garden is nothing of the kind. Yew, disliked as a sombre and depressing plant and distrusted as poisonous to browsing cattle, was for centuries kept out of the garden entirely. On a terrace below the lawn and walk, or in the next hedged enclosure if the site was flat, was a level space, usually an oval, where the people of the house could ride or drive for recreation round a central boskage of geometrically or fancifully clipped box or privet and just possibly sometimes bay laurel. This riding place was called the *gestatio* and beyond it were meadows and woods and perhaps some planted clumps of

III   Bodnant. The English yearning towards a romantic paradise of nature perfected is served by the great richness
of Chinese and Himalayan rhododendron species

native shrubs. After about AD 300 there would be a vineyard as part of the garden, at least in the south.

I see no reason why Pliny's description of a Roman garden should not hold more or less true for the gardens of Romano-British villas. Such a garden, apart from the nucleus just described, was a place of walks among ivy-clad plane trees; of colonnades whose columns were Italian cypresses; of paddocks with fruit trees regularly planted; of water, in small streams and fountains; of seats shaded by vines grown over pergolas of masonry, originally an Egyptian device. There could have been gardens like this in 'Vectis,' in Sussex and Kent and Dorset. There is no doubt that the Romans did introduce some of their plants to Britain; the Oriental plane is hardy in this country and the Italian cypress grows well in many southern counties. The argument has been advanced that because these plants and others used in Roman gardening were not, save the vine, found here in, for example, Bede's day, they were never here. But nothing is more common than for exotic trees and shrubs to disappear when the garden is neglected although they will survive when it is tended. What, after less than half a century of semi-neglect for which nobody is to blame, remains, for example, of Canon Boscawen's astonishing collection of exotics at Lugdvan in south-west Cornwall ? I think I saw about six of them still left when I went there a year or two ago. The fact that a south European shrub or tree was unknown in the English gardens of AD 900 or AD 1900 by no means entitles us to say that it was not flourishing here in AD 400.

Of the period between c. AD 450 and AD 1066 writers on gardening too easily despair, claiming that we know so little of the subject during those six centuries that we had better say nothing. I think, with respect, that we know a little. Two sources of factual information and one of what I will call specula-tive knowledge are commonly overlooked. There are the *Leges anglo-saxonicae*; there are the several Welsh *Dwlls*, or codes of law; and finally there is the well-attested fact that despite the wars of the Heptarchy, despite the Danish conquest and later the troubles between Saxon rulers and the great men of the old Danelaw, yet England was a more peaceful, better-governed, and therefore a richer land in Edward the Confessor's day, and even in Harold Godwinson's, than almost any in Europe.

Anglo-Saxon garden law The Anglo-Saxon laws in Alfred's day (849–901) legislated for certain horticultural disputes. Most significant is the fact that vineyards received special attention; for vineyards entail a degree of skill in gardening which, in my belief, entitles us to assume that where there were vineyards there were orchards, vegetable, and herb gardens. '. . . Si quis damnum intulerit alterius vineae vel agro, vel alcui ejus terrae, compenset sicut quis illud aestivet . . .' etc. (Wilkins, *Leges anglo-saxonicae*, London 1721). Such small gardens were much cultivated by the monks and late Saxon England was rich in mona-steries for not only was Edward a bigot if not a saint, but even the warlike Harold was a deeply religious man, as witness his Waltham Abbey. As for the Celtic part of these islands during the post-Roman pre-Norman centuries, there is evidence in plenty for orchards and it seems to me improbable that there would be orchards and no other kind of gardens whatever. There is an ancient poem of Merddin the Caledonian which begins: 'To no one has been exhibited at one hour of the dawn what was shown to Merddin before he became aged, namely seven score and seven delicious apple trees, of equal age, length and size, which sprang from the bosom of mercy. One bending veil covers them over. They are guarded by one maid with crisped locks. Her name is Olwedd with the luminous teeth.' This Merddin was Judge of the North, and a bard, in the sixth century. In the same century St Teilo, bishop of Llandaff, crossing over to Armorica to spend some years with his erstwhile fellow-student bishop Samson of Dol, planted not a mere orchard but a whole forest of fruit trees; it is said to have extended over three miles. It still existed, known as the *arboretum Teliavi et Samsonia* five centuries later.

Tenth-century pomology Interesting evidence for the technical advancement of Welsh horticulture long before the Norman Conquest is to be found in the *Dwll Gwynedd*, a code of laws enacted by Howel Dda c. AD 910. For example: 'A graft fourpence without augmentation until the kalends of winter after it is grafted.' First, it is obvious that the tenth-century Welsh were practising grafting; this art was brought to Italy

by Syrian slaves, imported by the Romans with the trees which the slaves were to plant and tend. That the Welsh, i.e. the Britons, had the art from Italy is clear, for both the verb *to graft* and the older word *to imp* are of Greek derivation and have Latin equivalents. In the second place the practice, implied in the above law, of withholding payment for the young tree until it was certain that scion and stock had made a good union, is remarkably sophisticated. The next phrase of the law is: 'And thenceforward an increase of 2d is added every season until it shall bear fruit and then it is three-score pence in value. . . .'

This price seems to have been remarkably uniform at the time: the *Dwll Dyfed*, the West Welsh code, gives the same value for a bearing tree and so does the *Dwll Gwent*. Even in the later *Leges Horocli Boni* we find: 're dulcis pomi $X \div LX$'.

In short I find it hard to believe that England was without gardens between Roman and Norman times if only because the care of fruit trees is a sophisticated part of gardening. It is at least possible, though I can offer no evidence, that Roman villa gardens were imitated about the great halls of the Saxon nobility. It is too easily forgotten that these halls were attributes of a settled and prosperous land and that their replacement by Norman castles, the fortresses of a hated occupying power, were, from the point of view of 'civilization', retrogressive. However, although the manners and even the wealth of the upper-class laity in England probably declined for some decades after Senlac, the so-called battle of Hastings, number and wealth of monasteries increased, and with monasteries came more gardens, of a kind. They were herb gardens, fruit gardens and vineyards. They were, in short, 'Latin' gardens.

Climatic change   By the second half of the twelfth century Alexander Neckham, headmaster of Dunstable School and later a professor at the Sorbonne, was describing in *De Naturis rerum* what a garden was like. His writings have been dismissed as not really derived from observation in England at all; the evidence advanced for this is that some of the plants he mentions are relatively tender and would not grow in our climate. But here two things are overlooked; if I printed a catalogue of what I have growing in my garden, it could be shown that I was a liar on the same grounds; plants which will not survive untended in our climate will live a man's lifetime if the gardener be careful. In the second place, evidence for a considerable climatic change is ignored. By the year AD 1300 vineyards, for example, had extended as far to the north as Finland. About the middle of the fourteenth century, however, there was, apparently, a big change in the climate of north-west Europe. It is discussed by Rachel Carson in *The Sea Around Us*; we find the vine, a key plant when we are considering climate, rapidly falling back until it has retreated behind the 50th parallel of latitude. Is it not at least possible that Neckham's tender plants might have been cultivated here before 1350, even though after that date they would have been killed by cold?

Evidence from monastic and cathedral chapter accounts, the only kind we have at this stage, refers only to produce of the garden that was bought and sold, so that we know that apples, pears, grapes, mulberries and cherries at least were grown, and such vegetables as leeks, carrots and peas, as well as medicinal herbs. If any flowers were grown; if these small gardens had design; if the beds were edged by clipped box, we should not know it. But in his *Gardening in Britain*, by far the best book on the subject yet written, Miles Hadfield, a cautious historian, cites the interesting case of the Tresco Abbey daffodils: when, in 1872, T. A. Dorrien Smith began the commercial growing of daffodils in the Scilly Isles, the two varieties used were those found naturalized among the abbey ruins, thereafter named 'Scilly White' and 'Soleil d'Or'. These must have derived from old garden plantings; and as far as I can discover daffodils have no medicinal value.

By the fourteenth and fifteenth centuries noblemen as well as the regular clergy had their gardens of fruit, some vegetables and perhaps a few cultivated native flowers: mazes of clipped evergreens, usually box, were fashionable. The English gardens of this period were orderly and very formal, in fact as 'unnatural' as possible. They were simply European gardens which happened to be in Britain. It is true that by late republican times in Rome a taste for 'wild', for 'natural' corners in the gardens had developed. But this

V   Tresco. Sub-tropical sempervivums, agave, and aloes in one composition

taste is possible only to a people who have built, cultivated, imposed order on so great a part of their landscape that there is a reaction in favour of the wild. Before men love the wild they must feel safe from it, it must have become clear to them that they have power to tame it. This was far from being the case in fifteenth-century England where a couple of million people lived in relatively small enclaves of civilization set in a land still Nature's.

The argument of this work will be illustrated by reference to actual and still existent gardens; each will be, as far as that is possible, representative of a whole class of English gardens. But as has been pointed out elsewhere the very fact that the English are active and enthusiastic gardeners means that very few gardens remain for long of one form or fashion; it is true that from time to time an attempt is made to restore a garden or part of a garden to the fashion of an earlier time: it is also true that a number of the great picture gardens of the eighteenth century, to which we shall come in due course, have been kept more or less as they were intended to be by the artists who made them. In their case a particular difficulty arises in that they were composed and made in the same spirit as that in which a *paysagiste* paints a picture, and in some cases with astonishing success. But paint is dead, whereas the material of the landscape artist is alive and continually escapes from his control: a garden whose trees are thirty years old does not look like the same garden with trees a hundred years old. However, from the eighteenth century onwards it is possible to present gardens representative of each change of fashion in gardening, each development towards the ideal of English gardening still, until Robinson's day, latent, dormant, unrealized in the English soul. For the late fifteenth and sixteenth centuries, then, the nearest we can get to a specimen garden now is that of Hampton Court.

Hampton Court
a pre-English garden

As everybody knows, Hampton Court was built and laid out by Cardinal Wolsey. As a fairly representative Renaissance prince of the Church, Wolsey's taste, like his diplomacy, was Italianate. But Hampton Court garden was certainly not Italianate as we now understand the word. It was, as far as one can tell from the very small amount of information available, enclosed, a place of walks and resting-places, arbours, geometrical in design, with its alleys probably lined with fruit trees and nut

Plate 10

trees, with knots rather than borders; and, as for flowers, if the exiguous contemporary records of garden-material is reliable, only rose trees were planted. After Wolsey's death, when Hampton Court became one of the royal palaces, Henry VIII enlarged the gardens. He built a Mount on a foundation of bricks and earth, planted this with hawthorns and crowned it with a pavilion. He crammed it with

Plate 20

heraldic beasts, that being the fashion, cut in stone; they were often, however, made only of wood; lead does not seem to have been used until later. It is entertaining to reflect that at this very time in still unknown Peru the gardens of the Sapa Incas were adorned by beasts, birds and even plant-portraits made of pure gold and silver. Henry's Hampton Court contained more flowers – probably nearly all native flowers – planted in beds surrounded by palings painted white and green. As well as stone animals there were wooden cut-out effigies of more heraldic creatures and devices stuck up on poles. There was, apparently, a kitchen garden for the production of pot-herbs and salads; the fruit trees included apricots, almonds, peaches and figs. Until as late as the eighteenth century nature in the raw, even the mild English raw, was still 'horrid'. In such conditions the garden must be as artificial as possible to please the prevailing taste. In any case the prevailing taste was not native; the day was yet to come when the English would start feeling their way back to paradise. And although a 'flowery mead' might well be enjoyed on a fine summer day, there was hardly any need to make one in a land still only very lightly touched by human hand. It seems clear that in early Tudor times a garden was a pattern made of geometrically symmetrical walks, clipped evergreens, statuary and masonry; this material was as highly stylized in arrangement as if wrought of yarn in a tapestry or of wood in a rood screen. The beauty of a planting was in its regularity. In later Tudor times this was still and so much the case that there was virtually only one garden design, with local variations. Evidence that there was more of art than nature in it is to be found in that essential feature, the Mount, such as the one Henry VIII had added to the garden of Hampton Court. A Mount was a geometrically regular

VI Tresco. Many Canary Island, African, Mexican and Australian plants are naturalized

artificial hill topped by an elaborate pavilion reached by a spiral pathway; it was ornamented, or to our taste rendered grotesque, by massed statuary, including effigies of heraldic beasts. Without the latter embellishment, where had this feature occurred in gardening before? The Mount is singularly like the *ziggurats* of Babylon, and were not the 'Hanging Gardens' *ziggurats*?

Grotesques and exotics

Hentzner, in his *Travels in England in the reign of Queen Elizabeth*, describes Hampton Court in such terms that it seems a forest of pyramids, fountains, stone or metal stags, goddesses and nymphs. (True, the great Palace of Nonesuch included in its grounds the natural woods.) These late Tudor gardens also had elaborate summer houses for garden dining. This period also saw the first great increase in plant material: how much of this came from Holland where Clusius was only the greatest of several who were beginning on the task of producing specifically 'garden plants', artefacts of living tissue, it is hard to say. There was no gardener equal to Clusius in England, nor were the ordinary run of gardeners equal to their Dutch equivalents. New species, as well as newly made varieties, were arriving in some numbers. William Harrison, Dean of Windsor, whose life spans the later two-thirds of the sixteenth century, wrote that plants were arriving from all over the world, particularly from India, the Americas, the Canary Islands and Ceylon. Most of them naturally failed to survive their first introduction, but it is not at all impossible that Harrison was speaking the truth when he claimed to have seen citrus fruits and even olives growing in England. The Carews of Beddington near Croydon had an orchard of orange trees which, apparently, flourished and which, like the citrus terraces of Sorrento today, were covered in cold weather with some kind of wooden structure, and in addition, unlike the Sorrentese orchards, were warmed by braziers.

The knot gardens of this period help to make my point about the gardens of the time being used to produce reassuringly stylized patterns as 'unnatural' as possible, and in no sense a manifestation of English taste. The pattern was 'drawn' either in clipped dwarf box or some other clipped evergreen, such as rosemary, in a rectangular frame; it might be an abstract design; or it might be a picture, say the effigy of a unicorn. 'The designs', says Mr Hadfield in *Gardening in Britain*, '. . . that have come down to us are abstract and geometric, they often seem to have an affinity with the architectural decoration known as strapwork, that importation from Antwerp which appealed so strongly to the Elizabethan mind. One may guess therefore that the knot came from Italy via Holland.'

I suppose that the nearest thing of the kind one commonly sees now are those beds, in municipal gardens, densely planted with coloured-foliage or flowering plants so as to spell a name or reproduce a town's coat-of-arms.

Hatfield House
Elizabethan Italianate

The greatest of the Jacobean gardens, and model for the rest, was Robert Cecil's at Hatfield House. It was altogether a 'Latin' garden, it tried to be a Mediterranean garden. The elaborate waterworks were designed by a French engineer, de Caux. Once again we have effigies and statuary all over the place. The several flights of steps from the railed terrace before the house were embellished, though it seems hardly the right word, with gilt lions made of wood; the statue surmounting the great fountain which did not work very well was 'painted to represent copper'. The very fish in the basin were made of lead. On the other hand Cecil's garden and other gardens of this time, although they depended so much on mason's work and really rather shoddy ornaments, and in general on a remote imitation of the Italianate garden style, were richer in plants than former gardens. John Tradescant, first of the great plant-collector cum nursery-gardeners was working for Cecil and he sent many new bulbs and roots and seeds back from Holland, probably the most advanced country, horticulturally speaking, in the world at that time excepting China and Japan. Later, the Tradescants collected plants in North America. The French queen sent Cecil five hundred fruit trees. The vineyard at Hatfield House was the largest planted in Britain until 1875; it must have covered seven or eight acres even if we allow for the overcrowding then common in vineyards, for thirty thousand vines were imported to fill it, at a cost of £60.

Paths in Jacobean gardens were of brick, setts or pebbles, arranged in symmetrical patterns; flower beds were knots; there was a lot of Italianate masonry. Clipped hedges were privet, box or thorn,

VII Stourhead. Approaching the Pantheon between flowering rhododendrons which, planted in this century, transform the garden in midsummer into something its maker could not have envisaged. For better or worse? Doubtless this great landscape made by art should have been left as Hoare completed it

never yew. Vineyards were commonplace, and elaborate summer-houses *de rigeur*. As much of the gardening fashion came from France at this time, I believe that pleaching, whether of limes or horn-beam, probably reached England in the first part of the seventeenth century. Also from France, and in the same spirit, came the elaborate pruning and training of fruit-trees to form espaliers and wall trees, peaches, figs, cherries and probably even pomegranates, although the latter seldom ripen in Britain and have done so only twice in the last half century. The art of deforming fruit trees was an ancient one; the Romans had it, as usual from Syria but it may have been practised by the earliest sophisticated cultures, perhaps at Byblos, a great proto-centre for pomology and viticulture. Pliny, a conservative, detested it, at least when it was carried to the extremes which he described. But he had odd ideas of what was possible, and so did even men of education in our own sixteenth and seventeenth centuries. It was believed, for example, that you could graft grape-vines on to cherry trees. I call this curious because the men who propagated such nonsense were nevertheless genuinely interested in their gardens and must have been on more or less familiar terms with the gardeners they employed, practical men who could have told them just what could and could not be done.

The influence of Le Notre

The dominant influence in English gardening during the Restoration and until the arrival of Dutch gardening with a Dutch king, was that of the French garden architect Le Notre. His method was to plant trees and shrubs in great number and according to a strictly geometrical pattern; or to cut an existing wood up so as to produce the same effect. This style was widely copied in Britain by such land-owners as could afford the very expensive waterworks, which often gave a great deal of trouble and did not always work properly, that went with it. Le Notre gardens are hardly gardens at all. They are rooms, or rather vast halls, out of doors. They are, at their best, stately and magnificent, but they are, to the English gardener, very dull. They are dull because they simply compose a single *coup d'oeil* which, having once impressed, is to be taken for granted. The important thing in a great French garden is not the garden but the fact that as a setting it enhances the importance of the people who walk and converse in it. It has no interesting detail; the visitors or the owners provide that, in their own persons. The channel through which Le Notre's influence reached Britain was John Rose, gardener to Charles II, author of *The English Vineyard Vindicated*, friend of John Evelyn, that lover of trees, and the first gardener in Britain to grow pineapples successfully on hot beds.

Glimpses of paradise

The first glimpse of native English taste, the half-conscious yearning for a natural paradise rather than a work of architecture without a roof, is to be caught at this time, when English gardeners began to make clever use of different levels in the garden. This is of the first importance; the ideal site for a garden is, in my opinion, the steep side of a hill, even a cliff face; good examples are the municipal garden at Torquay; and the very fine Vierra y Clavijo botanic garden on Grand Canary. This is the extreme case, but certainly some differences in levels over the extent of the garden are necessary to give three dimensions to a relatively small area under the immensity of the sky. Trees help, of course, but hills are better. Russel Page had discussed this problem most interestingly in his *Education of a Gardener* as it occurs when making seaside gardens. Where the meeting of sea and land is abrupt and steep, as in many French Riviera gardens, made, significantly, by Englishmen, or, for one very good example, in the garden of Overbecks at Salcombe in Devon, there is no problem. But where it is flat and unacci-dented, then the immensity of sea and sky seem to press all vertical 'movement' into the very ground and gardens look like postage stamps.

So it was, as I think in the seventeenth century that the English discovered their own, subsequently incomparable, genius and taste for gardening. More than one observer of the growing passion for this art remarked on it. Sir Henry Wotton, having admitted that other lands had the benefit of more sun that we could boast of, went on: '. . . yet I have seen in our own a delicate and diligent curiosity without parallel in other nations'. That is still true: Wotton seems to have been the first garden-lover since Roman times to insist that a garden should *not* be regular; or that if it was, then its regularity should be 'wild'. This was and is the English spirit.

VIII   Stourhead. Another demonstration of the intrusion of colour and plantsmanship into the masterpiece

Botanical gardens
New World influences

In the same century the first Botanical Garden was established, at Oxford, by Henry Danvers, Earl of Denby, who was the first great plantsman among English gardeners. It is possible that we have, in the increasing number of such collections of plants at this time, a case of the influence of Mexican gardening on European horticulture. The more intelligent of the conquerors of Mexico were greatly struck with the Mexican 'gardens of plants' and brought the idea of making such gardens back to Europe together with many of the plants discovered in the New World. The same influence was to lead, in due course, to the establishment of gardens of acclimatization, such as the great garden of Oratava in Tenerife, where plants from the New World could be planted and propagated and accustomed to conditions half-way between those of their original habitat and those which they would have to endure in European gardens. There is, perhaps, too much tendency to believe that the Americas, unlike China and Japan, provided Europe only with the raw material of gardening, new species, wild plants yet to be domesticated. Nothing could be further from the truth. Both the Mexicans and the Peruvians were skilled gardeners and long had been when their civilizations were discovered and destroyed by the Spaniards. Everyone knows that we had potatoes, tomatoes, tobacco and chocolate from the new-found lands; what ornamental shrubs came with them is less clear; the Peruvian *molle* trees were among them, but it seems to me very probable that others did come, even if they were lost and had later to be reintroduced. However, at this stage it is simply Mexican influence on the establishment of gardens of plants with which I am concerned. Lord Denby made at least two gardens of his own and it was under his influence that Englishmen began to shed all those fabulous beasts, nymphs, forts and such excrescences, and to simplify or at least tidy up their gardens. On the whole, simplicity has since been a virtue, although neither the English nor any other European people went to the lengths of the Zen Buddhist gardeners of Japan whose ultimate garden was a space of raked gravel and a boulder correctly placed . . . the art being in the placing of the boulder. English gardens of the late seventeenth century remained Italianate, and indeed, in a sense, they became more so; but in a purer, less baroque taste. For example, while masonry and waterworks were still important, they began to be used classically rather than whimsically. This classical tendency in the garden seems to have preceded, and perhaps even ushered in, the same tendency in architecture.

Gardening literature

The seventeenth century saw the first spate of gardening books since swollen to a twice-yearly flood. De la Quintinye's great book, fruit of his four decades as Louis XIV's head gardener, appeared in English as *The Compleat Gardener*. So sound was it that in our own time the late Mr Justin Brooke, the great fruit-grower of Suffolk, told me that he owed his success with his fig-orchard to following the great Frenchman's advice on the pruning of this fruit tree. The translator was John Evelyn, whose own *Sylva* is a classic of arboriculture. Isaac de Caux, son of the man who designed the waterworks for Hatfield House, and later redesigned the garden itself, published his account of *Wilton Garden*, which he had designed. Rea's *Flora, Ceres and Pomona*, Temple's *Garden of Epicurus* and Lawson's *A New Orchard and Garden* were published, and they were not the only ones. But in many ways the most interesting book of the period is one which, although it existed as a MS book from 1649, was not published until 1933 (by Gerald Howe): this is *The Garden Book of Sir Thomas Hanmer*. Hanmer was a Welsh gentleman who fought for Charles I in the Civil War, went on his travels in 1644, spent two years in France, and on his return settled, newly wed, at Bettisfield, a family property acquired in the early years of the century. The fact of England being under the Commonwealth kept this royalist in retirement, so he took to gardening: he did it so well that much of the herbarium material which Rea used in the *Flora* came from Hanmer, and Rea dedicated *Flora, Ceres and Pomona* to him. Hanmer became famous among gardeners for new tulips among many other things, and his book reveals not only the wealth of new plant material which was becoming available to gardeners, but the conversion of the English to plantsmanship, another stage in the progress of the English garden towards the ideal, the 'paradise'. They seemed already to be showing what one may call a scientific bias; this does not mean that they neglected the aesthetic aspect of gardening, of course, but it is a fact that scientific

IX   Stourhead. In the eighteenth century the verges of the lake were clear of planting

plantsmanship and gardening as an art are not immediately and easily compatible, and it was in Hanmer's time that the process began which has led too many English gardeners into practices such that they cannot see the garden for the plants. Hanmer distinguished the various kinds of ornamental plants by their roots, as the bulbous, tuberous, glandulous, fibrous; he made up artificial composts; it is of interest that he used the frass of rotten willow-stumps as a seed compost; he insisted that dung of man and beast be 'soe well rotted that it will pass through a reasonable fine sieve'. He made use of rotted leaves and of the sweepings of houses and streets in his composts. In winter he brought his tender shrubs which were planted in tubs, into a garden room: they included oranges, lemons and pome-granates, 'and many sortes of greenes', i.e. evergreens.

Surprising to many gardeners who have a vague idea that 'real' gardening began in the nineteenth century, is Hanmer's list of varieties; he has, for example, three climbing and one shrubby clematis; four white jasmines, of which three are tender exotics, and three yellow jasmines; they were probably not all of them botanically jasmines at all. He has many kinds of roses and several daphnes; daphne he calls Mezereon tree. Hanmer had the Judas tree (*Cercis siliquastrum*) and he remarks that the white-flowered variety (as now) was rare. He found the bay (*Laurus nobilis*) more or less hardy, but his strawberry tree (*Arbutus unido*) was housed in winter. Among his exotics, apart from citrus fruits, were yucca and oleander and (see above) molle, the favourite roadside tree of the Incas. He grew all kinds of hardy fruits and he was a skilful and experienced vine-grower with several varieties in his vineyard. His book includes an interesting account of Colonel Blunt's vineyard on Blackheath.

Up to this point, then, we have the English making their gardens on European lines, with little native modification; and we have them beginning upon that interest in plants for their own sake, both scientific and aesthetic, which it would be necessary to accommodate, to reconcile with the often con-flicting interest of garden design. We have, too, some slight stirring of discontent with the great models of Italy and France in which can perhaps be discerned the beginnings of two great movements in English gardening, movements which were, for a long time, to work against each other but which, in the long run, would both contribute to the making of English gardens in their final perfection as paradises. On the one hand there was a beginning of movement against order, against regularity; and on the other hand the planting of the first gardens of plants, collections for botanical purposes, or simply to satisfy the collecting instinct. Before these two different horticultural interests could be reconciled it was necessary that the English feeling for a 'sweet disorder' should become articulate, and should receive expression in the creation of gardens laid out to satisfy this native taste.

The ideal of a garden   As is very well known, landscape gardening on a heroic scale, involving the moving of vast quantities of earth, the making of lakes and the planting of woods, distinguished the eighteenth century in England. Landscape gardening was, perhaps, the first kind of horticulture which was specifically English and it transformed such large areas of the countryside that a good deal of England is 'made' landscape. The whole improving movement, beginning with Alexander Pope, from Kent and Brown to Repton and others, is so well known that it would be pointless to discuss it in detail here. There are two points I should like to emphasize about it: it was as much graphic art as it was gardening, that is to say the English Claude Lorraines were the 'improvers' and that they were doing, with earth and water and living trees and masonry, what the French artists were doing with oil paint, so that some of the 'improvers' ought to be ranked for talent with the great landscape painters. The second and more important point is that towards the end of this movement, these 'improvers', gentlemen amateurs as well as professionals, discovered what English gardeners would really like to be doing. What the Continental Europeans mean by an 'English' garden was yet to be invented, but the landscape gardeners of the eighteenth and early nineteenth centuries, the amateurs like Pope, as great a gardener as he was a poet, were moving, at last, in the direction which could lead to the development of an original 'English' garden, the re-creation of Eden, and the perfection of an art; they were moving away from Tudor baroque, from Jacobean Italianate, from Commonwealth and Carolinian Dutch; they were moving

X   Sheffield Park. The great landscape gardeners found their inspiration in seventeenth- and early eighteenth-century landscape painting. Here the scale is so large that later plantings have not greatly modified the original picture away from stylization towards style, thus taking the same course as English prose at the same time; they were moving away from a regularity which was not a native product and which as I have suggested, was a by-product of the dislike of 'nature' to be expected of men who were yet far from being able to impose their will on her. They were moving towards artistic control over the artificially irregular, very attractive to men who were becoming confident of their power to change the natural scene at will, and therefore were at last free to indulge their taste for its beauties and then to set about improving on the arrangement of natural elements, keeping only a simulacrum, an artifice, of nature's sweet disorder, in the pictorial or, in the original sense of the word, picturesque order they imposed. Finally, the movement was away from architecture; gardens had still their pavilions, fine walls, bridges and other features of masonry. But these too were to go, or most of them.

Chinese and English landscape gardens

Plates 5–8

Whereas English writers on English gardens tend to give the impression that the great landscape gardens of the eighteenth century were an English invention, an art form rising naturally out of the English spirit and drawing upon the several hardening traditions of European origin which the English had absorbed and modified, Continental European writers give a rather different impression: the real originators of the English garden, they claim, were the Chinese. According to these writers, the English invented nothing; they brilliantly applied Chinese gardening art to Britain. It will be worth while to examine this claim.

In his *Gardens of China*, Osvald Sirèn has this to say: 'The Chinese garden, considered as a special type of landscape gardening, may with more reason than most other types of parks or gardens be characterized as a work of the creative imagination, or in other words as something corresponding to the demands that must be made upon a work of art.'

Here, to begin with, is an axiom which is equally applicable to the English garden, whether the landscape garden of the eighteenth century or the same kind of garden as transformed in the nineteenth and twentieth centuries by the work and imagination of Loudon and of Robinson. Furthermore, Sirèn adds: 'This does not, however, imply that the Chinese have not followed certain rules and principles in shaping their gardens, but these have not led to the same degree of uniformity that characterizes the successive stages in the development of the art of gardening in Europe. As far as we are able to follow it, the Chinese garden has maintained a more intimate contact with untrammelled nature, and in its irregular and unexpected features appealed more to the imagination than to the reasoning faculty of the beholder.'

This, again, is true of the English garden. Now a third point: following other writers on this subject I pointed out above that what the English garden-makers were doing with soil, stone, water and plants was very much what the French *paysagistes* of the seventeenth and early eighteenth centuries were doing on canvas. They were creating landscapes with natural materials but with a degree of art in the arrangement which Nature rarely attains; the elements, the details, were all such as would and did occur in Nature. The artist, however, by bringing them together with art, achieved a more interesting, and above all a more moving result than is usually produced by Nature. The French did it with paint; the English did it with Nature's own materials; but both were making pictures. And this, too, apparently, was what the Chinese were doing very much earlier: 'Especially characteristic of Chinese garden art is its intimate relation to painting. It was in a very large part the great painters who created the typical gardens in China, and in this they were inspired by ideas similar to those which found expression in their painting. The gardens may, with almost as good reason as the landscape paintings, be referred to as *shan shui* (mountains and water), for also in these compositions of living material 'mountains' and water are the most essential elements.'

Sirèn cites a number of examples, as well as some of the instructions for accomplishing the desired results published in the *Yüan Yeh*, a gardening treatise of the seventeenth century by Chi Ch'êng. Perhaps a single representative example will suffice here: it is a very brief description of the Chi Ch'ang Yüan garden in Wuhsi: '. . . the garden contained a pond or lake of considerable dimensions, whose

XI   Bodnant. In no English garden is the brilliantly clever use of a vast wealth of plant material so evident as here.
The Laburnum Arch in late spring

deep bays and confluent canals were spanned with bridges. In the farther part of the lake appears an island or promontory with fantastically formed rocks. The shores rise in gradual gradient towards the background; on one side, where the dwelling-houses are situated, the slope is terraced; on the other side the bank rises in the form of a medley of deeply creviced rocks with narrow paths winding up through the crevices, and with trees and pavilions on the highest terraces. The wooded part is extremely rich and varied, comprising tall pines, several kinds of deciduous trees and clumps of bamboo. . . .'

The spirit of this garden is the spirit of Stourhead (see pp. 57–8). It was thus that Pope, Kent, Brown and others manipulated, or wished to manipulate, landscape. But the resemblance by no means ends with this. The Chinese were quite deliberately romantic, quite deliberately poetic in their making of gardens; nothing could have been more foreign to the European gardening spirit in which symmetry and straight lines (France) were the supreme beauty, and in which fine mason's work (Italy) was used to make the skeleton whose 'flesh' would be evergreens so clipped and so placed as to make of them, as it were, living masonry, geometrical shapes of leaves instead of stone. Not even the English went as far as the Chinese perhaps only because they were always, however slightly, restrained by their respect for the Mediterranean source of their own culture, and for ever being dragged back from the brink of romanticism by a more or less classical reaction. Thus one feature of the Chinese gardens, the stones large and small strangely wrought by time and water, which were collected and which acquired the value in the market of immensely costly works of art, was never a feature of English gardens. On the other hand there is a very similar spirit in the choice of plants; the Chinese planted conifers and deciduous trees, evergreens, some flowering shrubs (notably plum trees, Moutan paeonies, and camel-lias) and, in less informal parts of the garden near to the dwelling-house or to other buildings, a few herbaceous plants. So did the English gardeners of the nineteenth century. In the nineteenth century some of the influences discussed in the introduction led to the planting of many more flowering herbs, perennial and annual, and to the invention of the herbaceous border. Other ways of using flowers, of filling the garden with strong colour, were of Continental origin. But under William Robinson's influence (see below) the English reverted again to the 'Chinese' taste . . . irregularity, 'Nature', and not an ordered planting. It was impossible, by the end of the nineteenth century, to exclude the exotics which had been pouring into the country from all over the world; but Robinson and Miss Jeckyll found what I will, for the moment, call 'Chinese' ways of using them.

Rather than prolong this argument in words, I think it better to fall back upon pictures: is it not a Chinese proverb that one picture is worth a thousand words? Here, to begin with, is the plan of a
Plate 9 Chinese garden outside Pekin taken from *Plans des plus beaux jardins pittoresques*. And here, to go with it, is what Miles Hadfield says of 'Capability' Brown's way with paths; and with the layout in general: 'Brown worked to a formula: avenues, parterres, terrace, basins and canals – everything partaking of the old art and geometry – were obliterated. Nature – in Shenstone's definition of the beautiful rather than sublime species, for Brown's curves and serpentines were smooth and suave – was every-where. . . . If the canals and fountains were destroyed, water was still *l'ame du jardin*.' The *Yuan Yeh* begins every single one of its suggestions for a garden whether in town or country or village, with a reminder that the first essential is water . . . a stream, a lake, a canal. No fountains, though there may be 'natural' waterfalls.

English Confucianism So striking is the similarity in spirit although not in detail between Chinese and English landscape gardens that there would seem to be substance in the claim that the English did not invent the English garden but took the whole art from China and adapted it. But this is an appearance merely. The truth is far more interesting; it is, I believe, that a somewhat similar approach to life by the Chinese and English gentry, a similar highly secular poetry of Nature, a rationalism which took pleasure in things as they physically are and did not seek, or at least did not welcome transcendental philosophies and religions; a similar emphasis on manners; in short a similar 'Confucian' point of view, led the two peoples to the same kind of garden art. Another similarity which may have been important is to be

XII *Nymans in Sussex. The idea of the paradise enriched with plants which its maker, Colonel Messel, sent his own collector to fetch from the Andes and Australasia, is expressed with both art and science whose respective contributions have been wonderfully reconciled by time. The garden is also rich in Asiatic and American plants growing as if native to southern England*

found, perhaps, in the fact that both peoples were in advance, in their respective parts of the world, of others in getting the upper hand of nature in their countries. It is true that China suffered devastating floods; but on the whole her farmers had imposed themselves successfully on the land; so had the English. Both peoples had their land tamed; they no longer had cause to regard Nature with fear and could, therefore, regard her with love. They were not only not inclined to make their gardening a kind of architecture in order to reassure themselves; they were also not obliged to do so.

'English' gardens in Pekin

The fact, as appears in accounts of certain gardens, Alexander Pope's garden at Twickenham, William Kent's Stowe, the same artist's Rousham, Hoare's Stourhead (and there were others), is that 'Chinese' (i.e. poetic nature) gardening was well established in Britain almost half a century before the English had any but rather tenuous contacts with Chinese gardening. It cannot, indeed, be asserted that the English gentry knew nothing of the Chinese art before the Macartney embassy to Pekin of 1792; but it seems difficult to establish that any English capable of and willing to communicate any impression of what they had seen had any real opportunity to examine Chinese gardens before the people of Macartney's embassy did so. Sir George Staunton, a member of that embassy (Minister Plenipotentiary when his chief was indisposed), has a number of interesting references to Chinese gardens and from some of them it is perfectly clear that he was able to compare what he saw with gardens he had seen in England, and that this way of gardening was not a novelty to him, or was so only in some details such as the Chinese use of eroded stones already referred to: '. . . the villa . . . contained a garden laid out in serpentine walks, a rivulet winding round an island, a grove of various trees interspersed with patches of grass ground, and diversified with artificial inequalities, and rocks rudely heaped upon each other'.

The embassy had with them one or more 'botanical gardeners' who collected plants. The lists of their collection are not particularly interesting but a number of new ornamental plants were acquired; and considering the great simplicity, in terms of plant material, of the Chinese gardens, perhaps the number of these is quite surprising. They include polygonums, sophoras, euphorbias, water lilies, potentillas, antirrhinums, incarvillea, junipers, pines, honeysuckles, mulberries and other plants of an economic rather than an ornamental value. The embassy was obliged to travel into Tartary, beyond the Great Wall, to see the emperor who was at his summer residence in the country of his race. Palaces and villas were placed at their disposal on the way. At one such, where the country beyond Pekin began to rise towards the mountains of Tartary, the palace had a garden of which Staunton says: 'It stood upon an irregular surface near the base of a gentle hill which, with part of the vale below, was inclosed and divided into park and pleasure grounds, with a very pleasing effect. Trees were here very thickly dispersed but permitted a view through them of a stream running at a little distance. Beyond it the rising hills were some of them planted, and some left naked. The different objects seemed in their natural state, as if assembled here only by a fortunate chance.' In short, the date being 1793, the sort of thing which the English had been doing for nearly half a century. And, if we suppose, what is absurd however, the existence of some general canon of gardening laws by which 'progress' in the art could be judged, the Chinese, despite their very long start, for they had been gardening like this for about 1,800 years, were in some ways backward; for example, Staunton writes of the emperor's summer palace gardens at Jehol that the gardens were 'ornamented' with figures and statues, in places numerous, in a way which reminds me of Jacobean gardening of the worst kind: '. . . the figures in stone of a few animals stood in the flower garden beside monstrous and disgusting lions and tigers in porcelain . . .' and 'The decorations which most abounded and seemed to be most admired by the conductors of the party, were those of artificial figures of men and animals, *imported from Europe* [my italics], which by means of internal springs and wheels, produce movements apparently spontaneous. . . .'

The imperial palace at Pekin is briefly described, with its gardens: the gardens, says Staunton, '. . . include every variety of ground in miniature which the sportive hand of nature has created on the surface of the globe. Mountains and valleys, lakes and rivers, rude precipices and gentle slopes, have been

XIII Bodnant. 'Chinese' effects are often accidental

produced where nature did not intend them; but in such correct proportions and with so much harmony that were it not for the general uniform appearance of the surrounding country, a spectator would entertain some doubt whether they were the real productions, or successful imitations of nature.' Many gardens by Batty Langley, Launcelot Brown or Repton might have raised the same doubts. The greatest of these Chinese landscape gardens was the Yuen-min-yuen near Pekin, the circuit of the garden being, according to a mathematical member of the embassy, twelve miles. 'The grand and agreeable parts of nature were separated, connected or arranged in so judicious a manner as to compose one whole, in which there was no inconsistency or unmeaning jumble of objects; but such an order and proportion as generally prevail in scenes entirely natural. No round or oval, square or oblong lawns, with the grass shorn off close to the roots, were to be found anywhere in those grounds. The Chinese are particularly expert in magnifying the real dimensions of a piece of land by a proper disposition of the objects intended to embellish its surface. For this purpose tall and luxuriant trees of the deepest green were planted in the foreground, from whence the view was to be taken: whilst those in the distance gradually diminished in size and depth of colouring; and in general the ground was terminated by broken and irregular clumps of trees, whose foliage varied as well by the different species of trees in the group, as by the different times of year in which they were in vigour. . . .'

First intimations of Chinese gardens

Although I have said that, taking dates into account, it must be concluded that the English garden really was invented by the English and copied by other Europeans, and not simply copied by the English from the Chinese, it is impossible to assert that, until the chinoiserie mania of the early nineteenth century, and not taking any account of the introduction of Chinese garden plants also in the nineteenth century, Chinese gardening had nothing whatever to do with the creation of the English garden. Since late in the seventeenth century there had been publications, in Latin and in French for the most part, of translations of Confucius, and accounts of the country and life of China. The sources of the information were religious missions; not until later were there any useful lay sources, for example the Portuguese, Dutch and English merchants, the latter established in Canton. Osvald Sirèn, in his *China and Gardens of Europe in the 18th century*, refers to *Lettres édifiantes et curieuses écrites de Missions Etrangères*, 34 volumes of them published between 1702 and 1776; he refers to summaries of some Confucian books and descriptions of China and her history published in 1735 by Father de Halde; to the fact that the 'physiocratic' movement headed by François Quesnay in France found its inspiration in the belief that the laws by which China was governed and administered were 'natural' laws and that this was the rational way to arrive at a system of political economy, by finding out Nature's way and conforming to it. It is a curious fact that the illusions concerning the manner in which China was governed and the origin of her laws, for it was largely an illusion despite the influence of that great rationalist Confucius on Chinese official thinking, had at least some share in bringing about the French Revolution which so shocked and horrified the Chinese government when they heard of it that at least some of the suspicion and hostility which Macartney and his embassy had to face from some circles at the Chinese court were owing to England's near neighbourhood to France on the map. We can certainly agree, then, that the Chinese 'nature worship', a refined and subtle and very sophisticated descendant of the ancient Chinese animism, made a strong appeal to the European 'Back to Nature' movement, with its manifestations in both poetry and science, of the middle eighteenth century. But if it were no more than this, if all that England had from China at this time was, so to speak, encouragement for a state of mind in which the thinking English happened to find themselves, this is very far from proving that the English garden was really the Chinese garden. There was, however, a little more than this.

First, in the Jesuit Father Mathew Ricci's commentaries on the Jesuit mission to China, published in French in 1610, there had been a very small amount of information on one single Chinese garden which, from the description, does not even seem to have been typical of Chinese landscape gardening; it contains reference to the use of oddly shaped stones, and to a maze; but mazes were features of

European gardens before this time. Secondly, Sirèn refers to the account of Johan Neuhof, a member of the Dutch East India Company's embassy to China in 1653; the Dutch party was in China for four years; the account was published in 1669. There are, in it, some descriptions of Chinese gardens. Neuhof is not a reliable witness; for the most part he had not seen these gardens, he had merely been told about them. The Chinese conceived a poor opinion of the Dutch owing to the very eagerness with which the latter hastened to abase themselves when required to do so before princes and mandarins, in the belief that this would gain them their commercial ends. The Dutch were not, therefore, allowed to see much of what they subsequently described. The one feature of the Chinese gardens which caught Neuhof's attention was, again, the artificial mountains of eroded stones. But, as Sirèn points out, it was not necessary for these accounts of China to be accurate in order for them to be influential; the European gardener might well be fired by the idea of the Chinese garden, although the idea was communicated in false or exaggerated impression. Finally, there were, in the seventeenth and eighteenth centuries, very occasional Chinese visitors to London and Paris, who were made much of at court, and who could give some account of their country including, perhaps, its gardens.

What all this amounts to is this: the English do not seem to have had a really accurate account of Chinese gardens, with plans and drawings, until the end of the eighteenth century. By that time the English landscape garden was thoroughly in being. But it is very possible that the idea for such gardens, and no more than the bare idea, i.e. of a garden which should be natural, which should deny the paramountcy of architecture, had come to England from China. I cannot myself see the need to suppose any such thing, for it seems to be sufficient to say that both the poetry and the rationalism of the eighteenth-century English would give rise, as the same kinds of poetry and the same kind of rationalism had given rise in China, to the English school of gardening.

There is, however, a little more evidence to dispose of, notably that implicit in the use, by Sir William Temple in 1685 (*Upon the garden of Epicurus and of Gardening in the year 1685*), of the word *sharawaggi*. This word is not Chinese, it is gobbledegook; but Temple and others used it, seemingly to mean (in Sirèn's words in op. cit.) 'unsymmetrical or gracefully careless patterns or decorative arrangements, i.e. something that corresponded to or could be combined with the concept of the picturesque'. For Temple, and therefore after him for others, the word was used as if it were descriptive of the spirit of Chinese gardening; but, I insist, on what they conceived Chinese gardening to be, not what they knew about it which was nothing. *Sharawaggi* may (see the *Architectural Review*, December 1949) derive from *Sa-to-kwai-chi* (careless or unorderly grace); this is according to Mr Y. Z. Chang. Mr F. V. Gatenby, however, says it may derive from *sorowadji*, a Japanese word meaning an unsymmetrical design. Mr Ch'ien Chung-shu says the word is probably a corruption of *San-lan-wai-chi*, a widely scattered or disorderly composition or arrangement. Presumably the garbled word was brought back to England as sailors' jargon and seized upon: but seized upon for what purpose, as descriptive of a new, imported idea? Or, rather, of a new but native state of mind in need of a name? The latter, surely.

Chinese or chinoiserie? There was, and I think still is, another influence at work in creating the impression seized upon by Continental critics, that English landscape gardens were imitations of the Chinese: I refer here to fortuitously 'Chinese' effects unwittingly obtained by English gardeners because they were working in the same materials and in the same spirit. But I have put the word 'Chinese' between inverted commas because the effects in question are much more of chinoiserie than of real Chinese horticulture, and perhaps what certain scenes in certain English gardens look like is Chinese painting rather than Chinese gardening. The occurrences of such chinoiserie have become even more frequent since the introduction of so many Chinese plants.

Colour plate page 35 This notion of 'unwitting chinoiserie' having been discussed, casually, between Edwin Smith and myself, I was delighted when he returned from Bodnant (see pp. 205–12), with the picture reproduced as plate XIII, for it comes very close to being a perfect illustration of what I had in mind. And another picture, from the same garden, helps to make the case by overstating it to the point of pastiche. There

XV *Highdown in Sussex. A lush paradise garden on a chalk soil rich in exotic plants*

is, of course, much more in this than mere chance. The gardener in the Latin – the Italian or French tradition – sets about his work with, in mind if not on paper, a number of firm, hard lines within which he must create his garden; they are not necessarily straight lines, but straight or not and whether implicit in the shape of his plantations or explicit in masonry and clipped evergreen and fastigiate trees they are laid down more or less according to the rules, or at least in the spirit, of architecture. But the English and the Chinese, although the former are often so much influenced by the European tradition as to modify their Englishry, begin with the ideal piece of natural scenery in mind, a bit of countryside which by its shape and colour have upon the mind and spirit the same kind of effect as does a work of art; they then try to improve upon it. If the piece of land they have to work with does not of itself possess the attributes of the ideal, they begin by changing its shape and making it 'after' an ideal of nature, as for example at Hidcote (see pp. 151–5). If there are rules in this art they are such as natural scenes have suggested. It was pointed out, above, that among Chinese gardeners that man was an artist and honoured as such who sought and found – not made but *found* – a stone having the power in its shape to affect the spirit like a work of art. In an important sense, English gardening is on the same principle.

Elements of design   Even when the models offered by Continental gardens, the examples set by Italian and French gardeners, were ignored by English garden makers, the models offered by nature were not the only ones in the mind's eye of the designer. I use the word 'models' almost in the painter's sense, for neither the picture gardeners nor the paradise gardeners simply copied a landscape, even in different materials; they composed, using elements of natural landscape. But the scene in which the English gardeners found themselves was soon far from 'natural': it was stylized and formalized by farmers and builders. The use of rustic cottages (cf. Stourhead) and other buildings such as the Pin Mill at Bodnant, bear witness to the kind of landscape the designers had been influenced by. In the late seventeenth, the eighteenth and the nineteenth centuries cottagers in villages and burgesses in rising towns added ornamental plants to their fruit and vegetable plantings. The burgesses were soon being guided in their manner of making a garden by Loudon (see pp. 122–4), but the cottagers were left to themselves. The effects achieved from time to time by cottage gardeners whom nobody had told what to do, by the casual planting of a rose, a clematis, an aster, were artless, and to that extent 'natural', and often apt to suggest effects or even themes to the more sophisticated gardener in much the same way as was a piece of country untouched by horticultural man. But there was also the influence of farmland patterns. It should not be forgotten that until our own times when everything in the countryside gives way to the single consideration of productiveness for a quick return and to the methods of the urban industrialist, that farming was a craft not an industry, and like all crafts contained a considerable element of art, by which I mean that the farmer, consciously or not, sought satisfaction for his aesthetic sense in his work, as well as satisfaction for his pocket. The pleasing patterns of an agricultural landscape are as capable of suggesting effects and themes to the gardener as to the painter, where the farmer does not fell every tree which stands in the way of his plough, and grub every hedge. Geometrically regular hedges, those living walls, such as are used in hundreds of great and small English gardens, were invented by farmers not gardeners: and until very recently some of the most magnificent in the country, clipped hawthorn fifteen or twenty feet tall and with a surface texture like coarse tweed, were to be seen in no garden, but surrounding Kentish hop-fields. A striking example of the farmer's pleasure in formal patterns is still to be seen in the mountain farms of Grand Canary: in that country plantations and arable fields have to be irrigated; irrigation channels are drawn out with a wooden plough as old as Nineveh, pulled by cows or oxen. In making them the farmer does not confine himself to a design which simply fulfils the requirements of water-distribution, but gives some play to his fancy with the result that the hillsides are turned into vast, symmetrical abstract drawings. They take time to make, and that time is money lost but pleasure gained: the irrigation channels are in the same spirit as the rough carving or painting which still decorate the wooden yokes of their draft animals.

XVI Highdown. The cherry-blossom nears the end of its season

The farmland, and the cottage garden, must be thought of in our context as aspects of the 'nature' of the English countryside from which garden-makers drew their models. Gertrude Jeckyll (see p. 131) set the example of making use of cottage themes. Inevitably, there followed a sophistication of the primitive style, and cottage themes in great gardens have a pleasing touch of Marie Antoinette playing dairymaid. The origins of some of the admirable effects achieved by Lutyens and Lloyd at Great Dixter and by Sir Harold and Lady Nicolson at Sissinghurst (pp. 175–8) – in for example the corner illustrated in plate XIV – must be sought in the cottage garden. And in at least a dozen corners of Highdown the same influence is to be seen at work, even if grander ones predominate. Very often the modification introduced by the artist-gardener was in nothing much more than the choice of plant material: an effect achieved in the cottage with a common if still lovely rose was repeated in the great house garden with a rare new rose from China.

Colour plate page 37

What both English and Chinese gardeners could do, and still can for that matter, because the gardener's rules are not drawn from an architectural discipline but are picked up at need in the surrounding scene, was and is moreover to make use of the fortuitously artistic (i.e. meaningful, symbolic, suggestive) effects achieved by nature or by artless man; achieved, necessarily, by reason of the mere number of combinations of the same materials. (It is the old theory of the monkeys typing throughout infinite time necessarily writing the Bible or the *Encyclopaedia Britannica*.) Plate XVI from Highdown is a case in point but any good English garden has a dozen. It is particularly notable in such modern gardens as Mr Lionel Fortescue's at Buckland Monachorum, Sir John Heathcoat-Amory's at Knightshayes, and above all Mr Richard Grove Annesley's at Annes Grove, in Ireland. By the use of exotics you repeat in blue what nature has done in the nearest wood, but in white. You make a primrose path, a bluebell dell: but your primroses become some rare and exquisite crimson or gold or azure primula from the Himalaya, your bluebells Asiatic lilies.

Colour plate page 41

An identity of approach

To return, then, to the main argument: the similarities, in the eighteenth century, between Chinese and English landscape gardens derive from an identity or great similarity of approach and spirit, using elements of natural landscape, and I do not believe that China had much real influence on English gardening until the nineteenth century, until we begin to see manifest chinoiserie. I think that historians of gardening as of other arts, sciences, religions, philosophies spend too much time in seeking influences. I do not mean that this is altogether a waste of time; that would be a ridiculous assertion, obviously the style of one culture influences that of another, that is fundamental. But should we not consider whether foreign influences can, in fact, 'take', unless the style influenced is already somewhat on the same lines? Men under the same natural and economic pressures tend to find, time and again, the same solution to the same problem, without other help than their native ingenuity. Addison, Pope, Steele, all attacked the formal decorated style of gardening; Steele, in *The Spectator*, falls particularly foul of sculptures misrepresenting animals and men, and topiary work. Several decades later we find the greatest garden in China disfigured by such objects, shocking the taste of Staunton, Macartney and the gentlemen with them.

The English landscape garden was not the Chinese garden transplanted; it was a newly invented garden which its creators sometimes chose to believe was in emulation of a kind of gardening which they imagined Chinese gardening to be. As we shall presently see the dates between which Hoare created the perfect 'picture' garden, Stourhead, preclude all possibility of Chinese influence. As it happened, both peoples did, in some respects, create the same kind of gardening. That, at least, is what I believe to be the truth.

Notes on the Plates

1 PARADISE GARDEN

English gardens of the fifteenth century were copied from those of Continental Europe. No English representation of such a garden exists as early as this picture by an Upper Rhenish master. It represents a 'paradise' or 'flowery mead'. Identifiable plants include sweet rocket, lily of the valley, rose, lilium, a mallow, a flag iris. Fruit seems to have ripened out of its season in those days. *Photo by permission of the Frankfurt Städelsches Kunstinstitut.*

2 PARADISE GARDEN

Title page of the *Paradisi in sole Paradisus terrestris* by John Parkinson, 1629. Note the learned pun on the author's name.

3 PORTRAIT OF A YOUNG MAN

The background of this *Portrait* by Isaac Oliver (died 1617) from the Royal Collection at Windsor shows the strict geometry and predominance of building in the early sixteenth-century garden. *Photo by gracious permission of H.M. the Queen.*

4 A MUSICAL GARDEN PARTY

Tapestry picture. England, third quarter of the seventeenth century. *The Irwin Untermyer Collection, New York.*

5–8 CHINESE AND ENGLISH GARDENS

Plates 5 and 7, from Osvald Sirèn's *Gardens of China*, illustrate corners of great Chinese landscape gardens of the eighteenth century. Plate 6 is one view of Stourhead, an English landscape garden completed before the mid-eighteenth century. Plate 8 is a corner of Lord Aberconway's great garden of Bodnant at Tal-y-cafn, North Wales. Included here for comparison, they give colour to the view that the English garden was taken from Chinese models; but a study of the dates precludes such a conclusion, and the similarities arise from an identity of feeling and spirit. *Plates 5 and 7 by permission of Osvald Sirèn, Esq.*

9 CHINESE GARDEN PLAN

Plan of a Chinese garden outside Pekin, from J. C. Krafft's *Plans des plus beaux jardins pittoresques*, Paris, 1810. The 'serpentine' paths favoured by Capability Brown for English landscape gardens are attributed by some critics to Chinese influence but seem to have been fashionable in England before such influence could have been active.

10 HAMPTON COURT

Panoramic view of Hampton Court Palace by Leonard Knyff, 1650–1721. The predominant influence of architectural geometry and of the knot garden are apparent. *Photo by gracious permission of H.M. the Queen.*

11 BUSHEY PARK

Formerly part of the Hampton Court Palace pleasure grounds, now Bushey Park. Deer in a park being purely ornamental do not, unlike cattle, introduce 'the factor of use' and so vitiate the park's claim to be a work of art.

12 HAMPTON COURT

As it is today, the canal at Hampton Court which appears in the bottom right corner of plate 10.

13, 15 HAMPTON COURT

The geometrically ruled Broad Walk at Hampton Court, as it is now. As an example of the continuous evolution and change in English garden styles, the wall border is now planted to mixed roses and herbaceous perennials, a nineteenth-century gardening device, demonstrating the rise in the popularity of flowers and the decline in the taste for mere 'knots' of which Cavendish wrote 'The knots so enknotted it cannot be exprest' (1520).

14 HAMPTON COURT

An engraving by Parr after Rigaud, 1751. The wall, left middle ground, is the one which divides the picture in plate 13.

16 HAMPTON COURT

The design for these wrought-iron gates was commissioned by William III from Jean Tijou and the work was wrought by Huntingdon Shaw. This was after the king had recovered from that grief of which Switzer wrote '. . . gardening and all other pleasures were under an eclipse with that Prince; and the beloved Hampton Court lay for some time unregarded'.

17 HAMPTON COURT

Looking towards the south façade of the Palace. The wealth of foliage is in the modern, not the seventeenth-century taste.

18 PETWORTH PARK

J. M. W. Turner's 'Petworth Park; Tillington Church in the distance', for comparison with plate 19. *Photo by permission of the Trustees of the Tate Gallery.*

19 HAMPTON COURT

At Hampton Court today: the 'park' is in fact one of the original vast 'paterres' contained within double avenues of trees (see plate 10). In the canon of landscape gardening taste, deer and peacocks are admissible as ornaments.

20 HAMPTON COURT

One of the colossi on the south side of the Palace. He is cast in lead. The earlier ornamental figures in seventeenth-century gardens were made of wood; stone, and lead came later. There were at least two hundred carved wooden figures, mostly of animals, in the Hampton Court of Henry VIII.

21 HARDWICK HALL

This great house built in Elizabeth's reign had one of the first great Tudor gardens. It was swept away when succeeding generations re-gardened it to their own taste. This view is from the Long Gallery now.

2

3

4

5

6

7

8

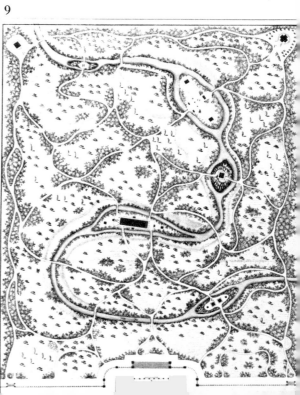

9

10

11

12

14

13

15

17

I HAVE SAID THAT THE DATES between which the most perfect and what also happens to be one of the first of the great picture gardens to be made was created, preclude all question of Chinese influence. It will be convenient, at this point, both to illustrate this argument and at the same time demonstrate the progress of English gardening towards this paradise ideal, by considering the origins of this noble garden. It was not the first of its kind. The Hon. Charles Hamilton's Painshill was a little earlier and perhaps there were others: I don't think so and it does not matter. Painshill, in any case, was not solely a picture garden. It included, for instance, a successful vineyard for the production of a sparkling white wine. Stourhead, on the other hand, was uncompromisingly 'picturesque'.

'The Lord of Stourton's place standeth on a meane hill, the soil thereof being stony. The maner hath two courts. The front of the ynner court is magnificent and high embattled castelle lyke. There is a park among hills joining on the maner place. The river of Stour riseth there of six fountains or springs, whereof three be on the North side of the parke, hard wythin the pale, the other three be North also but without the Parke. The Lord Stourton gyveth these six fountaynes on his arms. The name of the Stourtons be very ancient in these parts. The goodly gatehouse and front of Lord Stourton's house in Stourton was buylded Ex spolis Gallorum.'

Thus, John Leland, Henry VIII's Librarian, in his *Itinerary*. Stourton had, in fact, been in the same family's hands since before the Norman Conquest and remained in them even after Charles, the eighth baron, was hanged with a silk noose in Salisbury market place for the murder of one Hartgill and his son who had been so indiscreet as to back the dowager baroness' plea to her son to be allowed either an income or freedom to marry again. After Charles' death at the hangman's hands the family seems to have kept rather quiet and in 1714 the thirteenth baron sold the property to the trustees of Richard Hoare, son of the goldsmith who had founded Hoare's bank and been Lord Mayor of London. Henry Hoare, Richard's younger brother, bought the property from the latter's trustees for £20,000 in 1720. The new owner was the first of his family to begin the process of tearing down and changing the landscape which resulted in the landscape garden which we have now.

To make quite clear the significance of this garden for the whole art of landscape gardening, I want to begin, even before giving an account of the process of creation which produced the garden, by quoting from a critical essay 'Kent and "Capability"' contributed to the *New Statesman* (7 December 1962) by Reyner Banham when he was reviewing a number of books on the history of garden design and garden making. Dr Banham dismissed a claim, made by a correspondent, that the landscape garden was the great British contribution to world art. There are not, he says, enough masterpieces to add up to a contribution of significance: '. . . in fact there is only one total and authoritative masterwork surviving, and that is Stourhead . . .'.

Banham on Stourhead

Dr Banham finds that as works of art most of the great landscape parks are compromised by the factor of use. I do not agree with this. We are not yet at the paradise garden in which a herd of cows or a flock of sheep would be utterly out of place; we are at the picture garden stage. The cattle which graze a park – it was on this ground that the French critics of the last century dismissed the claim of English landscape gardens to be works of art – complete the work, they do not degrade it. A landscape garden is for use in the sense that a painting is for use – a painting is part of the interior decoration of a house or public building; it may happen, also, to be a contribution to spiritual and aesthetic enlightenment, that is, a work of genius; but this is a by-product. But of Stourhead, which Dr Banham excepts from his rule, he says: '. . . the poin there and now is the recognition that landscapes . . . came within Alexander Pope's category of "things of use". But not at Stourhead. There, a crafty choice for the position of the dam that holds back the waters of the lake and the landform of the valley whose floor the lake covers, combine to give a landscape composition focussed inwards on itself. It is not a prospect that is commanded from the house. . . . So, cupped in an irregular ring of hills, steered willy-nilly along a walk between the hanging woods and the shore, the visitor is conducted through a carefully composed sequence of views of trees, water and lakeside buildings. Each of these vignettes framed in green is, inevitably, *nature refaite d'après* Poussin, to invert the well-known Cézannism, only here it really is

Plate 23

Poussin. In general, the movement's taste ran towards the soft options of Claude rather than the tough architectonic disciplines of Poussin, and even where this was not the case, indifference and overgrowing have produced what the Knight of Glyn lately called such "neglected and bebrambled vistas" that more precise designs are now lost in thickset obscurantism. But Stourhead's steep shores permit no fuzz of undergrowth, and the foreground is normally clear water, functioning visually with the clarity of precision of Poussin's broad and open forescenes, while the doubling reflections increase the impact of the simple architectural forms of such lakeside structures as the "Pantheon". The simplicity of the architectural incidents at Stourhead is almost as conspicuous as their lack of pseudopoetic overtones. You don't have to read Thompson, Gay, or Dyer, or even Pope, to get the full flavour of the Stourhead scene. . . .'

This is very true. For my own argument it is important to emphasize that it is also quite un-English in spirit although wholly English in creation. As will appear as this narrative progresses, the fuzz of undergrowth had to be restored; not brambles indeed, but the exotic shrubs yet to be introduced were necessary to rid the English garden of a classic purity, a simplicity of line, an openness of character, a clarity of statement which excludes romance, the ideal; a possible world but not English. But we are not yet there; and meanwhile one might find, in the truth which Dr Banham states here, some justification for the claim that English landscape gardening was a plagiarism of the Chinese art. In the masterpieces of both countries the same aesthetic rules seem to have been applied. The Chinese, however, while they seem to have valued the 'impact' of the repetition of architectural incidents by reflection in the water, made a complete distinction, according to Osvald Sirèn, between landscape gardening and landscape painting manifest, for one thing, in the suppression of such reflections by the painter, analogous to their suppression of facial shadow in portrait painting. Dr Banham continues: 'The literary bit is concentrated in one single structure, the grotto with its water nymph and river god presiding over the springs, and the necessary occasional quatrain by Pope is right there in front of you on the basin which the nymph damply supervises.

'Yet right behind you as you read the lines is Stourhead's most stunning purely visual effect – the wall of the grotto is broached by a sizeable opening full of jagged teeth of rock and framing a view that is almost too beautiful to look at. The purely visual aesthetic of Stourhead, free of sentimentality and allusion, is what puts it in the class of European masterpieces, plus a controlling sensibility that combined toughness of conception with tenderness toward the "genius of the place" (Pope again, of course) in a manner that escaped Capability Brown for most of his life.'

'European masterpieces' – quite so. But what in due course the English garden was to develop into was a work which was peculiarly English as hardly to be in the European character at all.

Neither Capability Brown, nor any other fashionable consultant was, in fact, called in. The masterpiece, as we shall see, was Henry Hoare's own work. His was the taste and his the skill; as for means, I quote from the pamphlet on the place published for the National Trust, now the owners, by *Country Life*: 'The late seventeenth century had seen the steady rise into the landed classes of new families that were amassing vast fortunes through trade and expanding commerce. This led to speculations and stock-jobbing upon a colossal scale, whereby the Tory goldsmiths of Lombard Street (to become the rivals of the Bank of England, later established by the Whigs in 1694) had set up family banks such as Child's, Martin's and Hoare's. These goldsmith bankers formed in 1712 the South Sea Company of which Sir Richard Hoare was one of the original directors. The purchase by the Lord Mayor of London's affluent banker son of the ancestral estate of the Stourtons coincided with the promulgation of a new architectural phase, of which the sponsor was, it is true, the influential Whig, the Earl of Burlington. It was only natural that Henry Hoare should be influenced by the prevailing architectural fashion, even had he not been closely connected by marriage with one of its active exponents, as we shall shortly see. In any case Hoare at once proceeded to pull down the old Stourton house which had been situated on a knoll between the present house and the road from Zeals to Kilmington.'

The house which Hoare demolished is described by Aubrey as 'A gothique building which standeth on a great deal of ground, and this and Farleigh Castle are the two houses that are almost entirely the same as they were in the time of the old English barons. Here is an open roofed hall and an extremely large and high open roofed kitchen.' The house which replaced this was built on a new site and was a Palladian villa, the architect being Colin Campbell. Henry Hoare died almost as soon as it had been completed and before anything had been done to the grounds. He left a widow and a son of twenty, also called Henry who succeeded to the property on his mother's death in 1741. He made minor alterations to the house. And during about thirty years he worked on the layout and planting of the great landscape garden.

Here, then, is the creator of the part of the Stourhead estate we are concerned with, the man of whom Horace Walpole said that he had created 'one of the most picturesque scenes in the world', and of whom his grandson, Sir Richard Colt Hoare, the historian, wrote that he 'had the good taste and, I may add, the good sense, not to call in the assistance of a landscape gardener – a name unknown in those days. He saw with his own eyes and suggested improvements with his own hands.' Henry Hoare died in 1785, but before he died John Britton, in his *Beauties of Wiltshire*, was able to record that 'Mr Henry Hoare, at an advanced age had the heartfelt satisfaction of hearing his own creation universally admired and to see a barren waste covered with luxuriant woods.'

Henry Hoare's creation

Hoare was, in fact, the forerunner of the landscape school of the gardener-poet Shenstone and Capability Brown and it is certainly arguable that he was not only the forerunner but the supreme master, and that none of the professionals who came after this amateur (Brown was not working on Stowe until the late forties and did not set up as a professional improver until 1750) accomplished as great a work. What is more, Hoare had conceived and begun upon his garden more than ten years before Richard Wilson, returning from Italy in 1755, popularized upon canvas the landscape in the manner of Claude, Salvator Rosa and Zuccarelli which Hoare was carrying out in nature's own materials and, as Dr Banham says, in a style more difficult than any of these.

The focus of Stourhead garden is the three-armed lake. This had to be made: originally the valley held a chain of fish ponds. Henry Hoare built a dam across the south-west corner of the valley which was thus flooded to form the lake. The shores of this were planted with beech and fir. The beech planting is now in decline, nor have the firs survived as originally planted. The fringes of the water are today a mass of rhododendrons. They were planted by Sir Henry Hoare (1894–1947) the sixth baronet and this planting greatly upset the horticultural aesthetes. But it was inevitable that an attempt should be made to develop even this perfect garden in the direction of the whole gardening movement; I agree that in this case it was a pity. You cannot turn a Poussin into a mystery, a secret paradise; it is too 'Greek'. But as evergreens the rhododendrons seem to me unexceptionable and in no way to interfere with the creator's vision; it is true that in spring and early summer they transform the whole picture by spreading a flame of orange, mauve and white, with splashes of both red and crimson, over the lake shore. This was certainly not what the Henry Hoare who made the garden could have conceived; nor, probably, would he have liked it. During the time when the rhododendrons are in flower Stourhead is not the picture which Dr Banham describes; it is a different one, one on the way to the later English garden. The fact is that because the English are plantsmen, as well as being driven to attempt the realization of their dream, they find it very difficult to do what, for example, the Italians do, leave a garden as much alone as a satisfactory house; leave it as much unchanged as they leave their pictures unchanged instead of repainting them in a later taste. An English garden can be a masterpiece of art for a generation; but almost inevitably if the next heir be a gardener, it will be changed.

Hazlitt at Stourhead

William Hazlitt's description of the approach to the garden still holds almost good: 'You descend into Stourton by a sharp-winding declivity, almost like going underground between high hedges of laurel trees and with an expanse of woods and water spread beneath. It is a sort of rural Herculaneum, a subterranean retreat. The inn is like a modernized guardhouse; the village church stands on a lawn without any enclosure; a row of cottages facing it, with their whitewashed walls and flaunting honeysuckles, are neatness itself. Everything has an air of elegance and yet tells a tale of other times. It is a place that might be held sacred to stillness and solitary musing.' The gate into the eastern arm of the gardens is beyond this hamlet.

The 'architectural incidents'

The first of these you come to after entering the gardens by this east gate is the Bristol Cross. It was built to mark the junction of four Bristol streets in 1373. Somewhat later statues of four monarchs, John, Henry III, Edward III and Edward IV, all benefactors of the city, were placed in its lower niches and again, in 1663, statues of four more monarchs were added, Henry VI, Elizabeth, James I and Charles I. This entailed making the cross taller. Thirty-five years later it was gilded. But in 1733 it was declared to be unsafe and taken down. It was re-erected on College Green but again taken down in 1763 and stored, in pieces, in the Cathedral. As it was by then regarded as 'useless lumber' it was presented by the Dean, Mr Barton, to Henry Hoare who had it removed to Stourhead and there put up again. The Gothic greenhouse which stood near it has since vanished and from the description of it which survives its removal was as much a gain as the planting of rhododendrons was, in some opinions, a loss to the beauty of the whole. Another 'incident' which is no longer to be seen and whose removal was surely another gain, is the Turkish Tent. F. M. Piper, a Swedish visitor to Stourhead in 1779, made a series of drawings of the place and the Turkish Tent appears in one of these.

Plate 32

There is, at this point just beyond the Bristol Cross, a division of ways; you can go left over the bridge across the lake, or right along a path among trees with the lake on your left. That way you come first to the Temple of Flora. It has a Doric portico and contains busts 'after the classical Greek' and an urn representing Flora and her nymphs. From here you command a view, across the lake, of the other artefacts. Following the Temple of Flora path and passing a small lake on a higher level, you come to three more 'incidents', raised not for use, of course – that would, according to Alexander Pope and Dr Banham, condemn the garden as a work of art – but simply as ornaments. These are the Grotto, the Pantheon and the Watch Cottage. Grottoes were like Hermitages with living if phoney Hermits, a mania in the eighteenth century; the Stourhead grotto is probably the most complete thing of the kind still surviving. It is a tunnel whose roof and walls are pierced here and there to let in shafts of sunlight, so that the 'lighting' is theatrical. Half-way along the tunnel is the subterranean hall, the

Plate 28

Plate 26

sides and the interior of the dome-like roof being covered with rocks and spars. Here there is an alcove down the back of which water is made to drip, as a background to the reclining form of the Nymph of the Grot. It is from about here that flow the springs which are the source of the river Stour, their water being collected first into a marble basin. The inscription attributed by Dr Banham to Pope is in fact a translation from the Latin of Cardinal Bembo:

Plate 35

Nymph of the grot these sacred springs I keep
And to the murmur of these waters sleep;
Ah! Spare my slumbers, gently tread the cave,
And drink in silence or in silence lave.

Beyond and still in the tunnel is a statue of the River God with raised arm holding an urn from which water pours. Both figures are in lead, but whitened, and both by John Cheere who worked in that material. As you come out of the tunnel you are confronted by the Watch Cottage. It has a Gothic porch and a chimney and it was probably used as a rest place or summer house but there is no doubt that it was really there as an ornament.

Plate 34

The use of such statues as the Stourhead River God, not to mention the Nymph, did not meet with universal approval among the men of the new natural school. Possibly they were already trying to abide by a set of 'Chinese' rules which were supposed to exclude works of art from the 'natural' scene being created. (In fact, of course, and as we have seen, some of the great gardens of China even had animated statues made in Europe.) Batty Langley, one of the most fashionable 'improvers' in the period immediately following Hoare's pioneering work of garden art, included rules for statues in the canon of twenty-eight regulations he drafted for the correct designing of 'natural' gardens: the statues were to be used at the intersection of walks; you could have a Pomona in the orchard, an Harpocrates in the grove, and so forth. As Alicia Amherst, no particular friend of the landscape men, pointed out in her *History of Gardening in England*, George Mason was only one of the gardeners who shook their heads over those statues, as well they might for the art of choosing and placing them effectively is very rare indeed. Mason thought the use of statues 'a dangerous attempt in gardening' but not impossible: '. . . how peculiarly happy is the placing of the River God at Stourhead (Sir Richard Hoare's) in Wiltshire! . . .'

The Pantheon, which comes next along the path, was designed by Henry Flitcroft and inspired by the Pantheon at Rome. On each side of the portico which has Corinthian standards are niches holding, respectively, the figures of a Muse and of Dionysos. A vestibule is separated from the inner domed hall by a wrought-iron gate. The principal object of the hall is a statue, on a high pedestal, of Hercules by Michael Rysbrack (1756). On the right of this is another Rysbrack, a Flora. This is balanced on the left by a marble figure of Livia Augusta draped as Ceres, which was brought from Herculaneum. The other works in this hall are by John Cheere, two in lead, a Mealeager and a Diana; the rest plaster casts after the antique. Above them are reliefs in terracotta, artist unknown. Here is Horace Walpole's judgment on the Pantheon: 'In short few buildings exceed the magnificence, taste and beauty of the temple.'

The Pantheon
Plate 30

James Lees-Milne, author of the *Country Life* and National Trust pamphlet on Stourhead, quotes, by way of amusing contrast with Walpole's opinion, that of the Rev. John Wesley. He disliked the temple on the grounds that several of the statues were 'mean'; that he could not admire the statues of devils and 'we know the gods of the heathen are but devils'; and because he defied all mankind to reconcile statues of nudities either to common sense or to common decency. On me the effect of the interior of the Pantheon – the exterior is all that it should be – is much the same as the effect made by a Canova marble; it is cold and lifeless, and altogether void of meaning.

From the path beyond the Pantheon you cross the iron bridge to another lake, fourteen acres of water made by Sir Richard Colt Hoare, thence to the circular Temple of the Sun, after the original

Plate 31

at Baalbec. It is built on a hill and surrounded, on the lake side, by a dense stand of trees. There are more statues by John Cheere and below this temple is the bridge of five arches, over the lake, after crossing which you are back where you started.

So much for the architectural incidents which offer a series of destinations in the walk round the lake. Owing to the fact that this garden was the work of its owner there is nothing of much interest to be said about the plans which were drawn for it. There are two, neither of which were exactly realized; it may even be that it was dissatisfaction with professional suggestions which led Henry Hoare to do the job himself. One plan, in the manner of Bridgeman, and another of the garden more or less as it is but both by an unknown hand, are preserved in the library of the house. And that is literally all we have on paper of the garden's antecedents.

Stourhead is not a plantsman's garden; we do not mean that it contains no plants of interest for their own sake and not merely as elements in the production of an effect by planting *en masse*. Henry Hoare himself used native shrubs and trees and a great deal of a shrub which we now spend an immense amount of time and labour tearing out of Victorian gardens, the cherry laurel. Later plantings, of rhododendrons, azaleas, magnolias, notably *M. wilsoni* of which one of the rather rare perfectly grown specimens is to be seen beside the lake, have since been made. But there are half a hundred gardens of much greater botanical interest. The landscape movement was not interested in colour and it was not much interested in growing flowers. On the other hand it is not possible to exaggerate the importance of Stourhead not merely as the most perfect work of art in the school, but as an influence. It is one which is never sufficiently emphasized and in discussing it it will be worth while reverting to the discussion of that famous Chinese influence. First it should be said that if later critics who have made too much of this influence were French and Belgian rather than English, at the time, or nearly at the time, it was the English themselves who believed they were imitating Chinese gardens. Oliver Goldsmith was of the opinion that although the English did not come up to the Chinese in the creation of 'natural' landscape, they were making progress in the footsteps of their celestial mentors. 'The English have not yet brought the art of gardening to the same perfection as the Chinese but have lately begun to imitate them. Nature is now followed with greater assiduity than formerly; the trees are suffered to shoot out into the utmost luxuriance; the streams, no longer forced from their native beds, are permitted to wind along the valleys; spontaneous flowers take the place of the finished parterre, and the enamelled meadow of the shaven green. . . .'

Nothing could be further from the truth, of course: an enormous amount of money, time and energy was spent in making the 'natural' scene by artifice and the streams were forced out of their beds as never before. Goldsmith in fact knew no more about the art of gardening than about China. Needless to say, he had never been to China and as far as we can tell he cannot even have seen a drawing of a Chinese garden or read a description of one which could in any way be relied on.

The poet William Shenstone, in his *Unconnected Thoughts on Gardening*, suggests an artifice by means of which an avenue can be made to appear longer than its true length: 'An avenue that is widened in front and is planted there with yew trees, then firs, then with trees more and more fady, till they end in the almond willow or silver osier, will produce a very remarkable deception.'

True, it will. As we have seen the method was used and had long been used in Chinese gardening. But Sir William Chambers did not publish *A dissertation on Oriental Gardening* until 1772, did not include in it this trick for playing with the perspective, and was a thoroughly unreliable source of information in any case. The first account of this method of lengthening an avenue by arboricultural *trompe l'œil* appears in Staunton's *Authentic account*, etc., already quoted (pp. 34, 36) and that account was published after 1793. Shenstone died in 1763, at forty-eight. His own garden, Leasures, was a masterpiece by all accounts. The Chinese no more taught English gardeners perspective rules than how to make lakes. That art has too often been credited to Capability Brown because of the lake at Blenheim, his work. In fact, of course, Hoare was the originator here as in so many other respects.

In France and Italy, once gardeners had found out how best to create out of doors an extension of the house, roofless rooms as it were, they had done what they wanted to do. The Italian garden provided, and still provides, a setting for the drama of Man; the French garden provided, and still provides, a setting for polite intercourse. In both, plants were used only as a kind of building material. The English had to break away from this if they were to express the peculiar quality of English love of natural beauty. It is my belief that what the English aim at in a garden (the unattainable part of the ideal in English gardening), is a garden which is not meant to have anyone in it. It is not a setting for man's drama or man's manners; it is an arrangement of plants so that they shall be perfectly displayed. An English garden is an act of praise; it is a manifestation of poetry, and possibly even of religion. It is for this reason, which some will find very fanciful and far-fetched, that I believe that whereas gardening in continental Europe, as in China, is a fine craft, in England and Japan it is an art.

So much for what Dr Banham calls the one garden, the work of an amateur, which is worthy to be included in the number of European masterpieces. As far as I can discover, however, Stourhead did not set a fashion: it was in due course to be immensely influential but really to start this movement, European, un-English albeit an English accomplishment, and necessary as a step towards the 'final' English garden, a man practising garden design as a professional was required; and he should be a man of European training. Such a man was forthcoming.

I have not hesitated to call the men who made certain great gardens, in the past and in our own time, artists; but in almost every case their *œuvre* consisted of a single, or perhaps of two gardens and if they were proficient in any other branch of the arts, we do not hear of this. But a number of eighteenth-century gardens, the gardens or rather parks which first gave the term 'English garden' a meaning abroad, were created by men who practised and were better known in other arts: of these men William Kent was outstanding, so much so that it will be necessary to give as much attention to the man as to that example of his work which Mr Smith has illustrated in this book, the garden of Rousham.

William Kent's landscape 'painting'

William Kent was born at Bridlington in Yorkshire in 1684. Not much seems to be known about his family, but he must have been born into the class of master tradesmen, for after schooling he was apprenticed to a coach- and house-painter. He completed his apprenticeship, which was probably seven years, but during that time he evidently practised painting pictures rather than coaches and houses, for at the end of his 'time' he went to London with the support of some local gentry who raised a fund to enable the young man to go to Italy and there study painting, which they would hardly have done had he not shown promise. In 1710 Kent went to Rome and there he had the good fortune to meet and to please several gentlemen of the cultured land-owning class who were themselves in Italy for their education: these gentlemen, Sir William Wentworth, Burrel Massingberd and Sir John Chester, became Kent's friends and patrons. It was they who made him the allowance of £40 a year, plus irregular contributions amounting to at least as much again, which enabled Kent to remain in Rome and to continue with his studies of the visual arts, including architecture.

The Burlington House set

In due course Kent made an even more powerful and valuable friend. The third earl of Burlington, a Yorkshireman whose principal seat was at Londesborough near Bridlington, was in Italy for his aesthetic education, under the tutelage of a painter, Goupy, who had been engaged to accompany him and to guide his studies. William Kent made the acquaintance of this nobleman, who was a generous-hearted enthusiast of the arts and was to become a practitioner himself, showing considerable talent as an architect; he was no dilettante either, but perfectly well informed as a technician, a fact which earned him the contempt of those aesthetes and theorists of the arts who believed that no man of taste could safely meddle with mechanical technicalities. Lord Burlington became Kent's close friend and patron for many years, in a sense for the rest of Kent's life. They seem to have studied together and Kent readily adopted the ideals and theories which inspired his patron.

I am at a considerable disadvantage in dealing with the artists and thinkers of this period for I find that in reading about their ideas and their ideals, and in studying their works, I have an uneasy feeling of dissatisfaction. After Kent and Burlington had returned to England, Burlington House, the Yorkshire earl's London mansion, became the centre of an aesthetic movement which has a great influence on architecture and decorative painting, and on design generally. But the whole of this movement seems to me to have been self-consciously highbrow, for the first time in the history of the arts in England; and I am deeply distrustful of that state of mind and spirit. On the other hand there is at least one respect in which I feel entirely in sympathy with Kent and his like: Kent's birth, early training, and the influence of Rome, led him to practice not one art, but a whole group of arts; he was not merely a painter, he could turn his hands to work in wood or stone or plaster. Now I have always believed that all arts are one art. Kent has been sneered at and shrugged off by many critics whose opinion it is difficult to dismiss on the ground that because he worked not in one but in many materials, his work must have been superficial. This seems to me to be nonsense because I believe great art is a by-product. The great painters of the Italian Renaissance were universal craftsmen: Leonardo, Michelangelo and most of their contemporaries would work and did work in wood, in stone and in metal as well as in paint. Picasso, in our own time has made pots and toys as well as pictures. Kent was a 'tradesman' in the same tradition, and that tradition has never precluded the production of great works. Kent did not, in fact, produce any major work excepting Rousham; but that was not because he was trying to be a universal artist; it was because he was not an artist of the first rank.

In 1713 Kent won the Pope's medal for painting. This encouraged his patrons and friends and confirmed them in their financial support of him. He continued with his aesthetic and technical education until, in 1718, he and Burlington returned, bringing those designs by Palladio which were to transform the English country house, to London.

The Kent-Burlington ideal

It will be expedient at this point to take a look at the ideal, the notion, which was behind the work which Kent and Burlington, and others of like mind, wanted to do and, to a large extent, accomplished. And to see in what manner this led up to the design and creation of Rousham. The philosopher of their 'movement' was another nobleman, the third earl of Shaftesbury, and his philosophy, given elegant if rather cold and tedious expression in *The Moralists* (1709) and other works, was that of 'platonic idealism'. It was a contrived, an artificial system which is vaguely absurd; it was one of those systems which are more important in the history of intellectual fashions than in the history of thought; but at the time it was very important indeed in its influence on Burlington, and through him on Kent and other practical artists, and through them on the architecture, furniture, clothes, and finally gardens, of the first half of the eighteenth century.

William Hussey, in his introduction to Margaret Jourdain's admirable *The Work of William Kent* (Country Life), gives more briefly and clearly than I could do it, a description of 'platonic idealism' as follows: 'Shaftesbury's system of morals sought to establish the ideal spiritual condition for the soul. His cardinal point was that harmony, balance and proportion are the ultimate foundations alike of morality and beauty. . . . Beauty of life and beauty of form are identified as complementary aspects of the ideal. . . .' The artist, and the man of taste, must of course have 'right models' for the criterion of harmony, balance and proportion, and, as Hussey says: 'The "right models" in that age of classical precedents were inevitably drawn from antiquity.'

Lord Shaftesbury's ideas were not, of course, new. No doubt the Hellenic ideal of the golden mean was in some sort the 'right model' for them. In the publication of *The Moralists* in the first decade of the eighteenth century we have, moreover, evidence that it was not England's first glimpse of China, still to come, which influenced her aesthetic course, but such ideas as Shaftesbury's which prepared English taste for an enthusiastic acceptance of what seemed to the first English men of education to visit China some years later, to be Chinese 'platonic idealism'.

Kent, under Burlington's influence, was to attempt to give physical expression to Shaftesbury's ideal, copying the 'right models', of course, and thereby probably vitiating his own talents excepting when he could work in a field where no physical model existed and where, therefore, while being guided by a clear and admirable set of ideals, he could not be constrained or hampered by the existence of physical models. It would not be too much to say that Burlington might be considered the Producer of eighteenth-century classicism in architecture, decorative painting, sculpture and moulding; and William Kent the first Director.

It is not my business, nor am I competent to study Kent's work in fields other than garden design. He received his first commission in 1721 and carried it out, the decoration of the Cupola Room in Kensington Palace. That is to say, his first commission in England, for he had made various designs for his patrons, painted pictures for them too, while he was still living and studying in Rome. Thereafter he practiced decorative and 'pure' painting, architecture, designing of furniture and even dress-designing. He became the fashion, all the rage, he was enormously successful. He reached the zenith of eighteenth-century ambition, a 'place' in 1735 when he was appointed Master Mason, and thereafter deputy to the Surveyor General.

Meanwhile, how were Shaftesbury's theories and Kent's practice brought to bear on gardening? In *The Moralists*, Shaftesbury had written: 'I shall no longer resist the passion growing in me for things, of a natural kind, where neither art nor the caprice of man has spoilt the *genuine order* by breaking in upon that *primitive* state. Even the rude rocks, the mossy caverns, the irregular unwrought grottoes and broken falls of water, with all the horrid graces of the wilderness itself, in representing nature more, will be the more engaging, and appear with a magnificence beyond the mockery of princely gardens.'

Now this passage can easily be very misleading to the twentieth-century reader because the word nature has not, for us, the meaning given to it by either the theorists or the practitioners of gardening; nor was it even to have our ordinary meaning when we use the word, for it will be obvious to any reader of this book that even the creators of later gardens, men who had none of that classical education which coloured the minds and shaped the taste of eighteenth-century gentlemen, were working to an imaginary model of an idealized nature (Robinson at Gravetye, for example, Lord Aberconway at Bodnant and others), and not to the model of nature quite literally. Again I have recourse to Mr Hussey: 'By "nature" Shaftesbury and the landscape artists whom he inspired did not mean what nature signified to us. In this passage, with its reference to neither art nor man spoiling the genuine order of the primitive state, it is clear that he is using "nature" in the sense given it by classical critics; of a theoretical ideal, a nature as first created, without fault, and possessing divine order. It is important to grasp this meaning of nature to early eighteenth-century artists who were bidden to "imitate the Divine Maker and form to themselves, as well as they are able, a model of the superior beauties and endeavour to amend and correct common nature and to represent it as it was first created, which is the utmost mastery of human performance".'

The passage in quotation marks was written by Bellori (translated by Dryden) in *A Parallel of Poetry and Painting*. And this Divine Order, this first and since degenerated 'nature', pictorially revived for all to see by Claude le Lorrain in his landscapes, by Poussin and finally by several of their later English imitators, was not really to be knocked cockeyed until the publication of *The Origin of Species*; even after that attempts have been made to restore it; in, for example, Kropotkin's *Mutual Aid*, a vision of the Scheme of Things quite as artificial as Shaftesbury's.

A student and, as it were, popularizer of Shaftesbury's ideas was the journalist, Addison. He, in essay No. 414 in *The Spectator* (1712), took up Shaftesbury's notion of the natural garden: 'Why may not a whole estate be thrown into a kind of garden by frequent plantations? A man might make a pretty Landskip of his own possessions.' That is, turn his property into a landscape *painting*; make a Claude in real instead of in paint. Why not, indeed? Stephen Switzer, a practical garden architect, took the next step when he wrote, in *Iconographica Rustica*: 'All the adjacent country should be laid open to view and the eye should not be bounded with high walls . . . by which the eye is imprisoned and the feet fettered in the midst of the extensive charms of nature and the voluminous tracts of a pleasant country.'

The meaning of 'nature'

To these assured voices was added that of Alexander Pope, that great gardener: 'All the rules of gardening are reducible to three heads: the contrast, the management of surprises, and the concealment of the bounds. I have expressed them in these verses:

> He gains all ends who pleasingly confounds
> Surprises, varies and conceals the bounds . . .'

I do not propose to resume in detail the thinking which led up to Kent's practical work in garden design. As well as the ideas of Shaftesbury, Addison, Switzer, Pope, there were other contributions. The ha-ha, the sunk fence which enabled Kent to dispense with walls, was not one of his inventions; it was simply an idea borrowed from the classical French exponents of military fortification and Kent was not even the first to make use of it; it was used by Bridgeman. Kent's contribution was to think of the garden as part of the whole landscape view; of the landscape beyond the garden as being, visually, brought into the garden; of the garden and surrounding landscape as a picture; and of course as a 'restoration' of, a regeneration of Ideal Nature. The fact which, under the aspect of eternity, is rather comical, is that the natural *English* landscape was never for a moment seen as representative of this Nature, this in some way more 'genuine order' of Shaftesbury's. The model was an idealized Mediterranean, or Romagna landscape as created rather than imitated, by Salvator Rosa and Claude; and, more difficult, Poussin. When Dr Banham claimed that Stourhead is a Poussin, he was taken to task by critics less well-informed who insisted that the model was always Claude. But in fact even Kent, earlier than Hoare of Stourhead, had Poussins in his print collection.

Before he worked on Rousham, Kent had, of course, created or modified a number of other gardens. We cannot now see much if anything of what he did at Claremont and at Stowe, because there, where he altered or effaced the work of his predecessors Vanbrugh and Bridgeman, his own work was later effaced by that of Launcelot Brown. But from plans and from what remains Kent's method was to break up the symmetry of the gardens which came into his hands, to replace formal pieces of water by lakes of irregular shape; to replace straight paths by serpentine paths through plantings of trees and evergreen shrubs. The paths, of course, had to lead to some destination, and so he built temples after

Plate 38   the antique, temples of Venus, of Ancient Virtue, of Concord, of Victory, even of British Worthies. The 'absurdity' of all this, as of the building of artificial ruins, as of the making of grottoes and hermitages, is not such if one remembers what Kent and his later disciples were doing; they were 'painting' pictures, they were trying, very successfully in the event, to 'make it look like a fine landscape by Albano' (Horace Walpole). For the same reason much use was made, in that part of the garden which remained at least semi-formal, of urns and of statues. Too much.

There is no doubt in my mind that the influence of painters, and Kent was a painter and a collector, a connoisseur of paintings, excellent in its beginnings, was pernicious in the long run; but it was pernicious only in the sense that the good is the enemy of the best. It was almost certainly not possible for Shaftesbury's idea, the setting up of a 'Nature' such as she was conceived to have been in some imaginary golden age, to have been given physical representation without passing through a phase which falsified it. The great gardens of Kent and his successors were an astonishing achievement in painting landscape on countryside; but I doubt whether they realized Shaftesbury's idea; and they certainly did not realize 'the paradise' which the English were capable of imagining but which could not be achieved until the plant collectors and the scientists had done their share of the work. What was contributed at Rousham, Stowe, Chiswick and like gardens was a first essential step, a break with architectural lines, made by architects.

Rousham   Rousham was made between 1720 and 1725. The house belonged to a General Dormer who had already employed Bridgeman but must have disliked what he was doing, since he called in Kent and allowed him to efface Bridgeman's work entirely and start again. The piece of land which Kent had to deal with helped him: in the first place it is dominated by the shape of the stream, the river Cherwell, which takes two very sharp bends inside the bounds, that is, which is naturally 'serpentine'; in the second place the site is suitably sloping. The house itself stands level, however, so that a level lawn could be made up to the garden façade. Beyond that lawn Kent made, or modified, a hollow slope down to the river, and on each side of it planted trees, creating a falling vista between woods. All the rest of his work was done in the wood on the left-hand side of this vista. The raw material consisted of a series of pools. What Kent set out to do and succeeded in was to make a series of landscape 'paintings' in such a way that one could walk right through them, and as one reached one, the next opened to the view. To this end the pools in the wood were turned into Venus' Vale, a waterfall being contrived by making use of the slope. North along the river towards Heyford Bridge the way was opened by a green ride, evergreens were planted to form copses, and trees in picturesque groups. Two walks were driven through the wood, the Elm Walk, and, on higher ground, this green ride. These set off in different directions, but converge. Margaret Jourdain described it thus, after Kent had finished with it: 'the area was thus divided into three sections, the farthest from the river being merely a screen to the public road which skirts the grounds'.

The three were divided from each other first by Venus' Glade, then by Praeneste, the great portico, from which up the Elm Walk could be seen the over-size statue called the Colossus which terminated that walk; and thirdly that statue itself. 'In the other two [sections] winding paths were laid out. Then in the central section, now over-shadowed by dense old yews, there is an octagonal pool and a small, arched, cavern-like structure, called together the Cold Bath. To and from the pool, and following the path, water is brought by a serpentine rill descending to the Great Pond in Venus' Vale. This rill, formed of a masonry channel, is of interest as being the earliest concrete instance of the use of the "serpentine" line applied to garden layout. . . .'

Plate 48

It is worth noting, with reference to the discussion of the 'influences' which produced Stourhead, how very much earlier this is than any 'Chinese' influence can possibly have been. Long after the principal work on the garden must have been finished, 'In the winter of 1738–39 arrangements were made for the building of a Temple, called on the plan and ever since "Townsend's Temple", after the mason-architect William Townsend of Oxford. A plan and elevation for an elaborate version of this temple by Kent, is preserved at Rousham. In the view of this temple a lofty cedar and larch soar above the background of yew.'

Christopher Hussey, writing in *Country Life* (14 June 1946), points out that one of Kent's innovations was the use of conifers mixed with broad-leaved deciduous trees, not only to achieve variety of texture and colour, but because conifers (and the evergreen oak, *Quercus ilex*) did something to recall the cypress and ilex groves of classical antiquity. We are so used to conifers in both gardens and woods that it is not, I think, generally realized that only three are native to England, that of these three one is yew, hardly a conifer at all, and one a dwarf or at least very small tree, the common juniper. Thus spruce, fir and pine were exotics at this time. Kent used about a hundred Scots firs, and a lot of spruce, the latter having been introduced to nurseries, probably from Norway but possibly from northern Scotland. The cedars are from Lebanon or from the Atlas mountains. 'Early landscape designers sought "a considerable object to terminate the vista", ready-made and genuinely romantic if possible, if not fabricated. The bridge however [Heyford] seems to have been deemed insufficiently picturesque by itself, for a little way up-stream beyond it an old mill ["the Cuttle Mill"] was titivated, probably by Kent, into "the temple of the Mill" and on the skyline of the ridge a mile or so behind it a sham ruin was erected shaped as a wide gable with Gothic arches locally known as "the Folly". It was ingeniously called after its purpose "the Eye-Catcher".'

Plate 49

Miles Hadfield, in his section on 'Landskip' (*Gardening in Britain*) asks, was Kent's work gardening? I do not think it was. In the light of what was done afterwards, after these landscape artists had shown the way to the creating of idealized 'natural' landscapes, it was possible to go on to create the English garden in the artificial English landscape.

At this stage, having introduced the subject of the picture gardens of the eighteenth century and displayed a number of them as they are now to be seen, it may be as well to remind the reader once again of the theme of this book. In the beginning of gardening in England the owners of houses, great and small, lay and ecclesiastic, imitated the garden styles of France and Italy, having the same purpose in mind. For the civilization of all Europe was first Italian and then French, and the golden age of England, when the roles were reversed and other countries took to copying us, was yet to come.

Under the influence of such men as London, of the first great nursery firm of London and Wise, the first considerable plantsman, and of Loudon, the first English gardener to combine in himself the qualities of an artist in garden design, and plantsmanship, the Continental models of English gardeners were, however, modified to make allowance for that national taste for the 'natural' which was soon to assert itself in a thoroughly artificial style. That movement which began with Pope and which we have discussed and displayed as fully as is necessary, culminated in the very numerous works of Launcelot Capability Brown. Indeed, it is no longer possible to say exactly where that industrious artist did and where he did not work; for there are numerous gardens in England where you will be told that it is 'thought that' Brown laid out the grounds, or had a hand in laying out the grounds. It is probable that in many of these cases Brown had nothing whatever to do with it; but like all great and successful artists he founded a school without meaning to do so; he was imitated by lesser men and by often gifted amateurs; and works are attributed to him which were, in fact, done in his manner by others.

Capability Brown Launcelot Brown was born in Northumberland to what would now be called lower middle-class parents, in 1715. He lived sixty-eight years, not a short life in those days, and became head gardener to George III, Sheriff of Huntingdon, friend to William Pitt, friend to Lord Bute, and a man of consequence in more than one circle of important people who were shaping the time in which they lived. He completely swept away, or had a major influence in sweeping away, over one hundred gardens or parks in an earlier tradition, and had more to do with transforming the English landscape on a vast scale than any other single man, and perhaps than any ten men. He had a fair education, he became a gardener to Sir William Lorraine, went thence in 1739 to Wotton to work for Sir Richard Grenville whose sister had married Lord Cobham of Stowe. Within a year he had changed jobs again and was working in the kitchen garden at Stowe and making by his charm, intelligence and initiative, an impression on his employer and on everyone with whom he came in contact. Working at Stowe enabled him to learn something about the architectural design of gardens from William Kent, but nothing about gardening proper in which craft he was teacher rather than learner. Lord Cobham allowed Brown to go out and advise other owners of gardens and parks which needed 'improving'; it was thus that by 1749 when Cobham died, Brown had a new profession at his finger tips, and he went to London (1751) to practise it. As well as transforming estates by landscaping he taught himself to be an architect, designing houses and garden buildings with the utmost confidence and remarkable success. His success as a designer of landscape was really owing to the fact that he had just one idea, or set of ideas, based on using water to make lakes, and on giving walks and paths a 'serpentine' smoothness. With ruthless assurance he cut down great avenues and exterminated all the works of those who had gone before him.

So powerful was Brown's influence that it might very well have been pernicious if you take the view that gardens should change and grow. The adjective is admittedly tendentious, because what I mean is that if the respect in which Brown's gardens were held during and just after his lifetime had been maintained, then nobody would have laid a finger on them excepting in the way of maintenance thereafter. His gardens would have remained, as Hoare's Stourhead remained until it came into the hands of an active gardener, as unchanged as the great gardens of Italy to which, in many instances, nothing new has been added for centuries, the gardener confining himself to replacing dead shrubs and trees, and to keeping the masonry in good condition.

Now had this happened in England, that evolution towards an ideal, a dream paradise which I have postulated and which seems to me to have lain always in the English gardener's heart and mind, would have been sharply checked. If a garden was to be looked at as a picture, then obviously you could not do anything to it once its maker had finished the work. But, remarkable though the English landscape gardens of the eighteenth century were, and beautiful though they were, they did, in an important sense, lose a great deal by owing so much to landscape painting in their inspiration. It is obvious that such a garden must reach a point of perfection when its trees and other plantings were mature; and then decline from that perfection, decline from being the expression of an artist's vision; as they aged they might, of course, be even better than the garden which the artist had envisaged; they would certainly be different from that vision.

Moreover, the gardens created by Brown were peculiarly unsuitable for development along the lines which lay in the future and which were determined by the advances not of gardening as an art, but of gardening as a science, and also by the activities of the great plant collectors. You could not have introduced any of the vast range of new flowering shrubs – scores of rose species, literally hundreds of rhododendron species, more than fifty genera unknown to science in Brown's day, twenty or thirty new evergreens, several hundred new kinds of trees, and many thousands of lesser plants – plants which poured into Britain by way of Kew and the RHS in the century following Brown's death, you could not I say have introduced these or even one of them into a typical Brown 'garden' without turning that garden into something quite else. If the English garden as it now is, the English garden as envisaged by William Robinson, was to develop without too much of a violent change out of the English garden as Robinson and his contemporaries found it, then it was necessary that the firm classic line of Brown's work, the 'picturesque' but Italianate line, be softened and broken by someone who came after him to prepare the way for the new gardening of the post-Loudon epoch.

The man in question, the forerunner, was Humphry Repton.

'He had been visiting a friend in a neighbouring county, and that friend having recently had his grounds laid out by an improver, Mr Rushworth was returned with his head full of the subject and very eager to be improving his own place in the same way. . . . "I wish you could see Compton," he said, "it is the most complete thing! I never saw a place so altered in my life. . . . I declare that when I got back to Sotherton yesterday, it looked like a prison, quite a dismal old prison."

'"Oh! For Shame!" cried Mrs Norris. "A prison indeed! Sotherton Court is the noblest old place in the world."

'"It wants improvement, ma'am, beyond anything. I never saw a place that wanted so much improvement in my life; and it is so forlorn that I do not know what can be done with it." . . .

'"I must try to do something with it," said Mr Rushworth, "but I do not know what. I hope I shall have some good friends to help me."

'"Your best friend upon such an occasion," said Miss Bertram, calmly, "would be Mr Repton, I imagine."

'"That is what I was thinking of. . . . His terms are five guineas a day."

'"Well, and if they were *ten*," cried Mrs Norris, "I am sure *you* need not regard it. The expense need not be any impediment."'

It was Repton's good fortune that the expense need not, indeed, be any impediment: all over Britain there were not merely noblemen with vast estates on which they were prepared and able to spend fortunes even by our standards, but the smaller properties of gentlemen such as the owner of Jane Austen's *Mansfield Park* in which the above conversation takes place, who were also ready, and even as eager as Mr Rushworth of Sotherton, to lavish money. Repton by no means insisted on a vast estate, though Rushworth's Sotherton was seven hundred acres of ground. Dorothy Stroud, the biographer of Repton, suggests that Jane Austen had in mind a real place which had recently been 'improved' by Repton, and which was known to her, that is, Harlestone Hall, near Northampton.

Humphry Repton
'from classical to romantic'

Humphry Repton was born in 1752. His father was an officer of the Excise Department. At five the boy was sent to the King Edward VI Grammar School in his native town, Bury St Edmunds, at which the entrance fee was two guineas and the annual fee another two guineas, 'if taught Latin and Greek'. He attended that school until 1762 when his father moved to Norwich where Humphry went to the Edward VI Grammar School of that city instead. However, he did not remain there long because in 1764 his father decided that for the sake of his future career, whatever that might be, it would be as well for the youth to know at least one living foreign language as well as two dead ones, and as Humphry was destined for some branch of commerce, it was thought that Dutch would be the most useful tongue. At the age of twelve, then, he was taken by his father to Holland. They landed at Helvoetsluys and went thence to a village called Workum where Humphry was put to school with a Mynheer Algidius Zimmermann. Humphry was acutely miserable at being thus parted from his family. This was soon dissipated, however. As it was advisable to have a fellow countryman who could act *in loco parentis* on the spot, Repton senior had asked Zachary Hope, the great merchant banker of Rotterdam, with whom Repton had placed the money to pay for the boy's schooling, to act in that capacity. Hope and his wife had children of their own, so they asked Humphry to come and stay with them for a few days, and in that time became so attached to him that they invited him to continue with them and to share their son's schooling.

Nothing could have been better: the Hopes were not only very rich, they were people of taste with a tradition of luxury, and they moved in the best circles. Thus young Repton was brought into touch only with objects of beauty, and with minds which could form his own upon a good model. As Miss Stroud puts it in her biography of Repton: 'Thus what might have been two lonely years in a strange country were transformed into a happy and memorable stay during which he not only mastered the language as his father had intended, but learnt to take his place in society with an easy manner and quiet enjoyment which was to be invaluable to him in later years.'

He returned to Norwich when he was sixteen and for seven years worked as an apprentice, more or less, in the textile trade, meanwhile giving his real attention to poetry and music, but chiefly to drawing. He was to say in later life that it was to his early facility and love of the art of drawing that he was indebted not only for his professional success but for half the enjoyment of his life. He led an active and pleasant social life in Norwich, still one of the pleasantest cities in England. As a young man he was a consider-able dandy. In middle age, many years later, he wrote: 'In those days of my puppy-age every article of my dress was most assiduously studied, and while I can now smile with contempt on the singular hat, or odd shaped pantaloons of some dandy of the present day, I recall to mind the white coat lined with blue satin, and trimmed with silver fringe, in which I was supposed to captivate all hearts on one memorable occasion.'

At twenty-one he married a girl called Mary Clarke with whom he had been in love since he was eighteen. They set up housekeeping in the St Giles parish of Norwich, and with money provided by his father Humphry started in business as a merchant. He did not do well in business for his heart was far from being in it. A time of trial followed, for his wife bore him child after child (sixteen in all, but only seven lived), and the loss at sea of a number of ships in which he had goods, got him into financial trouble. He had decided to try some other business and some other city than Norwich when both his parents died and he inherited a small fortune. He bought a small estate at Sustead about twenty miles north of Norwich, and there he and his family settled down to live as country gentry on a modest but satisfying scale. Humphry was very happy; he had a pleasant seventeenth-century manor house of red brick, a garden and a farm, to the cultivation of which he applied himself seriously but in a gentlemanly rather than a yeomanly way. He wrote at this time to one of his friends: '. . . I don't wonder you should be at a loss to find Sustead in your map! It is so small a parish that I am obliged to enact the various parts of overseer, surveyor of the highways, and squire of the parish. Let me add, landlord of the Inn, by receiving you in the only one there is in the place; for there is not even an alehouse to disturb the peace. *I am impatient to show you the alterations in my house and lands.* The wet, hazy meadows which were deemed incorrigible have been drained and transformed to flowery meads. . . . Come and see how happy we are.'

The italics are mine. It is evident that Repton's first commission as an improver was received from himself. He was preparing himself, moreover, for the future he still had no idea of, in other ways. Among his friends in the neighbourhood was William Windham of Felbrigg, a man of learning and consequence with a fine library at Humphry's disposal, and at whose house he met, for example, Joseph Banks, later of Kew. Another friend was Robert Marsham, a contributor to the *Transactions* of the Royal Society and an authority on trees, and whose book on trees Humphry was to edit. (It was not published.) As well as learning about trees and meeting people like Joseph Banks, Repton spent much time sketching and drawing landscape, with particular reference to '. . . the picturesque disposition of trees and water, of buildings in relation to their setting, and the effects of light and shade'. Some of his watercolours were used to illustrate a history of Norfolk published at this time. What with good company, his art, his farm and garden, and his family, Repton seems to have had everything. Everything, that is, excepting money, for this pleasant life had to be supported on means which were really inadequate for the purpose. This is important for it seems quite possible that had his means been more considerable it would never have occurred to him to turn his taste and eye for landscape, and the sort of apparently pointless knowledge which he had been gathering, to account. But the profession for which he had been unconsciously preparing himself was not his first way out of difficulties which forced him to give up the agreeable life he had been leading for something very different. When his friend Windham was made Chief Secretary to the Lord-Lieutenant of Ireland, Repton wrote asking him if there was any way in which he could be of use. Dorothy Stroud quotes the following from Windham's answer: 'It happens very whimsically that your proposal is just an echo to a wish I was about to express to you (if you will allow me an image, when talking of Irish affairs, which makes the echo come first). From the moment this business was determined (with the determination of which I will not profess myself over-happy), having got myself into a scrape, my first thought was how I might bring my friends in with me; and in that light I had very early designs on you. . . .'

Repton was appointed Windham's private secretary and together they went to Dublin. Repton worked and played hard. So did Windham, but his health broke down and in any case he was not in sympathy with the Lord-Lieutenant's policy. He returned to London and resigned. Repton carried on in his place until Windham's successor was appointed, when Repton returned to his home preceded by a letter in which he wrote to his wife: 'And now my dearest Mary, what have I been doing? I have learned to love my home; I have gained some knowledge of the world; some of public business and some of hopeless expectancies; I have made some valuable acquaintances; I have formed some connexions with the great; I have seen a fine country in passing through Wales, and have made some sketches; I have lost very little money; I shall have got the brogue; and you will have got a tabinet gown. So ends my Irish expedition.'

Financially, it had not answered. In fact it became obvious that if he could not get more money, then a more modest way of life would have to be adopted. The latter course was the one chosen. He had seen a cottage which attracted him at Hare Street near Romford in Essex. He bought it and the family moved to it in October 1783. At the time this move was considered as a temporary measure. But Repton became so attached to the cottage and made so many improvements to this small property, that in fact he lived there for the remainder of his life. The move was followed by a series of undertakings which have all the air of expedients. For although Miss Stroud says that Repton kept his good temper and grace during his many vicissitudes, never losing heart at failure after failure, it is quite clear that he was for some time in serious straits. He was of very material help to John Palmer in the latter's schemes for improving the postal services by the establishment of regular mail-coach lines: Palmer eventually got a pension of £3,000 a year and £50,000 for his share in the work; Repton got nothing. He wrote two

Repton in Ireland

comedies which were not produced, he published a book of essays, he even became an art critic. At last, in 1788, in the course of a sleepless night – one feels that it was not his only one – the inspiration of trying his hand at landscape gardening occurred to him. In the morning he wrote letters to several friends to tell them about this notion. They were optimistic; and at last his optimism was justified. Capability Brown had been dead for five years. There were a number of lesser artists at work but none of Brown's stature. Repton was well acquainted with many of Brown's major works and Miss Stroud finds plenty of evidence that he based his own on them. But, as will appear, he did not imitate Brown; he had his own ideas and ideals, and it so happened that by giving expression to them in the jobs which were entrusted to him, he prepared the way for the more richly furnished, less classically austere gardens which were to come when the plant collectors and scientists had done their part.

Repton relaxes the rules   Whether or not Repton knew Capability Brown personally before the latter died, is uncertain. He did know Brown's son, and from him he had all Brown's maps or plans of the landscapes he had made. It was one of Brown's rules to bring the lawns, or at all events grass which might be rather meadow than lawn, right up to the house itself so that the house stood in a sea of grass and the first incidents in the landscape were at some distance. This was, of course, contrary to earlier practice. Both in the new works which he was to execute, and in the remodelling of Brown's works which very often came his way, Repton reversed this process. It seemed to him that the house and landscape needed tying together more delicately, more, as Miss Stroud puts it, subtly; instead of bringing the grass up to the house, Repton designed terraces, often with balustrades of stone piers or with urns carrying flowers, to link the house to the garden or park. Or he put in some parterres to join the house to the grounds; and that he did so is of the first importance. For it was very much easier to make a Robinson-Jeckyll garden, later when the time came for it, out of a Repton job than out of a Brown job. Repton, in fact, was moving towards the ideal English garden.

Nor was this the only way in which he was doing so: although his practice was not as thorough as his theory, in theory he wanted to get rid of the follies, hermitages, sham ruins and churches and whatnot with which the romantic landscape gardens were cluttered. All he would willingly tolerate were cottages with thatched roofs and fires kept burning in order to provide a nice plume of smoke to give life to the view! In his writings Repton was firm about this – he wrote a number of books subsequently famous on the subject which had become his profession – but in his works he was often obliged to spare the follies of the past, so to speak. Still, he did get rid of a great many such excrescences, and thus make way, again, for the new gardening which was to come after him.

In yet another respect, Repton was a forerunner of the garden of plants in place of the garden of trees, grass, water, space and masonry. This was in the disposition of trees, about which he had, as we have seen, learnt a great deal. It was Brown's practice to let the shape of, for example, a hill, appear nakedly, confining his planting to the setting of a small stand of trees (a 'cushion' of foliage) on the top of the hill. Repton used trees far more lavishly and, it must be said, with far more regard to the sort of thing which could happen in nature without the intervention of man. Nothing is more improbable than that a stand of trees should, in nature, be confined to the top of a hill. How, then, did such a notion become so very standard practice, after Brown, in so much landscape gardening? Here we must go back for a moment to the origins of the picture garden; it all began, as we have already suggested, and as has been pointed out by half a dozen authors in the past, in landscape painting. But in Italian landscape painting, even though the painter be French. Now it was a very long time indeed since there had been such a thing as a natural landscape in Italy. In Italy it was perfectly possible, and indeed commonplace, for a hill to have naked flanks and yet be crowned with trees. And the reason is that at some time in the past all the workable part of the hill has been cleared of trees to make way for plough, vineyard or pasture, and only that part left alone which was not worth the trouble of working . . . the windswept and much accidented summit. So that, at several removes, what Brown was doing in making his picture gardens was imitating not a natural landscape at all, but an Italian agricultural landscape. As R.S. Fitter points out in his *Wildlife in Britain*, there is no such thing as a 'natural' landscape in the sense 'primeval' in Britain either; but this is a refinement.

As we have seen, Repton, as he wandered about the neighbourhood of his little estate, had drawn and painted and therefore thoroughly observed the natural landscape. In his work, therefore, consciously or not, he modified the picturesque by reference to the natural. And one way in which he did so was by planting trees as they would grow if left to themselves, more or less. As Miss Stroud puts it: 'Repton's trees spilled like cream down the slopes to merge in the valleys.' She adds that for small groups he favoured a mixture of trees. I do not think that this means a mixture of species, however. His own reference to this is: 'No groups will appear natural unless two or more trees are planted near each other, whilst the perfection of a group consists in the combination of trees of different age, size and character....' Would Brown have wanted his work to appear 'natural'? Not, certainly, in the sense the word bears in this passage. Repton was moving away beyond the stage of making picture gardens, to something less restricted by rules. I do not claim that he knew exactly what he was doing; nor did he need to.

I do not propose to go into details of the progress of Repton's career as a garden maker. It was a phenomenal success. His method is interesting. It was Repton's practice to visit the client's property and to survey it and make notes and sketches. He would then prepare one of his subsequently famous Red Books. These are slender bound volumes containing a map or maps of what he proposed to do, plans, and a number of drawings or watercolours. Some of these Red Books are still in possession of the houses for which they were made. At least one has come upon the market and fetched a handsome price, for they are minor works of art. Repton was no doubt the best painter, with perhaps the exception of William Kent, of all the 'improvers'.

The Red Books

There would be no point here in giving a list of Repton's works: Edwin Smith here displays some representative examples which survive. His first great client was Coke of Holkham, he worked for William Pitt and for half the grandees of the period. Since despite his distaste for follies and bogus ruins he was in fact obliged to build features in some of his gardens, from designing landscapes he graduated to architecture, and from architecture to interior decorating. But we are not here concerned with his activities in these fields.

Miles Hadfield (in op. cit.) has a very enlightening passage on the subject of Repton's contribution to the English garden: 'But the most important development propounded by Repton was "the proper distinction between *Painting* and *Gardening*" – the difference between a scene in nature and on canvas. The principle may be summarized thus: first, the spot from whence the view is taken is in a fixed state to the painter; but the gardener surveys his scenery while in motion: secondly, the field of vision in nature is much greater than in a picture; thirdly, the light which a painter brings to a picture is fixed as he wishes it at a certain time of day – in nature it varies from hour to hour.'

Thus Repton's influence, which was enormous as time went on, so great in fact that he was often shown gardens he was said to have designed but which in fact he had never seen before in his life, was salutary. Picture gardening in landscape had produced one and perhaps several masterpieces; which was magnificent but not gardening. Repton was cautious, I think, in his innovations, but what he was doing can be roughly summarized as sidling away from the classical and towards the romantic. Others, his enemies, were to move farther and faster, but even then it was in the sense of 'literary' romanticism rather than that horticultural romanticism which would emerge later.

In 1793, by which time he was of course famous, Repton set about publishing his ideas on landscape gardening in a folio volume entitled *Sketches and Hints on Landscape Gardening*. While this work was still in the press, some of it still at the proof stage, came an attack on the whole theory of landscape gardening as practised by Repton, from two rich and cultured country gentlemen who were friends, who enjoyed embellishing their own respective estates, and who, it is apparent in retrospect, wanted to go much farther along the way which Repton had moved from Capability Brown, towards the 'natural' – the steps which had to be taken, in fact, before, by the introduction of exotics, the ideal English garden could be created. These gentlemen were Uvedale Price and Richard Payne Knight.

I have hitherto been using the word 'picturesque' by reference to the origin of landscape gardening in landscape painting. But it assumed, in the late eighties of the eighteenth century, a new meaning. That was picturesque which was imminently 'paintable', and that was paintable which was wild and rugged. Price and Knight were advocates of the wild and rugged school. The prophet of this school was the Rev. William Gilpin and its holy writ was his *Observations Relative to Picturesque Beauty* (1789): 'A piece of Palladian architecture may be elegant in the last degree, but if we introduce it in a picture it immediately becomes a formal object and ceases to please. Should we wish to give it picturesque beauty we must use the mallet. . . . From a smooth building we must turn it into a rough *ruin.* . . .'

Actually, there was nothing new in this, Repton had been clearing ruins out of gardens for years. But what Uvedale Price and Knight seem to me to have been after, in reality, although the cultural prejudices of the time kept their minds tied to reference to painting, and to notions of the visual arts generally, was to get away entirely from the Italianate, from the 'picture' landscape to something more like the English landscape. Their artistic prejudices forced them, in practice, to exaggerate absurdly: oaks had to be gnarled in order to be beautiful. The consequences of their thinking and propaganda are to be found in the absurdities of Marion Dashwood's romanticism. For her (*Sense and Sensibility*), a tree, to be beautiful, had to be dead – preferably blasted by lightning. Price published their theories in an *Essay on the Picturesque*. The principal target of a fierce attack was Capability Brown. But Repton, who had not departed from Brown's ideas nearly far enough to satisfy these gentlemen, also came in for a pasting. Knight, at the same time, published *The Landscape*, a didactic poem in which Brown, in his grave of course, and Repton very much alive, were attacked. Repton was in time to get an answer to his critics into his book, the monthly reviews and magazines joined in, and there was in fact a tremendous nation-wide controversy. It continued for many years. It did not hurt Repton, whose practice grew and whose views were established and respected. But just as he had moved away, albeit moderately, from the suavities of Brown's style, so the theories of Price and Knight and their supporters had enough influence and ultimately enough practical effect to carry the English garden further towards that natural composition of artificially assembled plants in an artificial framework which was 'after' nature, towards the making, in short, of a paradise.

Notes on the Plates

22 STOURHEAD

Monument in the parish church to Henry Hoare, designer and maker of the landscape garden of Stourhead.

23 LANDSCAPE BY CLAUDE LE LORRAIN

'Mariage d'Isaac et de Rebecca' by Claude le Lorrain, 1600–82. The landscape painting of Claude was the inspiration of many landscape gardeners, although Dr Rayner Banham has suggested that Henry Hoare followed Poussin rather than Claude. *Photo by permission of the Trustees of the National Gallery.*

24 AN ENGLISH LANDSCAPE

'The James Family' by Arthur Devis, 1711–87. In England men with a talent as *paysagistes* worked as often in the materials of real landscape as in paint; but English landscape painting came under the same European influence as English gardening. *Photo by permission of the Trustees of the Tate Gallery.*

25 STOURHEAD

View from the Pantheon, from an engraving by C.W.Bampfyld, 1777. Compare this with the photograph made in 1963 (plate 27).

26 STOURHEAD

The Pantheon across the lake. Rhododendrons at the lake edge are a nineteenth-century addition. Compare this with plate 32.

27 STOURHEAD

View from the Pantheon, across the lake to the Temple of Flora.

28 STOURHEAD

The Temple of Flora. Beyond, on the left, is the bridge. And on the height to the right of centre, the Temple of the Sun, after the original at Baalbec. The buildings in the garden were so disposed as to form stations and destinations of the several walks.

29 STOURHEAD

The path passes below the lake, entering by a tunnel of foliage, to emerge at the Pantheon (plate 30). The small tree on the right is an acer and would not have been available to Henry Hoare.

30 STOURHEAD

The Pantheon. The rhododendrons which were used to replace non-flowering evergreens or open grass greatly modify Hoare's original landscape when they flower in June.

31 STOURHEAD

This temple, on a height surrounded by trees, reproduces the Temple of the Sun at Baalbec.

32 STOURHEAD

In this drawing made by the Swedish artist F.M.Piper in 1779, the Temple of the Sun (plate 31) is seen on the left in the background, and the Pantheon (plate 30) right of centre. The ornament in the foreground is *not* the famous Turkish Tent, but the Chinese Parasol, since disappeared. *Photo by permission of the Royal Swedish Academy.*

33 STOURHEAD

The Grotto giving entry to the Temple of the Sun, and one of the innumerable points of view over the lake which is the focus of the whole masterpiece.

34 STOURHEAD

Neptune, or the River God, in the Grotto built about the springs which feed the lake. Some eighteenth-century clerical critics objected to Stourhead's heathen deities.

35 STOURHEAD

The Nymph of the Grot. These two statues are in white painted lead. Even garden design aesthetes who saw objections to the use of statuary approved the manner in which it was used here.

36 STOURHEAD

The Hermitage, with the Pantheon in the background. The more thoroughgoing of the eighteenth-century garden creators employed professional hermits to inhabit their hermitages.

37 STOWE

The Congreve Monument. The great landscape garden at Stowe was completed and at least partially made over by William Kent after Vanbrugh, Gibbs, Bridgeman and possibly other designers had worked on it.

38 STOWE

The Temple of Ancient Virtue. Alexander Pope wrote:
> Begin with sense, of every art the soul,
> Parts answering parts, shall slide into a whole,
> Spontaneous beauties all around advance,
> Start, even from difficulty, strike, from chance;
> Nature shall join you; time shall make it grow
> A work to wonder at – perhaps a Stowe.

39 STOWE

Boycott Pavilion, Oxford Bridge. There are two of these pavilions.

40 STOWE

The Queen's Temple. The Palladian style of architecture for both villas and garden buildings was brought to England from Italy by Lord Burlington, an architect of talent, and by his protégé, William Kent, who completed the making of Stowe.

41 STOWE

The Rotunda. William Kent's mark on this landscape garden is clearer than that of his predecessors. Of him Horace Walpole said: 'He leaped the fence, and saw that all nature was a garden.'

42 STOWE

The Palladian Bridge. Other bridges in this style are to be seen at Prior Park and at Wilton House.

43, 44 STOWE

The lake, with one of its two pavilions beyond; and the Elysian Fields. The inspiration of Stowe as of other landscape gardens was the Roman school of Italian and French *paysagistes*. But under the influence of Alexander Pope the 'genius of the place' was respected, with the result that the 'Englishry' of these gardens is obvious.

45 ROUSHAM PARK

At Rousham, William Kent wiped out the work already done by Bridgeman; it is in this garden that, in Miles Hadfield's words, Kent 'revolutionized the whole conception of garden design'. The statue, in lead, is by Van Nost.

46 ROUSHAM PARK

Cattle, like statues, were regarded as part of the picture by all but the purest aesthetes who could swallow a deer but strained at a cow.

47 ROUSHAM PARK

Bridgeman's Theatre. The statue-bordered path on the right leads to the avenue (plate 50).

48 ROUSHAM PARK

The Rousham Venus overlooks the pool or bath in her glade. The growth of trees, especially yews, has darkened and cooled the whole composition: all the tree-planting landscape-garden artists had to visualize their picture gardens as they would be after their collaborator, Time, had done its share of the work.

49 ROUSHAM PARK

The view beyond Scheemakers' sculpture affords an example of Kent's 'leaping of the fence'. The garden is on one side of the Cherwell only, but an artificial ruin was placed on the horizon, far beyond the garden, as an 'eye-stopper'.

50, 51, 52 ROUSHAM PARK

The Colonnade and the Glade of Venus. The statues are typical of the work of Jan van Nost at whose workshops in St Martin's Lane, London, were cast figures, urns and cisterns in lead for many of the great picture-gardens.

53 BLENHEIM PALACE

Bridge and view of the house. The first garden designer here was the architect Vanbrugh who built the palace of which, on first being shown it, Alexander Pope remarked:

> 'Tis mighty fine,
> But where d'ye sleep
> And where d'ye dine?

54 BLENHEIM PALACE

Henry Wise was first employed in laying out the gardens at the Marlboroughs' new palace of Blenheim. Later Capability Brown worked on the gardens. In the late 1920s André Duchêne created the new formal terraces and the *'parterres d'eau'*.

55 BLENHEIM PALACE

The lake had to be enlarged to live up to the massive bridge built by Vanbrugh for whom some wit suggested the epitaph:

> Lie heavy on him earth, for he
> Lay many a heavy load on thee!

56 BLENHEIM PALACE

The tree is the great cedar in plate 54.

57 BLENHEIM PALACE

The horse-chestnuts must be a later planting, although introduced from the Near East by way of Vienna in the seventeenth century.

58 BLENHEIM PALACE

In the new garden of the present Duke.

59 BLENHEIM PALACE

Cypresses in mown lawn. It was Capability Brown who brought the grass right up to the house itself. After his death Repton rescued many great gardens from the resulting coldness of line by putting balustraded terraces between house and lawn.

60 BLENHEIM PALACE

In the park-like gardens of such houses as Blenheim Palace, masonry, sculpture, clipped evergreens, grass and trees were the artists' materials, and flowering plants were of no importance.

61 LONGLEAT

The first gardens were designed and planted by the nurseryman George London and his partners, Cook, the Earl of Essex's man at Cassiobury, Lucre, gardener to the Queen Dowager at Somerset House, and Field, the Earl of Bedford's head gardener.

62 SHERINGHAM HALL

This landscape garden is a good example of the work of Humphry Repton.

63 CASTLE HOWARD

The landscape gardens were laid out by the Earl of Carlisle about 1700. The Earl had called in George London, the nurseryman, to advise him, but, rejecting London's geometrical patterns, became the originator of the new labyrinthine-serpentine fashion for Nature perfected. A pavilion by Vanbrugh seen from the bridge.

64 KENWOOD

Loudon described it as 'the finest country residence in the suburbs of London in point of natural beauty . . . and also of the main features of art'.

65 MELBOURNE HALL

It was here that Thomas Coke, Queen Anne's Vice-Chamberlain, advised by London and Wise, made a 'French' garden 'to suit Versailles'. Arbour by R. Bakewell of Derby, *c.* 1705–10.

Ye who have view'd in Pleasure's choicest hour
The Earth embellish'd on these Banks of Stour,
With grateful Reverence to this Marble lean,
Rais'd to the Friendly Founder of the Scene:
Here, with pure love of smiling Nature warm'd,
This far-fam'd Demy-Paradise he form'd:
And, happier still, here learn'd from Heaven to find
A sweeter Eden in a Bounteous Mind.
Thankful these fair & flowery paths be trod,
And priz'd them only as they lead to GOD.

IN MEMORY OF HENRY HOARE ESQ.
Who died Sept.r 8.th 1785, aged 80 years.

23

24

27

28

32

33

35

34

50

56

THERE IS A PASSAGE in Poe's *Domain of Arnheim* which seems to me so apt at this point that I shall quote it in full: having described his subject, Ellison, and said that he might have become a musician, poet, painter or sculptor, Poe continues: 'I have now mentioned all the provinces in which the common understanding of the poetic sentiment has declared it capable of expatiating. But Ellison maintained that the richest, the truest and most natural, if not altogether the most extensive province, had been unaccountably neglected. No definition had spoken of the landscape gardener as of the poet; yet it seemed to my friend that the creation of the landscape garden offered to the proper Muse the most magnificent of opportunities. Here, indeed, was the fairest field for the display of imagination in the endless combining of forms of novel beauty; the elements to enter into combination being, by a vast superiority, the most glorious which the earth could afford. In the multiform and multicolour of the flowers and the trees, he recognized the most direct and energetic efforts of Nature at physical loveliness. And in the direction or concentration of this effort – or more properly in its adaptation to the eyes which were to behold it on earth, he perceived that he should be employing the best means – labouring to the greatest advantage – in the fulfilment not only of his own destiny as a poet, but of the august purpose for which the Deity had implanted the poetic sentiment in man. . . .

'Mr Ellison did much towards solving what has always seemed to me to be an enigma: I mean the fact (which none but the ignorant dispute) that no such combination of scenery exists in Nature as the painter of genius may produce. No such paradises have been found in reality as have glowed on the canvas of Claude. . . .'

Yet note that there is in this passage an incompatibility between the beginning and the conclusion: '. . . the endless combining of the forms of natural beauty . . . the multiform and multicolour of the flower and tree . . .' cannot really be reduced in the end to a landscape by Claude. But the ideal is there, potential; the Claudian landscape as design; but the elements to be used far richer.

But before the advances of the seventeenth and eighteenth centuries could lead towards the English garden as it existed in the imagination of English gardeners, it was necessary to pass not only through the phase of picture gardening but also through the phase of what, on the analogue of high farming, I shall call high gardening, in which the important achievements were technical rather than aesthetic. The great technical advances, dependent upon enormous capital investment as well as on skill and knowledge, began early in the nineteenth century or even late in the eighteenth. The great flower-, vegetable- and fruit-factories were coming into existence. Consider, for example, Jane Austen's description, sketchy as it is, of General Tilney's Northanger gardens, but notably the greenhouses: 'The kitchen-garden was to be next admired, and he led the way to it across a small portion of the park. The number of acres contained in this garden was such as Catherine could not listen to without dismay. . . . The walls seemed countless in number, endless in length; a village of hot-houses seemed to rise among them, and a whole parish to be at work within the enclosure.

'[The General] . . . modestly owned that . . . without any ambition of that sort himself – without any solicitude about it, he did [not] believe them to be unrivalled in the kingdom. If he had a hobby horse it was *that*. He loved a garden. Though careless enough in most matters of eating, he loved good fruit – or if he did not his friends and children did. There were great vexations, however, attending such a garden as his. The utmost care could not always secure the most valuable fruits. The pinery had yielded only one hundred in the past year. . . .'

High gardening was a product of money, scientific and technical advances, the rise of the great and profitable nursery firms, and plant collecting. The first great nursery was that of London and Wise; by the end of the nineteenth century the name Veitch was not merely that of a business house, but of an imposing national institution. Also important was the organization of gardeners into horticultural societies and of one in particular, *the* (later Royal) Horticultural Society, with resultant swift exchange of new knowledge and plants. Finally, and equally important, was the rise of a gardening press. But among all these institutions the one which served horticulture most thoroughly by receiving from abroad, studying, acclimatizing new plants, was the botanic garden, the idea of which developed no doubt out of the medicinal herb garden of the Middle Ages, but more directly, as I believe, out of the Spanish reports of the Mexican gardens of plants, whole collections of useful or beautiful species, which the Aztecs, following their Toltec, and perhaps Maya, mentors, were accustomed to plant and to tend. Botanic gardens in Britain were to be relatively numerous; ultimately the three most important from the gardeners' point of view were those of Edinburgh, Dublin (Glasnevin) and, above all, Kew. And since it also happens that at Kew many of the landscape, many of the architect, gardeners had a hand in the making of the gardens, this will be a suitable point at which to glance at the career of that remark-able garden, botanically, and indirectly horticulturally, by far the most important in the world.

Kew Gardens   Kew Gardens, or more correctly The Royal Botanic Gardens, Kew, are a scientific, not an aesthetic institution. They exist for the collection and study of plants, both living specimens and herbarium material. As such, had they first come into existence in this century it is very unlikely indeed that they would have had any charm, any visual appeal whatsoever. The buildings would have been prefabs or Nissen huts. As it happens, however, they were started in the Age of Taste, and a number of horti-cultural artists of the first rank worked at the task of laying out these gardens. One of the characteristics of an age when the arts are declining, such as our own, is that of reverent care for the arts of the past. Just as the artistically impotent late Romans revered and preserved and collected works of art created by the Greeks, so do we revere, preserve, collect and even restore the works of art created by our own potent forefathers, and by the artists of the virile periods in other and alien cultures. As a consequence of this love and respect for the works of the past, the scientific activities of Kew Gardens have been fitted into an aesthetically satisfying setting: and with the model of what the past could do ever before their eyes, the Kew authorities do their best, when their laboratories, museums or libraries have to be extended, to respect the standards of taste manifest in their founders' works.

It is not precisely known when there was a first botanic garden at Kew: it is known, however, that the Rev. William Turner (*c.* 1510–1568), physician to the Duke of Somerset and 'father' of English botany, author of a famous herbal and of other botanical treatises, had a garden at Kew. Be that as it may, by the middle of the seventeenth century there was a house within the precincts of the present gardens, known variously as Kew House and as the White House, which belonged to one Richard Bennett. This gentleman had a daughter who married Sir Henry Capel, subsequently Lord Capel. The lady died in 1721 and as she had inherited the house from her father, it became Sir Henry Capel's property. Perhaps his love of plants led him to marry into the ownership of a place reigned over by the genius of botany; at all events he was a famous gardener, though not a botanist, in his day. He cultivated fruit, including oranges in an orangery which he built for the purpose, was a pioneer in the building of greenhouses, planted a myrtetum – English gardeners have always had a mania for myrtles – and collected flowering and evergreen shrubs. We do not in fact know much about his gardening activities; as Lord Deputy of Ireland, a place to which he was appointed after becoming Lord Capel of Tewkesbury, he cannot have had much time to spare for it. But he would appear to have been a plantsman rather than an architect of gardens.

After Lord Capel's death the Kew House property came into the hands of his great-niece, Elizabeth; she married the private secretary of George (later the Second), Prince of Wales, an active politician named Samuel Molyneux who, although a politician, seems to have been a man of intelligence and broad culture. He was particularly interested in astronomy and converted the east wing of Kew House into an observatory from which he and Dr James Bradley made the first observations of the series which led to the discovery of the aberration of light.

The Molyneux had no children and after both were dead the house came into the hands of the Capel family who let it in 1730 to Frederick, Prince of Wales. The age was one of faction and party in whose social and political strife no holds were barred, so that it may be the case that the contempt with which this prince, and for that matter the rest of the royal family, were treated by some contemporaries, was not deserved. Frederick seems to have been a chump rather than a knave, and the opinion some of his people had of him is perhaps best conveyed in a contemporary suggestion for his epitaph when he died:

> Here lies Fred,
> Who was alive and is dead.
> Had it been his father,
> I had much rather.
> Had it been his mother,
> Better than another.
> Had it been the whole generation,
> Better for the nation,
> But since it is Fred
> Who was alive and is dead,
> There's no more to be said.

Even if the prince deserved this rough handling, however, he had merits, for he was a gardener. His lease of Kew House began in 1730 and the prince then engaged the services of William Kent to lay out the grounds. This is the first piece of aesthetic good fortune we have to be thankful for; and another is that the Prince of Wales himself contributed, according to W.B. Turrill's account, more to the creation of Kew Gardens than has been generally recognized.

The initiation of scientific work in the gardens, however, and the introduction of the spirit of scientific botany, is owed to his widow. Frederick had married the princess Augusta of Saxe-Gotha in 1736 and it was with her help and sympathy that, when the couple settled down to live a quiet life at Kew House, he began his collection of exotic plants to fill in the outlines of the garden which he and Kent had sketched and begun to execute. Frederick died in 1751 and for the next twenty years, until her own death in 1772, the dowager Princess of Wales developed the garden which they had started. W.T. Thistelton Dyer, Director of Kew from 1885, in his account of the origins of the gardens, says of Augusta: 'She died in 1772, but in the preceding twenty years she gave to Kew Gardens the definitely scientific character which they have ever since retained.'

Turrill, however, treats this statement with some reserve: 'It can be agreed that the princess Augusta took a great personal interest in her garden. But the results of permanent importance achieved were more directly and in detail the consequence of the friendship of her husband, herself, and her eldest son who became George III, with John Stuart, third Earl of Bute, and of the appointments and associations made on his advice.

Bute as botanist

This Scottish nobleman and politician was a botanist of some distinction. His library included 300 folios devoted entirely to botany, as well as a great many lesser books. He had two houses at Kew. Turrill says that he was the author of a 'very rare' botanical work: *Botanical Tables, containing the different families of British Plants distinguished by a few obvious parts of Fructification rang'd in a Synoptic method*. The drawings and their engraving were done by Johann Sebastian Müller. About a dozen copies were printed at a cost of £10,000. Charles Johnstone, in *Chrysal, The Adventures of a Guinea*, accused Bute of having this work written for him by a hack and charlatan; but Johnstone is the most unreliable and spiteful of polemicists. Whether or no Bute was a botanical author, he certainly had a lot to do with the plantings at Kew. By the 1760's these had become considerable enough to call for a *Hortus*, and this, the first *Hortus Kewensis* (*Catalogue of Plants Cultivated in the Garden of H.R.H. The Dowager Princess of Wales at Kew*), was published in 1768. Sir John Hill, the author, was one of Bute's protégés, by profession an apothecary; he had, apparently, had some part in the superindependence of the Gardens.

Of more importance than Hill was Sir William Chambers, the architect. Chambers had been to China and was partly responsible for the introduction of chinoiserie into the English taste and, inadvertently, for the myth of English gardens being modelled on the Chinese. He was employed by Augusta at Kew in 1760 and in 1763 he published, at her expense, a book of *Plans, Elevations, Sections, and Prospective Views of the Gardens and Buildings at Kew in Surrey*. It was a joint work for which Chambers provided only the architectural drawings, his collaborators being Cipriani, Kirby, Sandby and Marlow, and a number of skilled engravers. Turrill says that probably Chambers had 'little or nothing' to do with the botanical side of Kew. His work lay in building the 'follies' which had come to be deemed necessary as objects of the various walks and vistas in a garden. Of the fancies he erected, the Mosque,

Plate 70

the Alhambra and the Gothic Cathedral have, happily, long since been demolished; the Pagoda, of course, remains as do a Ruined Arch and, a work of grace and merit, the Orangery. Several of his

Plate 68

Temples still survive, notably that to Bellona which, however, was moved from its original site and rebuilt on another half-way through the nineteenth century.

The two Aitons

First of the Gardens' really great botanists and Directors was William Aiton, a Lanarkshire Scot who came to England at the age of twenty-three and was employed in the Chelsea Physic Garden by Phillip Miller, one of the earliest and most prolific authors of gardening books, whose *Gardener's Dictionary*, in very numerous editions, was in use for at least a century. Evidently Augusta or Bute were looking for a professional garden superintendent and in 1759 Miller recommended Aiton for this post. He filled the post for the rest of his life and in 1789 published the second *Hortus Kewensis*, in which he listed the 5,500 species grown at Kew, classified them according to the Linnaean system, and gave such details as their country of origin and date of introduction: he, and his son (see below) are repeatedly referred to as early authorities by later and more scientific botanists and gardeners. Aiton made a name and reputation for himself, and was liked, frequented, and admired by distinguished men of his day.

William Aiton's son, William Townsend Aiton, was born at Kew in 1766 and lived to be eighty-three. He was brought up to assist his father in the gardens and was already a competent gardener in his early 'teens. On his father's death in 1793, W.T. Aiton succeeded to the post and held it for forty-eight years. Helped by Sir Joseph Banks, he brought out a new edition of his father's *Hortus*, this time in five volumes and containing over eleven thousand species.

During the greater part of Aiton's life the owner of the Gardens was George III, a lover of gardens and especially of Kew. He lived a great deal at Kew, at what had been the White House (or simply Kew House), but, with rebuilding, became the Dutch House until it was promoted to be Kew Palace. Meanwhile he employed James Wyatt to build him a new Kew Palace: this was a fanciful erection in the new romantic taste, 'a medieval, fortress-like dwelling or castle with numerous towers, turrets and similar appurtenances'. Turrill says that it was never inhabited; it was probably uninhabitable; George IV pulled it down. It is well known that the Georges and their eldest sons were always at war with each other, and it seems likely that George III's attachment to Kew and its Gardens was quite enough to ensure that his son would be indifferent to them. In any case George III was mad during the last ten years of his life and reign. These two circumstances are sufficient to account for the fact that W. T. Aiton had to see the Gardens half neglected during the latter part of his life of service there, and to witness, helplessly, the decline of the great work which had been carried on for so long.

It should be made clear at this point what territory was included in Kew Gardens. They began as Augusta's Botanic Garden, and it was of that Garden that the first Aiton was Principal Gardener. Turrill describes it: 'This in 1760 extended from what is now the Main (Kew Green) gate southwards to a little beyond the Chalk Garden, and was enclosed by walls. It was partly a physic garden, with herbaceous plants arranged according to the Linnaean system and most of the rest planted with trees and shrubs also scientifically arranged. The total area is said to have been about nine acres.'

The map will show this area, and the Pleasure Grounds of Kew House which were outside it. It will be seen that the western boundary of these Grounds was Love Lane. Across that lane began the grounds of Richmond Lodge, favourite residence of Caroline of Anspach, George II's wife. These grounds were laid out, with the fashionable 'follies' of hermitage, temples, pavilions and a Merlin's Cave, by the queen. When both properties fell to George III he threw them into one, obtaining Parliamentary sanction for the closing of Love Lane as a right of way. (It was a very ancient bridle path.)

George III pulled down Richmond Lodge and employed Capability Brown to redesign and lay out the grounds, in the course of which work Merlin's Cave and other nonsenses were removed. One of Brown's works in this garden was the Hollow Walk, which is now Rhododendron Dell; at the time it was made there were probably a dozen species of rhododendron in cultivation although I do not know that any were originally planted along the Hollow Walk; there are now about 800 species and varieties, some evidence of the overwhelming changes which have been wrought in gardening taste by the industry of plant collectors. While the Aitons remained in charge of the original nine acres of the first Kew Garden, a new Director or Superintendent – no official title seems to have been used at that time – was placed over them and the combined Gardens. This was the famous Sir Joseph Banks.

The reader may need reminding that Banks was born rich, heir to a great property in Lincolnshire, a London house and a fortune in the funds. He was, however, incapable of idleness; he accompanied Captain Cook on his voyage of discovery round the world; he paid a visit to Iceland; he became a biologist and botanist of distinction. When George III became the owner of the combined Kew Gardens, he removed Bute as garden adviser (no doubt needing him as Prime Minister, an easier post, instead) and appointed Banks in Bute's place. It was Banks who began the work of bringing plants to Kew from all over the world in a systematic fashion and not, as it has hitherto been done, any old how. Turrill tells us: 'Banks planned to grow in the botanic gardens plants from all over the world. To further this aim he arranged for trained collectors to be sent to various parts of the globe, he bombarded ministers and government officials with letters of advice and instruction and sometimes almost of command, and he spent lavishly of his own time, energy and money. It is said that during the reign of George III about seven thousand new plants from overseas were introduced into cultivation in England, the majority through the exertions of Banks, on behalf of Kew.'

As well as serving the Gardens in his own lifetime, Banks, albeit not deliberately, ensured their future. As a friend of the botanist William Jackson Hooker, Banks used his influence to get him the Professorship of Botany at Glasgow University. Hooker held this Chair for twenty years until, as will appear, he was appointed Director of Kew.

Although the decline of the gardens had probably set in with George III's period of insanity, it did not become serious until Banks died in 1820. The King died in the same year, and George IV was not in the least interested in gardens, plants or farming. There perhaps never was a more thoroughly urban

Joseph Banks

character. The Gardens did not, of course, go completely down. Aiton's assistant, John Smith, did a great deal to keep them going and got his reward when fresh interest and new 'management' set them on the upward grade again. A part of Kew Green was incorporated into the Gardens during the reign of William IV, and King William's Temple was built in 1837.

The most important thing which happened as a result of the neglect during two reigns, though fortunately short ones, was that Parliament took a hand. A Committee was appointed to enquire into the management of the Royal Gardens. It consisted of the most famous botanist of the day, Dr John Lindley; of the most famous gardener of the day, Mr (later Sir) Joseph Paxton, and a Mr Wilson, gardener to the Earl of Surrey. As a result of the impression made by this Report, a controversial document which did not meet with universal approval but was, in fact, as sound in principle as it was unfair in detail to individuals, the control of Kew Gardens was transferred to the Commissioners of Woods and Forests, which means that it ceased to be the property of the Crown and became the property of the Nation. This was done in 1840.

William Jackson Hooker

In 1841 Sir William Jackson Hooker, Banks' old friend and protégé, by that time Regius Professor of Botany at Glasgow University, was appointed Director of Kew: he was fifty-six years old. The gardens he took over covered fifteen acres, divided into sections by brick walls and his first undertaking was to pull these down, to renovate greenhouses, build new ones and instal the latest heating systems in the hothouses. He opened the Gardens to the public, he revived Banks' policy of bringing in plants from overseas and employing professional plant collectors, coming to an arrangement with the RHS to share the expense of this work. One of the collectors who began sending new species, as seeds, to Kew, was the Director's son, J. D. Hooker, who was already beginning his extensive travels. And the new Director began the policy of distributing plants from Kew to stock the plantations of new colonies overseas, one of the most important of Kew's works for the advancement of plantation crop farming as well as gardening. Within five years of his appointment Hooker had increased the area in his charge from under 20 acres to over 250, and had planted the now world-famous Arboretum; and within the same period he initiated the building of what is still the most graceful and was then certainly the largest greenhouse in existence. This was the Palm House, whose architect was Decimus Burton. It took four years to build, cost £30,000 and it is 363 feet long, 100 feet wide, 63 feet high at the highest point. To build it today would no doubt cost at least half a million. The Old Pleasure Grounds having been taken into the Gardens (accounting for a large part of the increased area), a landscape artist was employed to lay them out: this was W. A. Nesfield and his work is still visible, and enjoyable, in the main walks, vistas and avenues which carried on the tradition of being scientific in a visually seemly style.

In the following period of Hooker's activity, the Museum of Scientific Botany, now Museum No. 2, was built; the Herbarium and the Library were started; and, over a period of years, the lake in the old Pleasure Grounds was dug and filled with water from the Thames, the spoil being used to build the terrace for the Temperate House, another of Decimus Burton's works. Hooker died at Kew when he was eighty and was succeeded by his son.

Joseph Dalton Hooker

Joseph Dalton Hooker was a much-travelled man. While studying for his MD which he took at Glasgow, his father's old university, he used his spare time to learn botany in his father's Herbarium and Library. He developed a taste for books of travel, and in due course got himself appointed surgeon in the Royal Navy and posted to the *Erebus*, in which vessel he cruised the whole southern hemisphere under the command of Sir James Clark Ross. The use of the Navy in this way, for scientific surveys by officers not appointed officially for such work, was not unusual. Hooker made an enormous collection of plants for Herbarium material, which were sent to Kew, and are there to be seen still. The results of his field work were published in a series of books which became and have remained world-famous: *Flora Antarctica*; *Flora Novae-Zelandiae*, and *Flora Tasmaniae* (1847–1860). Hooker had, of course, returned home before these works were undertaken, and had been appointed assistant to the Professor of Botany at Edinburgh, and from 1846 to 1847 he was official botanist to the Geological Survey of Britain. He became a distinguished palaeobotanist and in 1847 a Fellow of the Royal Society. Thereafter he went to India, investigated the flora of the Gangetic Plain and Behar, and set off for the Himalaya. The years 1848 and 1849 were spent in exploring and collecting the flora of Sikhim, the eastern part of Nepal, and the passes into Tibet. He was seized and imprisoned by the Sikhim government, released after representations from the Government of India, and thereafter he made a botanical study of Eastern Bengal, the Khasia Hills and other parts of Northern India.

It was as a result of this journey that English gardens were enriched with the first of that flood of new rhododendrons which was to transform them during the following half century. In Sikhim, in the course of two journeys, he recorded and collected about thirty-five species, most of them new not only to horticulture, but to science.

Hooker was appointed assistant to his father at Kew in 1855, and after succeeding him, undertook more improvements to the Gardens. His creations are the Berberis Dell, the Rock Garden, the Thorn Avenue, the Holly Walk and the sweet Chestnut Avenue. He made various changes in buildings and layout which need not be detailed. He retired in 1885 but lived until 1911, an impressive and bewhiskered figure, a great Victorian if ever there was one, but evidently capable of relaxing for it is told by Sir Julian Huxley, who was taken to see the great man as a very small boy, that Sir Joseph's manner of entertaining children was to pull down his immensely long eyebrows until he could hold the ends between his lips, and then release them so that they sprang back neatly coiled into their point of rest.

I am deliberately not entering into any description of the scientific work which was done, increasingly at Kew, not only by the staff, but by botanists from all over the world who were welcomed to work there. This book is about gardens as works of art, not as scientific laboratories, but in the case of Kew, it is simply not possible to write straightforwardly of its creation as a work of art; too many people worked at it and for too long, and moreover the aesthetic quality of Kew is in a sense a by-product, a quality which has come into being simply because the scientists who made the gardens as a field for the study of botany were what few scientists of our time can claim to be, whole men, universal human beings and, therefore, among other things, artists. I shall confine myself to history, leave presentation of Kew's beauties to Edwin Smith, and of Kew's scientific work say only this: that in both the pure science of botany, and the applied science of economic botany, no institution in the world can for a moment be compared with Kew. The economic work was, of course, of enormous importance: it can be summed up by saying that what Kew did was to collect plants of economic value in one part of the world, find out all about them, and then distribute them to such other parts of the world as enjoyed climatic and other conditions in which the plant could prosper: rubber, tea, coffee, chocolate, bananas – the universal distribution of these and many other plants of less spectacular importance wherever they can flourish, this has been Kew's work.

William Thistelton Dyer

The Directorship of Kew became rather a family affair: the elder Hooker was followed in the post by his son, and the younger Hooker by his son-in-law. It was not a case of nepotism: these botanists tended to gather other botanists about them and men who were attracted to work at Kew thereby became fitted to direct some part of it. William Thistelton Dyer was the next Director. A graduate of Christ Church, Oxford, he was a teacher, but he was drawn into the Kew circle, he worked there, he helped Hooker with his *Flora of British India*, he became Assistant Director of Kew Gardens (1875) and he married Hooker's daughter. It was he who was responsible for the introduction of rubber and chocolate to Ceylon. Although he was concerned with his chief in the making of the Rock Garden, he was less a gardener and more an economic botanist than his predecessors, but Mr Turrill says that he did improve the Gardens aesthetically also, notably by laying out more informal vistas. Under his direction, the Bamboo Garden, the Sunken Rose Garden, and the Lily Pond were made. In due course, Thistelton Dyer was knighted, and in 1905 he retired, thereafter living to be eighty-eight.

David Prain At this point the family succession was broken. Thistelton Dyer's successor was an outsider. This new Director was a soldier-botanist of distinction, Lieut.-Colonel David Prain. He had taken a medical degree at Aberdeen University, joined the army, went to India in 1885, was in charge of the military hospitals at Allahabad and Lucknow, and meanwhile was becoming well-known as a botanist by his studies of Indian flora. In 1887 he was appointed to the Royal Botanic Gardens, Calcutta, where for ten years he served as Librarian and Curator of the Herbarium. After that he became Superintendent of this famous garden, and he was responsible for the establishment of the quinine-bearing tree in India. He made botanical journeys in both northern India and Tibet. He was appointed Director of Kew Gardens in 1905. His character has been so well and entertainingly sketched by Mr Turrill, that I cannot improve upon his description: 'He was direct in speech and incisive in style and disliked ambiguity or any compromise with principle. It was unfortunate that he often wounded the susceptibilities of many whose views he did not accept. In many ways he was an autocrat and even a martinet, and many stories of his treatment of the staff at the Royal Botanic Gardens have been told to the writer by old Kewites. Thus once, when members of the Herbarium staff approached him with a request that he would support an application for an increase in their very low salaries he replied that there was nothing valid to support the request. The cost of suits, among other things, was pointed out to him, and his answer was to visit a second-hand shop in Richmond, to purchase a suit for 7/6 ($1.50 at that time), and to parade the Herbarium dressed in it and proclaiming how cheap was the cost of living.'

Prain did not make many changes in the Gardens. He was in any case interested chiefly in economic botany, and in a major reform of the many and valuable Kew publications, for the Gardens had long been a source of a massive flow of scientific literature. Moreover, the times were becoming difficult. Among the other troubles the Director had to cope with were raids by militant suffragettes: there were two in 1913, in the first of which the glass of the Orchid House was smashed and fifty valuable plants destroyed; and in the second the Tea Pavilion was burnt down. Then came the war, during which strict economy prevented any costly improvements from being undertaken.

Arthur William Hill It had become customary by this time to knight Directors of Kew, and Prain received this accolade in 1912. His assistant, since 1907, had been Arthur William Hill, formerly Demonstrator in Botany of Cambridge University, Dean of Kings', and a plant anatomist of distinction. When Sir David retired in 1922, Hill succeeded. He, again, was a scientist first, a gardener second. His principal achievement was to form, during travels all over the Commonwealth, links between Kew and botanical institutions overseas. He had, however, the makings of a landscape gardener too, and he did make important improvements. He designed and carried out the building of the steps and seats to the south of King William's Temple; he partly rebuilt and considerably enlarged the Rock Garden. He is remembered as a kind-hearted and generous man whose good qualities were partially concealed by a pompous manner and a way of making somewhat cynical judgments. He was the only Kew Director to meet with a violent end, for he was thrown from his horse and broke his neck while he was riding in the Old Deer Park in 1941. For the next two of the war years Sir Geoffrey Evans was appointed Acting Director. The Gardens received their share of bomb damage, broken glass, of course, with the consequential damage to plants, and several 'incidents' involving incendiary bombs. A lot of valuable Herbarium material was removed to Oxford, and other material, books, documents, were scattered to relatively safe places all over the country.

Edward Salisbury The new Director was Professor E. J. (later Sir Edward) Salisbury. In some respects he is probably the Director of Kew best known to the gardening public for he has, in his writings, the very rare gift, at least very rare among distinguished scientists, of expressing himself with that perfect simplicity and clarity which is the height of literary skill and his books for the general reader have been popular. He was also, I believe, the first Director of Kew to be an ecologist. In addition to his scientific work at Kew, and to dealing with the war damage and war neglect, he made some changes in and additions to the gardens, building a new Australian House, making the Clematis Walk, and starting a Chalk Garden. Sir Edward retired in 1956 and his place was taken by Dr (now Sir) George Taylor who had been Keeper of the Department of Botany at the British Museum. He had done a good deal of botanical travelling, including in Tibet.

It will have occurred to the reader that the Kew Garden of the Princess Augusta was somewhat cluttered. It was, in fact, a representation of the Poetic or Rococo garden. The first features of this horticultural *bondieuserie*, so to speak, had been Merlin's Cave and Merlin's Hill, for which Bridgeman and William Kent were responsible. Derek Clifford, in his *History of Garden Design*, has a highly diverting description of the Cave as '. . . a thatched building of most peculiar design, a kind of nest of Indian wigwams with a Tudor front door'.

Kew follies

It was partly concealed at the heart of a maze, and when you reached it, it turned out to be a show of waxworks, being permanently occupied by a singularly mixed company, Merlin the Magician, his secretary, Anne Boleyn, Minerva, the Queen of the Amazons, Queen Elizabeth and her Muse. It is as well that they were of wax. The cave also included a library, with the poet-peasant Stephen Duck as Librarian who later drowned himself in a fit of depression, hardly surprising under the circumstances. The Hermitage, which I have also mentioned, was a romanesque building of rough-dressed stone; Kent had built the Temple, and the Queen's pavilion; Joseph Goupy had added the aforementioned Gothic Cathedral. Apparently Chambers' principal contributions were the Mosque and the Pagoda, the question whether he was in fact responsible for the other nonsenses which I have attributed to him above being an open one.

The Pagoda might almost be described as the outcome of a joke. As was pointed out in the brief historical sketch above, Chambers had been to China. Mr Clifford strongly bears out my contention that any resemblance between English and Chinese gardens in the first half of the eighteenth century was purely coincidental. One of the reasons for the belief, of French origin, that the English simply copied Chinese 'poetic' gardens, was Chambers' book *Dissertation on Oriental Gardening*. Now whether or not Chambers wrote this book as a kind of joke, as Mr Clifford maintains, what is quite certain is that his Oriental gardening was more or less imaginary. He wished to urge the claims of 'poetic' gardening; it would have a better chance of being granted if he gave it the prestige of China, which was becoming fashionable. In a later edition Chambers admitted that the hoax had been seen through and that there was no point in trying to keep it up. But meanwhile he built the Pagoda at Kew, as if, perhaps, to prove that he really did know something about China. In fact, however, there was far more resemblance between the gardens which Capability Brown was making and Chinese gardens, than between Chambers' idea of a garden and anything he can possibly have seen in China.

Chambers' chinoiseries
Plate 70

There is, however, a curious sort of *contredanse* performed by Chambers and Capability Brown in the work they did in garden design. Chambers, by helping to add to the clutter of 'poetic' rubbish at Kew does not seem to have been giving expression to that 'Chinese' garden idea he was supposed to be advocating and executing: Brown, when he was employed at Kew, promptly swept away the majority of the buildings there although he retained Chambers' two principal works; but Brown was, in his turn, overtaken by Chambers' theories, if not by Chambers' practice. For not until most of the buildings had been removed, and a simple, grandly conceived garden of the kind which Brown favoured and imposed on the whole nation created, could the garden as Chambers conceived but did not make it, be realized: 'The Chinese . . .' (probably Chambers' imaginary Chinese, yet it may be he had observed what follows in China) '. . . avoid all sudden transitions both with regard to dimension and colour. They build-up gradually from the smallest flowers in front through a rank of medium height, to the taller ones at the back. In the same style, colour is graded from white through primrose and yellow and so forth, . . . to the deepest blues, and most brilliant crimsons and scarlets. They frequently blend several roots together, whose leaves and flowers unite and compose one rich, harmonious mass . . . and the same method they use with flowering shrubs, blending white, red and variegated roses together; purple and white lilacs; yellow and white jessamines; altheas of various sorts; and as many others as they can with propriety unite. . . .'

I believe that the 'Chinese' who did these things were imaginary, and that Chambers was in fact putting over ideas of his own in this fashionable guise. I can find no evidence that the Chinese did garden in that way; and had Chambers seen their plantings he could not have failed to be struck with the usefulness and beauty of the principal flowering shrub of the Chinese gardens, the tree or moutan paeonies. But the point is that in this and other passages, Chambers was foreseeing the English garden as created by Robinson, as carried out perfectly at Bodnant, at Dartington, at Mount Usher and elsewhere, on the basis of the landscape garden as modified by Repton, but not for another two centuries. Chambers, in short, was putting the English dream-garden into so many words.

Plate 66 Decimus Burton's Palm House is better displayed here by Edwin Smith than I could do it. For many years Chambers' Orangery was not used as an Orangery; this building has been and is being restored to its original purpose by Sir George Taylor. In the building called King William's Temple there stood, for sixty years, two statues by Pietro Francavilla, an *Apollo* and a *Zephyr*. These, for some years on loan to the Victoria and Albert Museum, have been restored to Kew, but now figure in the Orangery. In 1929 the President and Council of the Royal Academy presented Sir Hamo Thorny-croft's *The Sower* to Kew; the pedestal was designed by Lutyens. A curious and interesting modern addition to Kew's buildings is the Japanese Gateway which stands on the Mosque Mound where Chambers' Mosque, subsequently demolished, originally stood. The Gateway is a reproduction, on a slightly smaller scale, of the Chokushi-Mon, the old Gate of the Imperial Messenger into the monastery of Nishi Hongwanji at Kyoto. It was presented to Kew after the Japanese-British Exhibition of 1910.

Kew Gardens design As I have, I hope, made clear, it is virtually impossible to write of design in connexion with Kew, a garden which has been the work of centuries, of many hands, and is not and can never be finished. However, if it can be said that the Kew we have now was designed and laid out by any one man, or at least that one man's mark is much clearer than that of any other, then that man is W. A. Nesfield, whose name has been mentioned in the foregoing historical sketch.

Nesfield was a soldier who had fought in the Peninsula and in Canada. But he was also a water-colourist of some merit. He did not rise very high in the army, for he retired with the rank and pension of a Lieutenant, but he then acquired some repute for his watercolour paintings of waterfalls and cascades, a curious manifestation of specialization. Later he worked in partnership with the architect Sir John Barry, as a garden design team. Derek Clifford thinks that Barry contrived the terraces and the sunk gardens which were necessary for the display of Nesfield's work, the walks, shrubberies and parterres. When I say that Nesfield has left his mark, I mean only in the basic lines of walks and shapes of borders or beds or plantation areas; the purpose for which these are used now, the plants displayed in them, are entirely different. Nesfield's own object was to make a flat picture in colour which, by virtue of Barry's shaping of the ground in three dimensions, could be seen as a whole. Very nasty these pictures must have been, too. Derek Clifford describes them: 'Barry-Nesfield gardens . . . are no more than the large home parterres of the Italian gardens adapted for the bedding out of half-hardy plants. . . . There was nothing of rest or seclusion or peace about such gardens. No shade was allowed. . . . Physic-ally, the difference was in the plant material used. . . . Certainly no Italian parterre of 16th or French of the 17th century disposed of such masses of vivid colour. . . .'

The detail of Nesfield's work was, in short, repulsive, and he was one of those responsible for that disagreeable kind of gardening known as 'bedding out'. He may have come, too, under the pernicious German influence in the later part of his career. . . . 'The masses of pure colour drilled among heavy defences of holly and laurel.' However, Nesfield's lay-out was perfectly sound; all that later Kew gar-deners had to do was to get rid of the 'riot of colour' idea, and plant differently.

John Claudius Loudon a foot in each world The man of genius, and of incredible industry, who linked the Pope-Brown-Repton era to the era of high gardening, who linked art and science, who linked aesthetics and technics, was John Claudius Loudon. His remarkable wife was hardly less important in the history of gardening. Among other things Loudon was a garden designer, nurseryman, landscape artist, encyclopaedist, journalist and editor, natural historian, botanist, agronomist and architect. He founded and carried on *The Gardener's Magazine*. If I had to sum up his achievement as a gardener in one phrase, I should say that he contrived to embody the new science of gardening in the old art. He was more of a plantsman than a picture-gardener, but he had the knowledge, the taste, the eye so to use his plants that the pictorial was not smothered. His wife, a novelist twenty-four years younger than himself, killed herself by carrying on his work after his death in 1843. The most historically significant act of their joint lives was the writing and publishing, in 1838, of *The Suburban Gardener and Villa Companion*. The small burgess was displacing the gentleman in social importance, and the Loudons realized it. Many great gardens were still to be made; but in future the smaller owner was to be more important in the development of gardening.

Loudon was a Scot and the son of a farmer. Naturally studious and hard-working, he taught himself to draw, to speak and write French and Italian, and after his schooling was apprenticed to a nursery gardener. At the age of twenty he went to London and he seems there to have had the entrée to the Banks' circle. At this time, the end of the eighteenth century, Lowland Scottish farming was probably the most efficient in the world, whereas the English farmers were somewhat backward. Although Loudon was in poor health, and was to be more or less ill all his life, he set up a school for teaching good farming and made a success of it. This was at Tew Park in Oxfordshire. He sold out profitably in 1812 and went travelling in Europe but on his return found himself ruined by the failure of the firms in which he had invested his fortune. He thereupon set about writing his *Encyclopaedia*, at the same time travelling again, this time in south Europe.

At forty-seven he married Jane Webb who was twenty-three and whose science-fiction novel *The Mummy*, a vision of life in the twentieth century, was enjoying a certain success. They were, thereafter, one of those rare couples who in their working as in their domestic life are inseparable, in the manner of Sydney and Beatrice Webb, for example. Their suburban garden at Porchester Terrace in Bayswater set a standard for what the new suburban gardening could be. Loudon, and Mrs Loudon, while they respected the work of Repton, had no strong and fixed ideas about what a garden should be like: it depended on the situation, the owner's taste, the money available. They were, in short, forerunners of the new eclecticism and the new common sense, a quality very different from Pope's horticultural 'good sense' which was almost entirely a matter of good taste. Loudon defined what he called the 'gardenesque' style as the production of that kind of scenery which is best calculated to display the individual beauty of trees, shrubs and plants in a state of nature; the smoothness and greenness of lawns; and the smooth surfaces, curved directions, dryness and firmness of gravel walks; in short it is the style best calculated for displaying the art of the gardener. Here we have a very clear definition at last of what the great English gardens were to become after Robinson, at whose career we are yet to arrive, had had his say. The word gardenesque provides me, since it has been defined in the above quotation from Loudon himself, with a means of referring to the kind of gardens which were soon to come into existence, and I shall make use of it hereafter.

Loudon was good at definitions: I think he needed to put clearly into words all the concepts he worked with; he had a very tidy mind. He seems to have been the first garden writer to state, unequivocally and in so many words, what was meant by the term 'English garden', which by that time had a definite meaning for foreigners; yet it was far from clearly defined, for Loudon says that what the words conveyed was: '. . . a vague general idea . . . of grounds and plantations formed in flowing lines in imitation of nature'. This seems to me equatable, to some extent at least, with his own definition of 'picturesque' gardening: '. . . the production in country residences of that kind of scenery which, from its strongly-marked features is considered as particularly suitable for being represented by painting'. It was, of course,

Mrs Loudon

more than that, if it be true that the English gardeners were, in fact, doing with plants and earth and water, what French *paysagistes* were doing with mere paint.

But with his neologism 'gardenesque' we are on the way – well on the way – to the 'English garden' of the English dream, the re-created paradise. It might be described as a style which was contrived to reconcile plantsmanship and the garden designer's art. But it can, and I think should, be put the other way round: plantsmanship and garden design were growing together towards the accomplishment of the ideal. But Loudon meanwhile was no bigot in any style, readily admitting the validity of several others, such as 'the geometric or architectural'. The style you favoured should depend on the site, the location, and the limitations of your skill and resources. It is in this catholic spirit that all the English gardeners, with the exception of the greatest, have worked, and still work.

One of the great strengths, as it was likewise one of the weaknesses, of the Victorian in all the arts, was vulgarity. Vulgarity is good because it is exuberant. Out of its copious productiveness men of a later and less excitable, less energetic generation, use taste to select what is good. Loudon, between two epochs, was an eighteenth-century man of taste as well as being a nineteenth-century man of science and business, a Victorian *avant la lettre*. Although he was as productive as a Victorian, most of what he did, or advocated in his voluminous writings, was modified by a natural intellectual elegance, even severity. Those who followed him had less of this quality, and sometimes lacked it altogether. Nevertheless, their services to gardening were enormous. Miles Hadfield (in op. cit.) says of a villa garden that he chooses as typical albeit outstanding for this period: 'The defect of the "Lawrencian villa" was its lack of repose: "the brilliancy of the flowers, the immense number of statues and vases, and the sparkling waters of the various cascades, produced an effect perfectly dazzling". This failing, indeed, makes the garden typical of the period, when elegance and some restraint, still advocated by Loudon, were beginning to fall away before the "perfectly dazzling", triumphantly sponsored by that young Proteus later to become Sir Joseph Paxton.'

The Lawrencian garden a riot of colour

The garden in question, whose owner Mrs Lawrence was also its designer and maker, and the greatest amateur of her day, showered with Horticultural Society awards and medals, had 3,266 varieties (not botanical varieties) of garden plants; it had greenhouses, forcing pits, compost and manure pits, and representations of every kind of gardening. No doubt it was admirable; it must also have been appalling, an early version of that 'riot of colour' which, to my mind, is the ruin of a garden.

A principal cause of the increase in plant material, more and more of which became available as time went on, was that rich industrialists, as well as the nobility and gentry, spent lavishly on their gardens. This period, too, produced the specialists, the tulip-fanciers who spent thousands on bulbs in a decade; the first alpine garden enthusiasts; the first orchid-fanciers and creators of that bonanza in orchid collecting which, according to Professor Kupper, actually led to the extinction of some species in the east and in South America.

The Royal Horticultural Society

Something more must be said of the Horticultural Society, whose example was followed on a smaller scale until there were thousands of such societies throughout the British Isles, the Empire and the United States, and many even in Europe. It was founded in 1804 by seven men: John Wedgwood, son of the great potter; Sir Joseph Banks, the pundit of science; Charles Greville, politician, courtier and connoisseur of all good things including exotic plants; William Forsyth, head gardener to George III; W.T.Aiton, Curator of Kew; R.A.Salisbury, the botanist and a notable gardener; James Dickson, nurseryman and seedsman and himself a creative gardener. Their Society was chartered in 1809, started its first experimental garden in 1818, and by the end of the century was a rich, respected and rather solemn learned society which had entered the company of those national institutions which includes such diverse bodies as the House of Commons, the Athenaeum Club, the London Library and the Zoo.

The Gardens at Wisley

During the first hundred years of its life the Society's gardens were at Chiswick but in 1904 this suburban situation was abandoned, for there was no room for expansion. Sir Thomas Hanbury had recently given the Society a small estate, in trust. This was a property of sixty acres at Wisley in Surrey, and there are the gardens of the Royal Horticultural Society as we know them now. It will be getting a little ahead of ourselves but will be otherwise convenient to deal with them here. Six acres only were under cultivation, mostly as a Wild Garden. In course of time more land was bought and at the present time the gardens cover about two hundred acres. The Wild Garden in question here had been created in the seventies by a former owner, George Wilson of Weybridge, a famous amateur gardener in his day, and Treasurer of the Society. Hanbury bought the estate when Wilson died and made it over to the Society on certain terms. The terms of this Trust define the Society's obligations at Wisley, they are:

To maintain a garden where Fellows of the Society and others may see growing
as full a range of ornamental plants as possible.
To carry out research work in horticulture and related sciences.
To provide advice to Fellows on horticultural problems.
To carry out trials of new varieties of flowers, fruit, and vegetables.
To train young gardeners in the theory and practice of horticulture.

There would be no point in dealing here with the scientific and educational side of the Society's work: it will be sufficient to say that it is of the first importance and that, for example, many thousands of Fellows' questions are dealt with by the scientific staff every year and an enormous number of trials of new varieties of plants are constantly in train. These trials, which result in new and improved stocks of every kind of garden plant being introduced into gardening every year, are of two kinds, called 'permanent' and 'invited'. The permanent trials are of established varieties planted in collections and of new varieties which, having been exhibited at the Society's London hall in Vincent Square and been picked out by the appropriate committee, have gone forward for trial at Wisley. An 'invited' trial is one to which Fellows, nurserymen and members of the gardening public are asked to send for trial seeds or plants of some chosen subject in a given year.

Of the features of Wisley gardens which are of the greatest importance at the present time, for their influence on garden design and management, the following have been picked out by members of the Wisley staff as outstanding.

The mixed borders

In nineteenth- and early twentieth-century garden practice, shrubberies were one thing and herbaceous borders another. This distinction has gone and not only have shrubs become by far the most important element of the new English garden, but it has been found possible and desirable to grow shrubs and perennial herbs together. Partly this has been a matter of garden economics, for example, it can be attributed to the shortage or high cost of garden labour. But also it is very much in the spirit of 'paradise' gardening, it is a kind of stylized version of wild gardening. The mixed borders at Wisley, one on either side of a path which leads south from the terrace towards Battleston Hill, are 140 yards long, 6 yards wide, backed by hornbeam hedges and separated by a grass walk 36 feet wide. The shrubs of these borders have been selected as being particularly suitable for growing with herbaceous perennials which are set among them. The shrubs, incidentally, include roses, always a problem to gardeners who still plant them under the illusion that they must have a place to themselves; here they are treated like any other flowering shrubs, and are the better for it.

Battleston Hill

Battleston Hill is a fine example of and model for woodland gardening. The trees are Scots pine, oak, sweet chestnut and birch; in 1937 the undergrowth of these was cleared and the whole area planted with rhododendrons, and at other, later times this planting has been extended. The plantings were not solely of rhododendrons; other flowering shrubs have been included in order to show how the flowering season of such a garden can be lengthened and how, too, they can be made to provide the right conditions for the rhododendrons. The latter are for the most part hardy hybrids which have been awarded the Society's First Class Certificate or Award of Merit. Underplantings include a great variety of the narcissus family and there are representatives of hydrangea, fuchsia, potentilla, and hypericum among the shrubs. Lilies, too, are grown here in conditions which suit them well, hostas are used in the shady parts and, where the sun strikes most of the day, agapanthus.

A problem which is faced by the gardeners at Wisley is that while it is necessary, to fulfil the purposes of the Society, to plant collections of species almost in the manner of a botanical garden but using garden rather than wild plants, it is also desirable to demonstrate the best ways of planting for orna-ment: it is an extreme case of trying to reconcile plantsmanship and garden design. On the whole the problem is solved satisfactorily; but it sometimes becomes insoluble as, for example, on that part of Battleston Hill where a collection of rhododendron species designed to display the variety and horti-cultural range of this genus has been planted, underplanted with a variety of lily species and hybrids. It is an important and valuable demonstration, but it is not quite gardenesque, so to speak. And the same problem recurs as, for example, in the flowering-cherry field beyond Battleston, approached by an avenue of *Prunus yedonensis*: it is necessary to enable Fellows to compare species and varieties, and to do so they must be more or less all in one place and not, as would be the case in a garden, used, perhaps in groups, but mingled with very different genera.

Another use of this kind of planting of shrubs and trees at Wisley is to display the crosses made at Wisley and, after trial, put into commerce; for this garden is a source of good garden plants (that is, plants which grow well and easily under a wide range of different garden conditions), in great number and for the whole gardening world of the temperate zones. (It is significant that American nurserymen covet the First Class Certificate or the Award of Merit for their plants above all other distinctions, since they are of very real value in the United States.)

The rose borders　The most important flowering shrub in gardening, now as in the past, is the rose. The revival of the taste for what are called shrub roses, that is, roses which make a large and shapely plant which can be treated as a 'shrub' and put into mixed plantings, is discussed in its place; but the hybrid tea roses, and similar kinds, roses which produce very beautiful flowers but which are not shapely as shrubs and which cannot be subjects of shrub-gardening properly so called because of the hard pruning which they demand and because of their stiff and ungraceful bearing, are still the most important of all. At Wisley they are growing in two very large rose borders which contain a representative collection of both established old varieties and the best of the new ones. These borders undergo a kind of slow and unchecked change, as old varieties which are superseded by better ones with the same general character are replaced. Fellows of the Society visiting these borders at the appropriate season can, therefore, make a choice of the roses they would prefer to have in their own gardens. A border of hardy and half-hardy annuals is maintained in the same spirit; so are the model fruit gardens and the fruit tree trials which need not be noticed here.

The Rock Garden　A relatively modern development in English gardening, imitated all over the world, is that of rock gardening. It is derived from the work of collectors sending back plants and seeds from the flora of mountain systems all over the world, the flora which are to be found between the upper limit of the tree line, and the lower limit of perpetual snow. Mountain climates being what they are, even moun-tains in the sub- and full-tropics yield species which may be hardy in Britain. Modern rock gardening is practised in the same 'paradise' spirit as woodland or gardenesque gardening. That is to say, an attempt is made to reproduce a natural alpine landscape in miniature, but to improve upon nature by the bringing together of species which, in the wild, live very remote from each other. This is an enor-mous advance upon the old 'rockery' gardening in which a heap of stones was assembled more or less anyhow, and planted, chiefly with ferns, producing an effect as hideous as it was unnatural. The Rock

Plate 77　Garden as we now have it at its best is based on stone very carefully selected and laid out to simulate a natural outcrop, water, usually with one or several cascades, and the use of alpine bulbs, shrubs and herbaceous perennials. It is by far the most exacting and recondite form of gardening, for the skill and knowledge required to persuade alpine plants to flourish, plants which are in nature confined to very special and local conditions, is great. Many of these plants, for example, seem poised in a scree of pure stone, yet have their roots constantly in slowly moving underground water. Others depend absolutely on almost precise amounts of snow lasting for a definite period of time. The fascination and difficulties of this kind of gardening have given rise to a special class of gardeners, with their own Society, their own journals and their own shows. Many of them cultivate their difficult and exquisite alpine plants in pans under glass, and in this sub-class of the art, gardening is reduced simply to the expert and very specialized appreciation of a small class of plants for their own sake. But alpine gardening at its best is a form of 'paradise' gardening. The Edinburgh Botanic Gardens have the most nearly perfect Alpine garden, but Wisley caters for the alpine gardener first of all with an Alpine House which displays a representative collection of these difficult plants perfectly grown; secondly, in the Rock Garden; thirdly, in the Alpine Meadow garden.

The Alpine or Rock Garden consists of a broad path winding between what look like natural hills of worn sandstone but what are, in fact, artefacts. The area was landscaped by a well-known practitioner, Edward White. Steps and smaller, winding and rising paths lead about among the rocks, so that the plants set here may be seen easily and the conditions in which they are growing inspected closely. In the rock garden the combining of pure gardening and instructional or demonstration gardening has been more successful than in any part of the Wisley gardens where it has been attempted. And the merging of the Rock Garden proper into the Alpine Meadow has been so successfuly contrived 'after nature' that the two gardens do seem part of a single, Alpine landscape. The Alpine Meadow, as its name implies, is an attempt to reproduce one of those high-mountain meadows which, in Switzerland or Savoy in the month of May, or for that matter in parts of the New Zealand Alps, or the high Himalaya, or probably the Andes in the equivalent season, are gemmed with the small bulb flowers of many genera and with primulas and their allies. The use of grass where it will not naturally remain short is, however, a difficulty. Not in the Wisley gardens, but elsewhere, it was brilliantly overcome by Clarence Elliot who substituted our native and very prostrate thyme for grass. The water of the Rock Garden streams is carried down to the water garden known as the Long Pond.

Wilson's original Wild Garden, basically oak and birch growing in a moist peaty soil, has been kept. But of course it has been added to and time has changed it. Exotic conifers which enjoy these conditions, and a whole range of ericaceous plants such as pieris, enkianthus, vaccineum and gaultheria have been set under the trees, also magnolias and rhododendrons, camellias in variety and such newcomers to the woodland garden as *Metasequoia glyptostroboides*, known only as a fossil of fifty million years ago until a live stand of these trees was discovered in Central China in 1947. Groundling plants able to naturalize themselves have likewise been added to the Wild Garden, notably wood anemones and many kinds of Dog's-tooth violets so-called. Here, too, our native ferns are collected both to beautify the garden and to demonstrate their use in a branch of gardening.

The Wild Garden

A collection of heaths and heathers in great variety, garden selections, hybrids and wild forms, is gathered into the part of the gardens known as the Seven Acres, where there is also a collection of conifer species in diverse forms. This is combined with a display of the deciduous trees which are best for autumn foliage-colour and for the winter colour of the bark of several genera. Here, again, demonstration and pure gardening have been quite successfully combined.

In the Pinetum, on the other hand, this combination has inevitably been less successful. This is for obvious and unavoidable reasons a collection for comparative study by the Fellows of the Society. As such it is a sort of living index of conifers which can be of use in the garden.

There are parts of the gardens which might almost bear a date label, but not because Wisley is run in the spirit of a museum; it is not. It happens to be convenient to gather together the principal hardy perennial herbaceous ornamental plants into the two long Herbaceous Borders; there they can be seen and noted by Fellows who, however, are unlikely to grow them in quite the same way, who are more likely to plant the kinds they choose in mixed borders with shrubs, or even as decoration to a wild garden. The borders might well be labelled Early Twentieth Century. But such borders are still to be seen in some English gardens. The Glasshouses, Stove and Orchid Houses too smack of the rich gardens of the late Victorian epoch; but if hardly any gardener can now afford 'a whole village of glasshouses', the automating of greenhouses by the use of electricity has revived interest in tender plants and the Wisley houses cater for the special interests of, for example, orchid collectors.

These gardens, then, have grown out of the rise to prosperity of what was originally an exclusive Learned Society and now has over sixty thousand Fellows. And it is important that the RHS grew fast and fat, because it disposed of money which was needed for plant collecting in many parts of the world. Their first successful collector was a gardener named Macrae who sent home hot-house plants from South America. North American plants were of much greater interest, especially those which came from the north Pacific coast whose climate resembles our own. Archibald Menzies, surgeon to George Vancouver during the latter's voyage of discovery and exploration round the world, was a sound botanist and he had brought home herbarium material from North-West America. The Horti-cultural Society employed James Douglas to go to California and adjoining regions to collect seeds of Menzies' plants, and anything else of interest.

Plant collectors Douglas had worked at the Glasgow Botanic Gardens under the great W.J.Hooker and the then curator, William Murray; these two gentlemen recommended the Horticultural Society to send him abroad. He was clever, brave and methodical; he made a series of remarkable journeys of exploration and plant-collecting until he was killed by a wild bull in Hawaii in 1834. One plant of his collecting, *Mahonia aquifolia*, having become a naturalized wilding in Britain, now figures as part of our own flora. Douglas gave us, among other things, clarkia, the scented (since become scentless) musk, the ornamental currant, and *Garrya eliptica*. The Douglas Fir was named after him to whom we also owe many abies, thujas and the Sitka spruce among our trees.

In due course not only the Horticultural Society, but rich individuals, and the great nursery firms, were employing collectors in many parts of the world. A tea broker named Reeves who lived and gardened in Macao sent us the Chinese paeonies, camellias and some azalias. The brothers Lobb, employed by the famous house of Veitch, were responsible for numerous introductions.

As early as 1772 Kew sent Francis Masson to collect plants in the Cape of Good Hope province. And in 1880 Kew, in collaboration with a well-known botanist, Sir James Smith, sent John Frazer, a draper who had acquired a knowledge and love of plants by frequenting the Chelsea Physic garden, to North America. Douglas, mentioned above, came after him in that fertile field. For Japanese plants, both cultivated and wild, English gardens owed most to a German, Philip von Siebold, whose name is commemorated in such plants as bear the specific name *sieboldii*. The Lobbs, working for Veitch of Exeter, I have already mentioned; their plant-country was Chile but William Lobb also collected for the same great firm in North-West America.

Robert Fortune Robert Fortune, first of the really great collectors to become known by name outside the closed circle of the Higher Gardening, was a Scot born in 1812, who received training at the Botanic Garden at Edinburgh and in the Horticultural Society's garden at Chiswick. The Society sent him to China and from that country he introduced some of the finest plants now in English gardens. But he did some-thing even more important by introducing the tea-shrub from China to the hill country of India whence it was introduced to Ceylon, thus founding an enormously important industry and changing the gastronomic habits of several nations.

Other collectors for Veitch should be mentioned: John Gould Veitch himself worked in the Far East sending plants to his firm and later in the century Charles Maries, born in Stratford-on-Avon, was working the same field for the same firm: to him we owe, among other things, *Hammamelis mollis*, the beautiful Chinese witch-hazel. E.H.Wilson first visited China under the aegis of Veitch and Son; he had had forerunners in the Indo-Chinese collecting field, two Frenchmen, Delavay and Farges; and the Irishman Augustine Henry. The latter was in fact responsible for Wilson's career, for he had sent herbarium material of *Davidia involucrata* to Kew and it was to fetch seeds of this plant that Veitch sent Wilson to China. He went through hideous dangers and atrocious hardships, and it was at the frequent risk of his life that he sent back not only Davidia seeds, but seeds of many other species. The great line of Wilson-Farrer-Forrest (of rhododendron fame) was carried into the forties of our own century by the late F. Kingdon-Ward whose collectings were innumerable and of the greatest interest; the last of his great introductions was the lovely Manipur lily (*L. macklinae*). And we still have collectors at work, notably Oleg Polunin.

The later collectors were simply enriching a store of plant material which, long before their dates, had become perfectly adequate for the creation of the 'Robinsonian' garden. But before coming to that manifestation of progress towards the English paradise garden, it will be necessary to go back a little and consider another gardener of genius.

Joseph Paxton was probably the most remarkable man whom the science, rather than the art, of gardening has produced. He was born into the working class in 1801; his childhood and adolescence were very wretched, yet somehow he contrived to educate himself and his real career began when he got work in the Chiswick experimental gardens of the Horticultural Society. There he made up his mind to emigrate to the United States; there can be no doubt that had he done so he would have become one of the great tycoons of the mid-nineteenth century era of rapid development. Meanwhile, while waiting to accumulate a little capital no doubt, Paxton was put in charge of the arboretum. The Society's landlord in Chiswick was the Duke of Devonshire, he often visited the gardens, and he came to know and respect the young arboretum foreman. When, on the eve of a journey abroad, the Duke found himself short of a head gardener for Chatsworth, he offered Paxton the job (£6 a month and a cottage). Paxton, then twenty-five, accepted. At thirty-seven, after having made Chatsworth the most famous garden in the world, he was offered £1,000 a year (say £7,000 of our money), to become head gardener at Windsor Castle; he refused the offer.

In his transformation of Chatsworth, Paxton earned the approval of all but Loudon. He was wholeheartedly a scientific, even a mechanical, gardener. He became, in the course of his gardening, an architect, a village-planner and builder, a company director, a Member of Parliament and the designer of that 1851 Exhibition Hall of steel and glass which subsequently became known as the Crystal Palace. I have read that the structural principle of that building, forerun by the great greenhouse which he built at Chatsworth, was suggested to him by the structure of the leaf of the great *Victoria amazonica* water-lily. Paxton was knighted; he ceased to be a gardener; this left nothing of real interest for him to do, so he died. He had made the most remarkable garden in the world by technical skill, industry, business management efficiency; and without taste. The gardens modelled on his style might, indeed they did, *épater*; but what Paxton contributed to gardening lore were ingenious contrivance, a sort of horticultural engineering, and a number of new orchids.

The first great gardener after Loudon to recombine art and science, to make use of the whole past to open the way into the future of English gardening, was William Robinson, the creator of Gravetye and the part-creator of the English garden as it is now.

It is, I believe, in Robinson's work that the English dream garden, the paradise as improved by man, the Domain of Arnheim as conceived by Poe's Mr Ellison, has its first clear realization. For what, often very unsuccessfully, Robinson was to try and do once he had put himself into a satisfactorily prosperous state to afford it, was to 'naturalize' into an English landscape plants more spectacular than any which the native temperate flora could furnish. This is by no means to create a paradise; it is, quite often, to create a mess. Before the paradise gardens could be made it was necessary to go a step farther, to cease from trying merely to embellish, after carefully ordering the natural scene, and to create, 'after' nature but according to art.

Robinson was born in 1838 in Ireland. His parents were Protestants, obscure and poor. Nothing is known of his boyhood, until he became gardener's boy to a clerical baronet of the Ascendancy. By the

Joseph Paxton

Plate 82

William Robinson

age of twenty-one Robinson was in charge of the gardens. He left the job in the most extraordinary circumstances, after conduct which has never been explained. According to Geoffrey Taylor in his *Some Nineteenth Century Gardeners*, one night in the bitter winter of 1861 Robinson opened all the lights of his employer's hot-houses, drew the fires and bolted for Dublin. This can only have been in revenge for some wrong, real or fancied, done to him; it shows the passionate temper which was to be troublesome to his associates during a large part of his life. It is significant that David Moore of Glasnevin did not hesitate to send Robinson to London with a recommendation to Marnock, Curator of the Botanic Gardens in Regent's Park. Moore must have known of Robinson's fantastic act of sabotage; but he must also have known that Robinson had somehow been provoked to it. Marnock, a friend of Loudon's, gave the young man a job in the herbaceous section of the gardens. The plants in it were all natives and one of Robinson's tasks was to collect specimens. In the course of so doing he conceived a passion for the English countryside and above all for the simple cottage-type garden. Out of this passion arose his vision: he saw a garden in which nature, so mild and lovely in England, should not be coerced and deformed, but aided and abetted to do her best by the planting of suitable exotics not merely in but, as it were, *into* the native scene. The result, at its most glorious, and beyond Robinson's own achievement, can be seen in such gardens as Mount Usher, Castlewellan, Caerhays, Lochinch, Bodnant, Knightshayes, Garinish Island and Trengwainton.

Robinson's 'Alpine flowers'

Meanwhile, Robinson was educating himself; he learnt to speak and read French, and was sent to Paris as representative of both Veitch and *The Times* for the great Exhibition. Later, he made other visits to France, notably to the alpine provinces. He had learnt to write excellent English prose; his first book was *Alpine Flowers for English Gardens*. Presumably he learnt botanical Latin, for he was elected a Fellow of the Linnaean Society. In 1870, the year his first book was published, he went to America. On his return he wrote *The Wild Garden*, in which his vision, the native scene embellished with suitable hardy exotics, was expounded.

Meanwhile, and with this same vision always before him, he missed no opportunity to attack the formal garden schoolmen to whom Loudon, a man of broader vision and less passionate temper, had always conceded some virtue. Above all, he campaigned against Paxtonism, against 'bedding-out', against all that kind of horticulture which he damned as 'pastry-work gardening'. Miles Hadfield (in op. cit.) says, however, that Robinson was not, at least at first, an extremist; and that his watchword was Pope's Good Sense.

Robinson's journals

Next, Robinson started two gardening journals; *The Garden* (1871) a lavish glossy with fine colour-plates and contributions from some of the brilliant amateurs who were beginning to practise Robinsonism; and *Gardening Illustrated* (1879) for small gardeners. The latter is still in being as part of the *Gardener's Chronicle*, the trade paper of the professional gardener and now in its 122nd year. Probably no journal has contributed so much of value to gardening in Britain as the *Gardener's Chronicle*: it was founded by Joseph Paxton and Bradley, the publisher of *Punch*, and its first editor was Professor Lindley. Its present editor, Roy Hay, has had the extremely difficult task of retaining both the old professional trade interest; the scientific integrity; and, in order to survive, of appealing to the amateur gardener. In this he has succeeded; the paper is still the best weekly in the field. For many years Robinson's *Gardening Illustrated* was its rival for both public support and advertising revenue; united, they should stand a few more centuries. It is significant as evidence for the triumph of English gardening heralded by the foundation of these two magazines, that one of the mass circulation French weeklies employs Mr Hay to write its gardening article; just as, for twenty years, the greatest of the French nurseries, Vilmorin-Andrieux, employed a distinguished English artist, Russel Page, as their garden designer. From the beginning, *Gardening Illustrated* made money for Robinson, which *The Garden* proceeded to lose for him.

Like all men of genius Robinson had chosen the right time to be born. We have seen that plant collectors were pouring new plant material into England; that the RHS had become a power in the land; that the great nurseries were rising to their zenith; but furthermore, there were many rich men still and more than ever ready to spend huge sums on making gardens; and labour costs were very low. They were going to rise soon, and to make the kind of very elaborate gardening which entailed the employment of scores of gardeners, of 'whole parishes' as Jane Austen put it, quite out of the question. And it was at this juncture that Robinson was ready with his vision, the garden which did not require anything like so many men to maintain it. In two other ways Robinson showed that he was indeed a man of genius: he never lost sight of the source of his vision, the cottage garden; and he contrived to meet the right collaborator, Gertrude Jeckyll.

It seems to me that in this necessarily sketchy history, I have not paid nearly enough regard to women in English gardening. But it is always so: men make so much more noise about their achievements: in gardening, as in other fields, it is sometimes a case of much cry little wool; while women get quietly on with the weeding and other necessary tasks and by a suggestion here, a tactful hint there put the man who is to become famous on the right course. Mrs Lawrence, Mrs Loudon and others were as important as any of the men I have mentioned and I suspect that in the very beginning it was a woman who started the whole thing, some pre-historic food-gathering matron who saw the advantage of transplanting food plants to her own backyard instead of traipsing all over the place in search of its fruits. And surely it was a woman who first suggested having a few flowers among the beans and cabbages.

Gertrude Jeckyll

Gertrude Jeckyll was a gentlewoman of education and culture. She learnt her wild flowers, her native shrubs and trees, in childhood, much of which she spent in solitary but happy wanderings out of doors, while indoors she lived in a household where the arts were loved and practised and taught. She became a painter, she travelled, she learnt and practised several of the fine crafts. She met Robinson, and she agreed with his ideas, shared his vision at least in its broad outlines. She set about making a Robinsonian garden in Surrey and she started contributing to *The Garden* whereby her name became known and her ideas respected. Finally, she began to design gardens. Her influence on Robinsonism, though not on Robinson, was salutary; she checked its excesses; she was severe in selecting only the best from the over-abundance of new plants; she had a unique talent, which was wanting in Robinson himself, for selecting also the right colours to marry with the native scene of woodland and water which was her chosen, but not her only, canvas.

Anti-Robinson

Since Robinson, that passionate visionary, was incapable of measure, it is fortunate that there were other men interested in gardening who could write almost as persuasively as himself and who defended the formal garden in some of its best aspects; had this not been so it might, when the time came to make the perfect 'English' garden at last, have been necessary to rescue the formal traditions from obscurity. As it was, they were never lost sight of. Thus an architect, J. D. Sedding, did a great service to the future by writing his *Garden-craft Old and New*; another of the same profession reintroduced a formal, Italianate element into his gardens out of his own love for old Italian gardens; this was H. A. Peto who was employed by Ramond l'Estrange Bryce to design the very beautiful gardens of Garinish Island in West Cork, still one of the most nearly perfect of 'English' gardens. Reginald Blomfield's *The Formal Gardens in England* would have been chosen by me as the most effective anti-Robinsonian blast; but Mr Hadfield's criticism (in op. cit.) of this book has revealed an unsoundness which I confess I had not realized.

Gertrude Jeckyll herself was the first Robinsonian to concede something to the opposition and so to wed formalism to naturalism: she shared the designing of her own house and garden at Munstead with Sir Edwin Lutyens. Lutyens also had a hand in another garden of this period, which was a product of Gertrude Jeckyll's modified Robinsonism, Nathaniel Lloyd's Great Dixter.

Notes on the Plates

66 KEW GARDENS

A view of the great Palm House built by Decimus Burton.

67, 68 KEW GARDENS

Laid out in the seventeenth and eighteenth centuries, Kew, although it became a scientific botanical garden as early as George III's reign, had the benefit of being created in the Age of Taste. Many of the great garden designers and architects worked in it. Time has rid us of the least attractive 'follies' and left only the best of them. Plate 67 shows the Temple of Aeolus, plate 68 the Temple of Bellona.

69 ROYAL BOTANIC GARDEN, EDINBURGH

The Edinburgh Botanic Garden owes the wealth and lushness of its vast range of exotic plants, especially Alpine genera, in part to the superior genius of Scots gardeners, but in part also to a humidity of climate to which this picture bears witness.

70 KEW GARDENS

The Pagoda is one of the few remaining features of Kew Gardens attributable to Sir William Chambers, whose *Dissertation on Oriental Gardening* however was more chinoiserie than real Chinese.

71 ROYAL BOTANIC GARDEN, EDINBURGH

One of the New Zealand tree-ferns, seen from the gallery of the Palm House. In Cornwall some of these tree-ferns grow in the open (plate 146).

72 KEW GARDENS

The Temple of Aeolus (plate 67).

73 ROYAL BOTANIC GARDEN, EDINBURGH

The Palm House at Edinburgh has not the beauty of Decimus Burton's at Kew (plate 66). The gardens were started in 1670. Their greatest contribution to horticulture has probably been in the cultivation of Alpine rock-garden plants; and in the study and ordering of the great genus rhododendron. The tree in the foreground is a viburnum.

74 ROYAL BOTANIC GARDEN, EDINBURGH

Bronze reclining woman by Henry Moore on the lawn outside the Scottish Museum of Modern Art, formerly the Curator's house.

75 ROYAL BOTANIC GARDEN, EDINBURGH

The city from the Rock Garden. This Rock Garden is one of the largest and probably the best in the world. It was designed and started in 1908 by Sir Isaac Bayley Balfour.

76 ROYAL BOTANIC GARDEN, EDINBURGH

The Pool. The woodland, pool, heath and rock gardens at Edinburgh compose a better representation of the romantic paradise garden than is to be found in any other botanic garden.

77 ROYAL HORTICULTURAL SOCIETY'S GARDENS, WISLEY

The Rock Garden. Wisley has been of more importance than any other in the trial, improvement and ordering of plant material for the English garden.

78 CHATSWORTH

Chatsworth is the principal seat of the Dukes of Devonshire. The gardens as they now are were first planned at the end of the seventeenth century by the 3rd Earl and in 1688 the 1st Duke called in George London to execute his own and his father's plans for improvement.

79 CHATSWORTH

By 1700 Chatsworth was already famous for waterworks.

80 CHATSWORTH

Both this and plate 78 are views from the main terrace of the House.

81 CHATSWORTH

Water, placid or playing, was always of primary importance at Chatsworth. In 1700 Dr Leigh was writing of it: 'The gardens, very delightful, pleasant and stately, adorn'd with exquisite waterworks; the first we observe is Neptune with his sea-nymphs from whence, by the turning of a cock, immediately issue forth several columns of water. . . .' The south façade of the House.

82 CHATSWORTH

Chatsworth and its waterworks. Jan Sieberecht's painting of the 1st Duke's house and garden from the east. The painting is in the collection of Lord Sandys at Omberly Court. *Photo copyright 'Country Life'.*

83 CHATSWORTH

Head of the Staircase of the water cascade viewed from the temple in the foreground of Sieberecht's painting (plate 82). Not everyone admired this magnificence: thus Mrs Thrale, writing of Shenstone's more natural garden at Leasures,

> From Kedlestone's offensive glare
> From Chatsworth's proud cascade
> From artful Hagley I repair
> To thine and nature's shade . . .

70

71

72

73

74

75

80

81

82

English Gardens Now

In the preceding pages we have sketched, briefly, the origins and traditions which went to the making of English gardens into the nineteenth century. The intention now is to describe and display a certain number of gardens which can safely be called representative of the ideal, the paradise so long sought and worked towards: representative, however, of styles and methods and skill, but in no sense 'average', for each is an outstanding example of its kind. Here, however, several points should be made and emphasized: the number of superb gardens in England, Scotland and Wales is so large that it would be impossible to display them in less than a dozen volumes as large as this one. It has been necessary to leave out very many gardens which are quite as fine, of their kind, as those which we have included. But if a man knows the gardens we have included, then he knows what modern English gardens are like, which is what chiefly matters. We have also made an attempt to get away, again briefly, from the 'great' gardens, gardens vast in extent as well as superlative in execution, and to show how the smaller English gardens, the gardens of the village, of the suburb, even of the city, have likewise been given their twentieth-century character by the work of the five preceding centuries.

The great gardens of Britain today are, very roughly, of three kinds. In the first place there are the museum pieces – the words are used in no denigratory sense – the gardens of the eighteenth century which are preserved in their original form, as far as that is possible in a work of art whose materials are alive and growing: with some of these we have already dealt and we shall not return to them. Next there are the gardens, the most important class now, in which a balance is struck, in style, between anti-Robinsonism and Robinsonism, between the earlier, formal or Italianate styles, and the less formal, wilder garden. Such gardens might very well be considered as a tribute to the memory of Loudon and his sensible, catholic taste. Thirdly, there are the woodland gardens, in some ways the most romantic, the nearest to the 'paradise' of the English dream, gardens in which plants, for the most part shrubs, of the most gorgeous and exotic beauty, are so set as to simulate a 'natural' woodland scene, although in nature no such plants are found growing all together. Such gardens are the product of two influences, that of the great plantsmen and plant-collectors; and that of Robinson's *The Wild Garden*. We shall come to them in their place.

Of the great, relatively modern gardens of mixed styles but complete integrity, the most important, artistically, and to some extent also botanically but that is less interesting in the broad context of 'aesthetic' horticulture, is Hidcote Manor. For this garden set a style, created, out of its success, a number of rules which could be followed, with interesting local variations, in other gardens.

Let us first glance, very briefly, at the position of gardening in general at the time when Lawrence Johnston began to make Hidcote Manor gardens.

Robinson's own garden had been made at Gravetye in Sussex. The house was derelict when he bought it. As for the garden, he went at it with such passionate impatience that garden historians are now a little apt to shrug their shoulders over his goings-on. I, for one, understand and sympathize; I believe that Robinson was one of those men who are haunted by a keen and frightening sense of the passage of time: *ars longa* is true in a special and distressing way in the garden, for no man's lifetime is long enough to enable him to accomplish what he sees in his imagination's eye; the painter can finish a picture, the novelist his trilogy; the gardener, dependent on the rate at which his plants grow, cannot finish his garden. When Robinson had vast quantities of earth moved, when he planted fully grown trees, when he planted not a few hundred bulbs to increase naturally, but bulbs by the hundred thousand, he was trying to make a garden as he envisaged it within what remained of his lifetime. It is, of course, folly; I share in it. Why, gardeners begin to wonder, was Robinson such a great figure in the history of gardening? His success as a gardener in practice was not comparable with Loudon's, Paxton's, Jeckyll's; he failed as a farmer; he was rude, noisy, impatient, extravagant and arrogant. What of it? There are men who cannot but strive to realize their vision; there are others, more fortun-ate, who manage to envisage no more than they can accomplish and are not driven to strive to do too much. But it is the first who persuade the second to envisage anything at all. Arthur Young, in the related field of agriculture, had a vision of what farming should be; he failed dismally as a farmer, he was a chronic bankrupt, but he transformed the whole of European farming for the better. I have not a shadow of doubt that Robinson was a great gardener.

Plant collectors, and the increasing number of breeders of new garden plants, were making it neces-sary, by the beginning of our own century, for gardening to borrow from another fine craft, dress-making, the device of annual fashion changes in order to absorb the energy of the craftsmen and women. The newest plants brought forward, and given an accolade by the RHS at its shows, displaced the older ones, not always because the new ones were really better, but simply because they were new. It was almost as necessary for the socially conscious gardener to have the newest hybrid rose, the latest bearded iris, as for the woman of fashion to have her waist in the socially, rather than the anatomically, correct place. The RHS Award of Merit system gave authority to a plant's claims for space in the garden, as the Society's system of awards to gardeners, the highest being the Victoria Medal of Honour, set a mark upon the gardening elect. But it is probably true to say that never have awards, both to plants and to men, been made with such consistent integrity.

There came a strong reaction against the man-made garden plants. It is true that they continued and still continue to be preferred by the majority of gardeners, and that they represent a magnificent achieve-ment; moreover, the process of creating them still continues, and lilies are, today, undergoing, chiefly at the hands of Jan de Graaff in Oregon and Dr Yates in New Zealand, the transformation which other genera, for example tulips, daffodils, rhododendrons, have long since undergone. But there were to be gardeners who began to see more grace, and above all more fitness for the 'natural' English garden even when modified by a measure of formalism, in the botanical species than in the garden hybrids; and if not in botanical species, then in the less spectacular hybrids. Men like Graham Thomas and Bertram Park in due course revived interest in the 'species' and the old shrub roses; species tulips became better garden form than the hybrids; as for rhododendrons, there exists a special class of shrub gar-deners, in some sort the cream of the cream of the horticultural cognoscenti, who have always rejected all but a few hybrids which contrive to look like botanical species. Great amateur artists in gardening, for example, the late Lady Nicolson (Victoria Sackville-West) who wrote a weekly column on gardening for the *Observer*, did most to propagate the new and sophisticated simplicity by setting the example of it in her own garden at Sissinghurst (see p. 164).

The achievement up to the time of Robinson's death, the progress towards a paradise, can, then, be summed up: the grip of alien, notably of Latin and Dutch influences had been broken; English designers and gardeners had discovered the rules of composing an aesthetically satisfying 'natural' landscape, whether on a large or small scale. They had made a start on the work of transforming this into a dream landscape, an ideal quite beyond unaided nature to attain, by the introduction of exotics into such frameworks. In the smaller garden they had learnt, or Miss Jeckyll had taught them, how to incorporate the element of 'folk' art in gardening, the native taste of the cottager, into more formal and larger gardens, by deducing craft rules from the results which the cottagers had accomplished empirically. Meanwhile the great nurseries, the Royal Botanic Gardens at Kew and the Botanical Gardens of Edinburgh and Dublin (Glasnevin) had accumulated, through the work of exploring plant collectors, a vast fund of plant material of exotic beauty. It remained to discover the art of using this, of introducing it into the English garden as it now was in such a way that the garden would not be a mere collection of plants but the materialization of the English dream, the paradise envisaged as possible but nowhere to be found in nature. This was to be the achievement of the late nineteenth and early twentieth centuries, and it is ironical that it was accomplished at the very moment when social and economic pressures were such that the art, no sooner perfected, had almost to be abandoned. The techniques perfected could be applied, certainly, in smaller gardens, the millions of gardens of the affluent society. But the millionaires of the new epoch were not to be the kind of men who make gardens. This, and not want of money or labour, is the real explanation of the fact that the making of great gardens has nearly come to an end. Many great gardens, final products of the progress I am here sketching in outline, were made in our century: Bodnant, Highdown, Sissinghurst, Great Dixter, Garinish Island and others – these are but a few of them. If I choose to begin with Hidcote and its maker Lawrence Johnston for special note, even before describing Nymans in Sussex, it is because it seems to me that no man ever came nearer to perfection in joining garden design – the architecture, the bone-structure of a garden – with plantsmanship and nature.

Major Johnston made two gardens, Hidcote in the Cotswolds and Serre de la Madone in the south of France. He began work on Hidcote in 1904. His material was a good old stone manor house, pleasantly accidented country, a cedar tree, and a stand of fine beeches. 'The master-plan was this. The rising land was levelled and ascended from time to time by flights of steps; it was enclosed by a variety of hedges, and formed into a series of geometrically designed gardens, each with its own delights such as gazebos or pleached limes. All are symmetrically placed on an axis with a clear vista through, ending in the piers of a fine gateway.

The emergence of the modern garden

'The valley was turned into a wild garden; a path winds above the stream which is shaded by rare trees, its banks planted with shrubs, lilies, primulas and other naturalized plants. This little valley diverges somewhat from the main axis of the vista, and it is in this broadening space that we see the true genius of design, for it is packed with a number of little hedged compartments into which one descends, each different and each a place of enchantment, to make one's exit into the valley.

'One broad, grassed vista closed by high hornbeam hedges goes as it were to unite both parts at right angles to the main axis; at its head one sees, through iron grilles, nothing but the sky. It is the sky too that one sees as one mounts up the main walk to the cedar – slowly, because of the continued diversions as one passes. When one at last goes through the terminating gateway into a grove of ilexes, there is suddenly disclosed that view to which I have referred: no less than the vale of Avon leading into that stretch of land in which lies the heart of Shakespeare's poetry. . . .'

Plate 116

Thus Miles Hadfield: it is impossible to improve on it.

Some of the most respectable critics of gardening as an art, if not always a fine art, consider this garden of Hidcote Bartrim Manor to be the master work of the twentieth century; and, as such, bringing together in itself an expression of all the principal styles and traditions of English gardening in a brilliantly successful combination.

Hidcote Manor

Hidcote Manor is in the Cotswolds, remote from any great city but conveniently near to those famous examples of English domestic architecture, Broadway and Chipping Campden. The manor house, itself, is a typical Cotswold house of its class, of the well-known golden-buff freestone, roofed with stone shingles, having a forecourt in front of it and, on one side, a chapel. The place stands in the middle of a home farm and there is a hamlet of thatched cottages. In 1905 when Lawrence Johnston bought the property there was no garden of any kind: there were fields, a specimen cedar which was and is exceptionally large and well-grown; two groups of fine beech trees. Nothing more. And it was not even an encouraging site for a garden; it stands high and is described as being wind-swept. It has no basic, natural 'shape' to suggest any particular treatment or line of development; the soil is heavy clay; it is cold, and as the late Victoria Sackville-West, having created a garden in somewhat similar conditions but a better climate, wrote of it, 'There was nothing in the way of old walls or hedges to afford protection', the protection which she herself had benefited from in the old walls of Sissinghurst Castle.

Lawrence Johnston's plan

Important to the design is the relief of the site which Johnston started with: from the great cedar which seems to have been used as a sort of starting point, the land rises at a steady slope to the ridge of an escarpment. Then it falls away again, shallowly at first, then steeply. Beside this broad, rising plot of fields, as they then were, is a little valley, parallel but descending, beginning roughly at the cedar, and with a stream at its bottom. This valley widens as it falls away.

The first task, after the artist had visualized what he wanted to do with this material, was one of earth-moving on a large scale: in the decade before the First World War it was still possible for a man of means to employ the labour necessary to such operations: at that time the operation entailed the employment of many hands, picks, shovels, horses and carts. The cost of labour has since risen by approximately 1000 per cent. Yet the claim that no man, nowadays, could 'afford' to make such a garden in such conditions as Hidcote, is almost certainly unjustified. The ingenious and efficient earth-moving equipment we now dispose of, costing, with the operator's skilled services, from £3 to £5 per hour, will do in each hour as much work as fifty labourers. The fact is that garden making on the scale undertaken by Lawrence Johnston is simply not in the *zeitgeist*. In 1905 all men were sure that the sun would rise tomorrow; in the second half of the same century many men doubt it.

Plate 119

Johnston cut the rising land from the cedar to the escarpment into a series of wide, level terraces. These were connected by flights of stone steps at each rise. These terraces were made upon a single straight line so that a vista clean through the garden would be possible. On each terrace Johnston planned to have one or more geometrically regular enclosures opening into the next; each terrace was hedged with some good hedging plant, or otherwise defined with shrubs or trees, such as pleached hornbeams. The vista through this rising series of gardens culminates in a stone-piered gateway closed by fine wrought-iron gates. From this the observer commands a tremendous view over the heart of England. From the cedar to the gateway was the main axis of the garden.

I have said that the little valley beside the rising sweep of land runs parallel with it: this is not absolutely true: it diverges from its nearest point at the cedar to its farthest at a point level with the gateway which terminates the vista along the principal axis. Thus the land between the two is a triangle with its height much greater than its base. Johnston linked the high garden with the valley by a series of small hedged enclosures each with its own theme, through which you descend into the valley. The valley itself was dealt with on strictly Robinsonian lines, that is, it was made into a wild or woodland garden by the planting of a discreetly chosen collection of exotics, from small bulbs and herbs, to exotic trees, some of them rare. The whole garden covers about ten acres so that it is not among the largest; yet so cunningly is it designed and contrived that it gives the impression of being much larger and however long you linger in it it is difficult to convince yourself that you have seen it all.

What sort of garden is this? Referring both to the very large range of exotic plants and to the success of the design as a whole, Miles Hadfield (in op. cit.) writes of it: 'Here the ancient worlds of China and the Mediterranean lie side by side as do, equally happily, those once bitter enemies nature and formality.'

As I have already suggested, then, a brilliantly successful combination of the two major and divergent garden styles, a success of the kind which was also achieved, a couple of decades later, at Dartington Hall (see below). But what about the components? If Hidcote, for all its striking originality as a work of horticultural art, clearly shows the influence of William Robinson in the valley, elsewhere it shows the influence of Gertrude Jeckyll. Reverting to Victoria Sackville-West's description of the garden: 'Would it be misleading to call Hidcote a cottage garden on the most glorified scale? It resembles a cottage garden, or rather a series of cottage gardens in so far as the plants grow in a jumble, flowering shrubs mingled with roses, herbaceous plants with bulbous subjects, climbers scrambling over hedges, seedlings coming up wherever they have chosen to plant themselves. Now in a real cottage garden, where limitations and very often the pattern – for example, the curve or the straightness of a path leading from the entrance gate to the front door – are automatically imposed upon the gardener, the charming effect is both restrained and inevitable. . . . It is very largely accidental. But in a big garden like Hidcote great skill is required to secure not only the success of the planting, but of the proportions which can best give the illusion of enclosure. . . .'

Plate 120

To my mind this passage is misleading. The fact that the way in which plants have been used at Hidcote is in the tradition of the English cottage garden, has no significance for the 'feel' and the significance of the garden as a whole. In detail, aspects of the cottage garden were, indeed, used by Johnston as by Gertrude Jeckyll; but only in the sense that architectural sculptors used, for example, the acanthus leaf or the grapevine as a motif, stylizing these forms to suit their purpose. It should never be overlooked that the unquestionable charm of the cottage garden was originally as fortuitous as the charm of a woodland glade. And that sophisticated gardeners who were far from being cottagers used the cottage garden as a motif in exactly the same way as they used a woodland glade as a motif; that is to say, that in so far as the cottager planted at random and achieved his effects by accident, his garden was a work of nature and not of art. There is nothing whatever unself-conscious about Hidcote – and is not the above description reminiscent of Chambers' idea of a 'Chinese' garden?

But there is an even more important difference between Hidcote, or rather the spirit of Hidcote, and the spirit of the cottage garden. This difference is a social one. An enormous gulf separates the spirit of Hidcote from the spirit of the cottage garden, and this is of such importance that I shall try to develop it and explain exactly what I mean by it.

The cottage garden, where it is not as it usually is nowadays, self-consciously such, can be seen to express a spirit of community; it was one of a number side by side in the hamlet; in it the gardener did not garden exactly as he pleased although he, often rather she, might give proper expression to his own taste in detail. He gardened first in competition with the neighbours but also, willy-nilly, in a sort of subconscious collaboration with them. 'Enclosed' is just what a real cottage garden never is: it belongs as much to the passing road as to the house, as much to the neighbours as to the owner; it is as much a part of the whole village or hamlet, or if it be isolated, of the countryside itself, as to the gardener who makes it. It is, in short, a 'folk' entity and harks back to a time when the community in which men have to live and are probably 'meant' to live was not obscured by the cult of the individual mind and spirit. The cottage garden is open and unsecret and it is as much a thing for people, a thing of use, as the house itself, or the furniture in the house. By a definition that was insisted upon first by Alexander Pope and, in our time, by Reyner Banham (see p. 60) the cottage garden is not a work of art.

Hidcote is; and not only is it a work of art, it is, for me, perhaps the supreme work of English garden art because it is so very enclosed, despite the openness and even barrenness of the site which Johnston had to struggle with; Hidcote is a secret garden, a stillness. I repeat a deliberately overstated point which I made at the beginning of this work: Hidcote is not meant to have any people in it any more than the beholder of a landscape painting is meant to get inside it. For practical purposes the English garden invariably has to compromise with the spirit in which it is conceived; there are, there have to be, steps at Hidcote from terrace to terrace, ways through from enclosure to enclosure, but it would almost be as well to pretend that they are not there and to insist upon ignoring the fact that you are using them. This garden is not a setting for man; it is something to contemplate but not to intrude upon; something to be moved by, as by any other work of art, because it has been accomplished.

The Courtyard The principal section of the garden in the immediate neighbourhood of the house is the Courtyard. Here there is an interesting collection of plants used in masses and not in excessive variety. Outstanding are the hydrangeas, the hypericum, which has become famous among gardeners everywhere as 'Hidcote' and which is surpassed in beauty only by the 'Rowallane' hypericum, which is too tender for the Cotswolds; finally, for evidence of Johnston's plantsmanship: garden architects and designers are apt to be suspicious of plantsmanship because it leads to planting botanical collections instead of gardens, to using plants for their own sake instead of as materials in a work of art. But Johnston, who had travelled very widely and looked at plants wherever he went, and who created, in the Serre de la Madone in the south of France, a warm-climate garden with quite a different flora, never, so to speak, lost sight of the wood in looking at the trees. His botanical erudition was of positive use. Consider, for example, in this forecourt, the use of *Schizophragma hydrangoides* to clothe a wall. The number of evergreen plants with the close-clinging, climbing habit of ivy is small; nine out of ten garden designers seem never to have heard of any of them; ivy is made to serve the purpose every time, and without regard to the fact that schizophragma, *Pileostegia viburnoides*, or *Ficus stipulata*, all with the same quality of clinging close without adventitious help to stone or any other vertical surface, give a change of texture, of colour, of habit. By having a far wider knowledge of what plants were to be had than most gardeners, and by making a much more catholic use of botanical authorities, Lawrence Johnston was able, time and again, to achieve perfectly an effect which a lesser man would have fallen just short of.

Plate 124 A hedged way, beyond which the kitchen garden and glasshouses are concealed, leads to the vast Theatre Lawn, an oval focused upon two great beeches rising out of a mound which, in spring, is coloured by crocus and narcissus. Beeches, of course, grow magnificently in the Cotswolds since they enjoy lime. The Cotswold soils are calcareous, being on limestone which is often very near the surface. This usually imposes a very severe limitation upon the choice of plants, since hundreds of the most desirable species and their hybrid or selected offspring are intolerant of lime. In practice a great gardener accepts this limitation and creates, as Sir Frederick Stern has done at Highdown in Sussex, a garden of plants which prefer limestone or are indifferent to soil acidity. At Hidcote, however, Johnston overcame the limitation by abolishing it, creating, where he needed it, a soil to suit what he wanted to grow, as we shall see.

The Old Garden The Old Garden, that is, the part of the garden near to the house and focused on the cedar gives access to the grass walk through the main axis of the rising terraces which ends, as already described, in the great gateway and the view over Shakespeare's country to Bredon. Thus the link of small enclosed gardens which joins the Long Walk to the valley garden lies on one's left. This valley garden is called the Wilderness.

Before coming to a consideration of detail, what is the general effect of Hidcote? I have already said that, for me at all events, it is secrecy, self-sufficiency; it is the product of a single mind and spirit. What is important about Hidcote is not that it exists, but that it was made; in the same sense that what is important about the works of, say, Bach, is not that we have them, but that there once lived a man capable of composing them. Hidcote, too, is a place for plants; it is an extraordinarily full garden, a garden in which the plants have taken over and colonized places for themselves and been restrained only so much as will prevent them from inconveniencing each other and prevent the weak from being overcome by the strong. About the cedar there is a small paved area and some stone steps to a higher level, enclosed by clipped hedges and some topiary work: the topiary is of the simplest kind. If, in walking round the gardens, you begin at this point, that is, if you see it before the spirit of Hidcote has entered into you, no harm is done: but I recall coming back to the cedar after long wandering in the rest of the gardens and feeling disconcerted by even the small measure of discipline imposed on the yews. It was entirely irrational, of course, since there are in fact miles of clipped hedges, but one comes to think of them as walls, although walls with a degree of interest in their texture and colour which masonry does not achieve.

A note on these hedges, which are so important in giving the quality of secrecy to the garden, will be in place. Lawrence Johnston did not confine himself to one or two species. At the top of the main vista, by the gateway, hornbeams were used, two double ranks, pleached and clipped into a hollow rectangular mass of foliage. Yew and box, the latter the oldest hedging plant in English gardens and, of course, a native; the former also native but not used for clipped hedging until comparatively modern times. Holly, too, perhaps the finest of all hedging plants in cold climates, has been used both alone and mixed with other species to give a diversified texture. There is one tapestry hedge: hornbeam, yew, beech and holly were planted mingled together and clipped; the mixture of textures and colours is very pleasing. Of the copper-beech hedges, Victoria Sackville-West wrote: '. . . they may not inaptly be compared to an Ispahan carpet, with their depths of rose-madder and violet, and the tips of young growth as sanguine as a garnet seen against the light'.

As well as being one of the most gifted artists in garden design in the history of English gardening, Lawrence Johnston was not only, as I have said, a great plantsman, he was a botanist and a plant collector who fetched plants from all over the world and who had correspondents everywhere sending him plants to try. One of the surprises at Hidcote is the success of plants which I should have thought too tender for that rather cold quarter of England. The Courtyard has among other plants the yellow Banksian rose; *Magnolia delavayi* with its gigantic evergreen leaves; hoherias; the tender Chilean climber *Solanum crispum*; and Italian cypresses, as well as numerous hardier species. A complete plant catalogue of Hidcote plants would occupy this volume, but I propose to mention a few of the more interesting plants noted in the rest of the gardens. Two which perpetuate the name of the garden or its maker all over the world are the *Hypericum patulum* 'Hidcote' already mentioned and the rose which M. Pernet-Ducher who bred it named after Lawrence Johnston, and which is also often referred to as Hidcote Gold. There are good collections of ceanothus and of tree paeonies, half a dozen magnolia species and some camellias. The hedge of the white garden – an enclosure planted with a variety of species with white or near white flowers – is grown through and through with that flaming Chilean climber *Tropaeolum speciosum* and it is surprising to see the white variety of agapanthus, a plant which I had supposed confined, in Britain, to the warmest districts; it is, of course, South African. Another plant which perpetuates the garden name and which I had overlooked is the 'Hidcote' lavender used in various ways, including as a wall plant growing in crevices between stones. A usually tender plant in the enclosure called the Pillar Garden is *Abelia grandiflora* and in the terrace garden I made special note of *Eucryphia nymansensis* and a fine specimen of the Moroccan *Cytisus batandieri*. Hidcote is certainly not a rhododendron garden but Lawrence Johnston did not entirely deny himself the use of the best of all flowering shrubs and some special beds free from the native lime were made to accommodate *Rhododendron augustinii* which has blue flowers.

Again, in the garden beside the stream, densely and cleverly planted with exotic and less exotic shrubs in association, a lime-free area has been used to grow camellias and *Rhododendron yunnanense* with some other rhododendrons. This was not possible in the Wilderness, but there the best possible use has been made of hydrangeas, not the florist's hortensia, but the much more attractive *H. villosa*, and 'Lacecap' varieties allowed to reach their full size as shrubs but flowering white or pink, the soil making blue flowers impossible. The rose properly called Hidcote Gold, not, that is, 'Lawrence Johnston' but one raised in this garden is one of the delights of the Pine Garden. The garden is very rich in species roses, and the early shrubby hybrids, mostly of French origin, known as 'old fashioned' roses.

Hidcote was, perhaps, the first perfectly successful 'paradise' garden. But, at about the same time, a

The plants

little earlier and a little later, others were in the making. Lawrence Johnston, like another great amateur in an earlier gardening style, Henry Hoare of Stourhead, happened to be a considerable artist. But there were other gardeners of talent: there was, notably, Colonel Messel of Nymans.

Nymans

Of the great late-Victorian gardens in which the influence of Gertrude Jeckyll and William Robinson, and of the rise of the plant collector, combined to urge and enable a great gardener to advance towards the realization of the dream, the 'paradise' towards which the English garden was evolving, Nymans in Sussex is outstanding. Its makers were Mr L. Messel, his son Colonel L. C. R. Messel, and their head-gardener James Comber whose son, born and bred and trained at Nymans, became a great collector of plants in the Andes and elsewhere in the Southern hemisphere. The Messels created the framework, supplied the eye, the taste, and the knowledge of what could and should be done to give a garden shape and bones. But as these bones were to be fleshed with exotic plants from all over the world, they needed the help of one of those gardeners who are plantsmen, skilled and sensitive propagators of plants who succeed even with rare and difficult species of which nobody has any experience.

Nymans is between Handcross and Cuckfield on the Haywards Heath–London Road, on a fertile and well-drained sandy loam and in a climate which is relatively mild. As in all good English gardens the garden is divided into sections which, however, so merge into each other that although each is a garden with its own sense and integrity, each is also a part of the whole. There are five of these gardens; a sixth is apart from and does not merge with the rest. House and garden have their junction in the Forecourt; but in the forties the Great Hall, a fabric, like the rest of the buildings, of soft grey stone, was burnt down. Curiously enough, the plants growing over its face and which served to make the link between house and garden, were not killed by the fire and now clothe the ruin which it left. (There is another notable example of this phenomenon at Trehane, in Cornwall.) The principal plants of this face are *Magnolia grandiflora*, the Banksian rose, and the tender *Rhododendron burmanicum*. Wistaria and bignonia share the wall with these and with other climbing roses. Myrtles, daphnes, clematis and still more roses cover the forecourt walls.

The lawns

This forecourt of grey stone and a great number of exotic plants grown together into a prosperous community in the manner of a natural community of plants in the wild, sets the tone for the whole garden and justifies my claim that Nymans is an advance towards realization of the paradise.

The Forecourt, and the façade of the Great Hall (now a picturesque ruin), face south-west. To the east of them and embracing both is a vast area of lawn, itself contained in raised banks densely planted with shrubs, and containing in its south-east corner a Sunk Garden, itself enclosed within banks of shrubs. Now this simple plan, of enclosing a large lawn within banked shrubs, themselves often backed by trees, is good standard landscape practice which could be found in many an eighteenth-century 'picture' garden. It is, indeed, much older for it is to be found in descriptions of Roman gardens. But whereas earlier generations would have used such evergreens as the so-called laurel (*Prunus lauro-cerasus*), or possibly clipped box, the embanked shrubs of Nymans are rhododendron, azalea and hydrangea. Not, of course, the rhododendron which springs to the mind of most continental Europeans when the name is pronounced, the rather dismal mauve-flowered evergreen which has run wild in so many English woods, but a representative collection of the 850 species and their hybrids which, between 1849 and 1950, collectors from Sir Joseph Hooker to the late Frank Kingdon-Ward poured into Britain from Sikhim, Nepal, Tibet, West China, North Burma; from the Caucasus and from Siberia and Manchuria. Nor are the hydrangeas simply those small, rounded, over-flowered, pot-grown 'hortensias' beloved of florists and caterers with a large room to decorate. At Nymans, as in other woodland gardens, they are large, woody shrubs as they are in nature, although in Sussex they do not attain the ten or twelve feet which is commonly to be seen in Cornwall. These banks of shrubs, in which the predominance of botanical species over garden hybrids ensures a discretion in the display of colour and a distinction in the forms of the foliage, are so planted as to be 'natural', here advancing over the edges of the lawn, there retreating to form a bay in which flourish Regal, Formosan and other lilies, and great clumps of that 'lily' which is not one, the arum.

The development and care of the lawn in English gardens has often been, and most commonly is, attributed to the fact that the climate makes good lawns possible and even easy. And it is true, if we consider the lawns of public parks, the small lawns of cottage and suburban houses, the small enclosed lawns which make the floor of all the secret enclaves which one comes upon when walking through the great woodland gardens, that the relative ease with which lawns can be made and maintained in our climate makes them the pleasantest floor which we can give to our gardens, more agreeable to both the feet and the eyes than the stones, flags or mosaics of Italy or than the raked gravel of France. But the very large lawns of Nymans, contained in embanked shrubs, should be considered in another light altogether: the pattern we see in that garden is very frequently repeated in great shrub gardens: it is a feature of Castlewellan in County Down; of Mount Usher in County Wicklow; of Chilham Castle in Kent, and of many others that will occur to the reader. Nor is it by any means a feature only of the older gardens of this period: it has been used, with a difference, at Dartington Hall; and in the great garden which Mr McIlhenny is remaking at Glenveagh, County Donegal. And what this great, green expanse does is to substitute for water where it is either impossible or inconvenient to have a lake or lakes. That this is so can best be realized by considering the gardens of Sheffield Park, also in Sussex. These gardens (I shall come to them in a minute) are formed round four lakes, but the manner in which these lakes have been contained in plantings is the manner in which the great lawn at Nymans has been contained in plantings. The vast lawns of English woodland and shrub gardens are to the lakes of those better provided with water, what the steppe is to the sea. There is a parallel in Japanese gardening, in one branch of which subtle and highly developed art, the same water-substitute, the same provision of a considerable open space contained in plantings, is sometimes accomplished by making an area of raked sand which, by its shape, reaches and moves the spirit through the eye.

Beyond the lawn at Nymans, south-east to the boundary, is the Heather Garden. It is a place of small (some artificial) hills, and large rocks which were cleverly 'let in' to the soil to give the effect of natural outcrops; what, in short, was created here was a small piece of moorland. It is not, however, confined to heathers which are represented as ground plants in very great variety and ranging in colour from white through all the shades of puce and cyclamen, to crimson. Other ericas share the setting, notably the prostrate and dwarf types of rhododendron which, in the high Himalaya, replace the heather of our native highlands, one or two other and more rare kinds of the same genus, and, most striking feature of this part of the gardens, groups of *Pieris forrestii* in the variety selected and propagated at Wakehurst and named after that garden. The young foliage of this evergreen shrub is not green, but a translucent salmon red, while the flowers are great pendulous racemes of white bells like oversize lilies-of-the-valley. In striking contrast with the large and small ericaceous plants is a planting of *Callistemon citrinus*, one of the hardier of the Australian 'bottle-brush' shrubs. Nymans was one of the first gardens in which Australian, notably Tasmanian, plants were grown with success in Britain.

A Laurel Walk marks the whole south-east boundary of the gardens, overlooking the park and the downs. This walk takes you behind the house, and coming out on the south-west side of the house and forecourt, you can make your way into the Walled Garden. This is the nearest thing to formal gardening in the whole place. Originally an orchard, and still retaining some of the ancient apple trees, it is considered by the Countess of Rosse, who lives for part of each year at Nymans and cares for the garden which her grandfather and her father created, to be the heart of the garden. Its central focus is an Italian fountain at which four paths, which divide the Wall Garden into four equal segments, meet. The meeting place and the fountain are contained by four magnificent clipped yews, splendid examples of the ancient Roman horticultural art of topiary. Roman? The only art the Romans invented, or at least so improved as to deserve the credit of inventing, was that of constitutional government. Topiary

The Heather Garden

Plate 114

The Walled Garden

Plate 118

157

they learnt from their Syrian gardeners and taught to their British slaves when they made their villa gardens in England.

The four yews of Nymans are restrained in design: no heraldic animals painfully clipped out of the living foliage offend the eye. The borders beside the paths are old-fashioned herbaceous borders originally designed by William Robinson, although Gertrude Jeckyll, a frequent visitor to Nymans, very probably had her word to say too, for it is an historical fact that Robinson's tendency to run wild was checked by Miss Jeckyll's development of the English cottage style of planting, and by her eye for soft colour and the elimination of the garish. The forefront of the borders are set with thousands of spring-flowering bulb species; the background is formed by trees and shrubs. It is impossible, and might be tedious, to enumerate these, but something must be said about the more remarkable ones. Here are *Magnolia campbelli* bearing, in March, flowers like great rose-pink bowls nearly a foot across and cast in translucent wax; here are eucryphias from the Andes, including the parents of the chance hybrid *E. nymansensis* which has been distributed and planted all over southern Britain and much of the world overseas; here are davidias from the Far East, stewartias from the southern United States, many kinds of magnolia, the great white and red flowered cornels of China, the camellias and rhododendrons of China and Japan, Tibet and Sikhim, rhododendron species in variety, the winter-flowering witch hazels of China, asteranthera from the island of Chiloë, with its waxy tubular flowers of blood-red. Both hemispheres and every continent have contributed to the making of this enclosed paradise.

This garden is fully enclosed. The way out of it and into the next is through a carved Italian archway overgrown with clematis, roses and passion flowers. This is a woodland belt, by-passing the rose garden to which I shall return, by means of a meandering path through one of the most successful realizations of a dream of exotic woods which have been accomplished in Britain. The rhododendron which here dominates the scene is *R. sino-grande*: this plant is a primitive, a living fossil. Its oval leaves are as thick and strong as leather and two feet long by a foot wide, dark, glossy green. It is a tree, not a shrub, and its inflorescences are colossal, mighty clusters of pale yellow bells shot with crimson. This species is planted in numbers. They evoke the world as it was about fifty million years ago when this rhododendron reached perfection and decided to change no more: there are, in the mountains of China and Indo-China, long, narrow valleys at great altitudes where this plant dominates the whole flora and has done since long before the human race had even been implied in some evolutionary change in some small and unimportant branch of the fauna. Among these rhododendrons are planted *Lilium giganteum* (or rather *Cardiocrinum giganteum* as the botanists now call it). This lily, with its spire of huge, narrow white trumpets, may be twelve feet tall and is usually about nine feet. It is extremely difficult to grow well so that its flourishing colonies at Nymans are one of the garden's triumphs. The Countess of Rosse has an entertaining story about these giant lilies. A distinguished visitor to the garden during her youth was Bunyard the nurseryman, one of the very few men who have ever perfectly understood the training and use of the senses so to respond to the natural beauties of the world, whether the form of a tree, the colour and shape of a flower, or the flavour of a pear or a claret, as to be a true 'sensitive'. His praise of all he saw at Nymans was therefore balm to the soul of Colonel Messel who was the more disconcerted when Bunyard marched past the display of giant lilies, probably unique in the whole world and certainly very spectacular, without a word or more than a glance. Asked to admire them, Bunyard replied: 'I cannot. I cannot bear to look at them, they are like very beautiful women utterly ruined by thick ankles.'

The Top Garden

Following the path among these marvels, you come to the Top Garden, guarded by a pair of tall cypresses rising from a thicket of azaleas. The Top Garden is contained, again, in great banks of shrubs, including the Chinese enkianthus which turns flame and gold in autumn, cornels, kolkwitzias from Japan and the sweet scented osmanthus. These surround and completely conceal from outside a hidden garden formed of old-fashioned roses about an ancient well. These roses came, in many cases, from French and Italian gardens. For one of the disadvantages of the English passion for gardening is

Plate 112

that the gardens are for ever being changed and replanted, so that good plants tend to be lost; whereas in Italy and France, where the heir to a garden is content to enjoy it without himself becoming a creative gardener, beautiful old varieties of garden plants are often preserved for ever, or until they die. Beyond the Well Garden is what was once a stone quarry and is now a natural wilderness of camellias and leptospermums, lilacs, hydrangeas and magnolias, yuccas from Mexico and Chusan palms. At a lower level are paeonies in large masses, iris and, among the shrubs, the flame trees of Chile, eucryphias, the Sicilian genista and the North African *Cytissus battandieri* with its great, heavy racemes of fragrant, golden flowers.

Both the Pinetum and the Woods at Nymans are gardened in the spirit of that dream I have evoked, of a landscape at once natural and such as nature never made. At the centre of the Pinetum is a small temple. About it tower conifers which have come to astonishing size in less than a century. A generation ago they had so crowded the old paddock in which Mr Messel originally planted them, that his son decided to thin the trees. In this way clearings in the wood were formed. Similar open glades were formed in Rhododendron Wood of enormous ancient oaks across the road. To walk through such woods, and to come, from time to time, suddenly upon a wide and softly grassed enclave entirely enclosed by trees and with, in the skirts of the wood, here and there a group of some exotic flowering tree or shrub from China or Peru but looking as if it had been there for centuries is to be taken into the dream. This device of woodland gardening was achieved in its highest perfection in the great Cornish garden of Heligan which I saw in the late forties before it fell into neglect. At Nymans the decoration of the glades was achieved with the eucryphia which sprang as a selfsown seedling between the first specimens of *E. gluttinosa* and *E. cordifolia* to be planted in the garden and from which many more were propagated. It is a small, light, very delicately drawn tree which, in late summer, becomes completely covered with great saucershaped white flowers with yellow centres. To help it went the rhododendrons which Forrest and KingdonWard were sending from Yunnan and from the Himalaya, and here and there great clumps of hydrangeas which, in this garden, flower blue or purple whereas in less favoured ones they flower pink. In the wood, also, is the only water which this garden can boast of, the old hammerponds of the ancient Wealden ironfounders linked together by a stream which winds and chuckles over rocks and stones.

In the 1920's Harold Comber, son of the Nymans head gardener, began to send back plants from his collecting expeditions in the Andes, and in Tasmania. By this time the garden was about as full as it could be. More land, across the road, was taken in, the gorse coverts were burnt off, and a new garden, since known as the Reserve Garden, was made. The planting of that part of it, known in the family as 'Tasmania', provides a catalogue of southern hemisphere species whose names would be of more interest to botanists, but whose exotic forms and flowershapes and colours make of this also a place of enchantment. There are parts of this garden where, for example, the dwarf rhododendrons of the northern Indian mountains have colonized the ground like our native heaths and callunas, and where the scented, whiteflowered rhododendrons of northern Burma seem native where they grow.

This achievement, of recreating by art and with the restraints of art, and combining together a series of exotic natural scenes belonging in nature to remote places, is repeated in a different manner, with other materials and on a different scale at Sheffield Park.

The Manor of Sheffield belonged in the thirteenth century to Simon de Montfort and it was near this property of his that he fought the battle of Lewes. Matthew Paris says: 'A great part of the baron's forces lay at the village of Fletching about six miles from Lewes, where Simon de Montfort, Earl of Leicester, their leader, spending all night, according to custom, in offices of religion and prayer, and exhorting his men to make true confession of their sins; and William de Cantelupe, Bishop of Worcester, thereupon giving them absolution, and enjoining them for the remission of their sins to fight stoutly next day in the good cause, and promising all that died in it an entrance into the Kingdom of Heaven; they marched themselves in the morning before sunrise.'

The Pinetum and the Woods

Plate III

Sheffield Park

159

De Montfort was killed at the subsequent battle of Evesham and Henry III then granted his Manor of Sheffield to one William Bardolf. From him it passed, presumably by purchase, to the Lords de la Warr (the family name was West), but in the mid-fifteenth century it was seized from them by Henry VI, and for three centuries it was held by a series of obscure persons. In the eighteenth century it was back in the hands of the de la Warrs but they sold it to one of the 'new men' of the time, John Baker Holroyd, MP, President of the Board of Agriculture, friend and editor of Edward Gibbon, and ultimately Earl of Sheffield. The date of the sale was 1769 and the price paid was £30,000. The grounds about the Manor contained a number of lakes. In the early seventies of the century, the new owner set Capability Brown to work to 'landscape' these grounds and make him one of the fashionable 'picture' gardens, while James Wyatt was employed to build Holroyd a neo-Gothic house. Brown's work was not, as far as I can discover, one of his outstanding jobs, but he provided a frame and setting for a later owner, a setting for the making of a 'paradise'. The second and third Earls of Sheffield did nothing to the gardens; they maintained them in good order, satisfied with the land-and-water scape which Brown had created for the founder of the family fortunes.

A 'natural' paradise
Plate 109

In 1909, when the third earl died, Sheffield Park was sold to Arthur G. Soames. It was he who, working steadily for twenty-five years until his death in 1934, embellished and transformed Launcelot Brown's picture garden into a 'natural' paradise. The scale he was working on is large, one hundred acres.

Although it is more or less true that the second and third Earls of Sheffield did no more than maintain the gardens, and that Soames was their creator as they now are, the third earl seems to have been interested in trees. Brown, of course, had used only native plant material, but the third earl diversified the colour and texture of the arboreta – for they are nothing less – by planting exotic trees. The blue Atlantic Cedar, many kinds of pines and firs from North America and from the Mediterranean, Lawson

Plate 110

cypresses, notably the golden form, arborvitae, willows in variety, maples for autumn colour, tulepo trees, were among his plantings. This was fortunate for Soames, for though a gardener envisage what a garden will look like when his trees have grown, he cannot, unless he start work rather earlier in life than is usual, live to see his garden as it should look if he must wait for the trees to reach maturity.

To give an idea of the taste, not to mention industry, which went to the planting of this garden of trees about lakes – there are five lakes – it would be necessary to give a long list of names, and for the reader to be familiar with these names and to know where the species were brought from. Since these conditions cannot be fulfilled, it is not possible to give any idea of the, as it were, horticultural workmanship of this garden. As to the effect achieved, since to most people a tree is a tree, all they will be aware of in visiting the garden is a brightness, a diversity, a variety of texture and outline which are beyond anything which could possibly be accomplished with native material. The visitor will know, will see and sense, that he is within a work of art (after nature), and his pleasure will accordingly be heightened. Only the fully informed will realize how it has been done and appreciate the quality of the work.

Shrubs and groundling flowers are much less important at Sheffield Park than at Nymans. Conscious or unconscious, the gardener's object has been the same as at Nymans, to make a natural scene whose power to affect the spirit through the eyes has been multiplied manifold by bringing trees into the picture from the four corners of the world. In Sheffield Park the gardener has worked with a large brush and sweeping strokes, encouraged thereto by the size of the canvas and by the sketch of a garden which Brown had created for him. At Nymans, on the other hand, far more use has been made of detail and of colour. In both the final achievement is the same: a world as beautiful as it might have been if the work of creation had not been spread over so vast an area of space and time, and if the creator had had in mind the small measure of man.

Since the beginning of this century a number of gardens, smaller in area than the foregoing, but combining, in the same successful way, all the principal styles of English gardening, or such of them as are suitable in the locality, in a single expression (what theologians call a syncretism), have been made. Two which are outstandingly beautiful, but also outstandingly successful as 'integers', are, in chronological order, Great Dixter on the Kent and Sussex border, and Sissinghurst Castle in the Weald of Kent. The process of making such gardens continues. One, for example, which has become famous although not yet twenty years old is that of Mr L. S. Fortescue at Buckland Monachorum, in Devon, a garden in which an astonishingly wide range of plants have been combined together into an integral pattern on a hilly site and with its bones made of Leyland cypress hedges. The maker of this garden is a remarkable plantsman whose garden demonstrates the results which can be achieved where extremely strict rules in the matter of distinction or quality in the variety of plants chosen, colour, grouping and form, are made and kept. At the heights of its several flowering seasons, the Buckland Monachorum garden is spectacular. The two we now come to are less so; but it is probably true to say that, by the greater restraint exercised in the choice of plants, and in the broader, more open plan, also in the greater use of architecture, a serenity not to be found in Mr Fortescue's garden is accomplished: his garden is an excitement; the others, a retreat from excitement.

In the middle of the thirteenth century Dixter near Northiam in Sussex was a moated manor house. A century later it was held by one Hamon-at-Gate and it was not, apparently, a very considerable holding since it was valued at forty shillings and the holder was bound to find only a single bowman for his feudal overlord in respect of his land at Dixter (Dicksterve, as it then was). Its value increased, for in the time of Hamon's daughter when her husband held the land it was valued at £20. By the end of the fifteenth century the property had passed, by marriage as dowry, into the hands of the Lords Windsor and there it remained for something over a century, although the family do not seem to have lived in the house for much of this time. It was, instead, let to various tenants: one of them, John Harrison by name, in the time of the third lord, has left a record scratched on a beam in the parlour:

Great Dixter

JOHN HARRISON DWELT AT DIXTERN
XXXVI YERS AN VI MONTHES
CAME THE FERST OF ELISABETHE RAIN

In 1595 the manor was sold to John Glydd. It had, until this time, been a great open hall with a central fireplace and no chimney. The new owner built in two floors and a big kitchen chimney. The old solar was made into three rooms and the parlour into two. More changes were made in the eighteenth century. But they were inconsiderable, affecting only doors and windows; and it was thus something very like the original ancient manor house bought by Nathaniel Lloyd in 1910.

It was necessary for the new owner to make certain alterations and additions, but to make them with discretion, for the idea was to restore the house to something nearer its original form. For example, the hall bays and oriels of the solar were to be restored and the partitions which divided much of the interior removed. Moreover, Mr Lloyd had found, at Benenden in Kent, an early sixteenth-century hall house which was going to be demolished. He bought it and removed it to Dixter to be added to his own house as a separate wing. For all this work he would need a good architect and the man he chose was Edwin Lutyens. It is not my business to describe what Mr Lloyd and Lutyens did to the house. But Lutyens was also employed to design the 'bones' of the garden. As far as I know he had done no garden designing before this time.

Lutyens at Great Dixter

The history of the Great Dixter garden is very short for the reason that until Mr Lloyd began to make it in 1910 there was absolutely nothing of the kind. What surrounded the house was really farmyard, with farm buildings in red brick, the local building material. In front of the house were a bay laurel and a wild pear, both beautiful trees still surviving; in an orchard behind the house were a few ancient, and therefore picturesque, apple trees. There was also, and this too is still with us, an old Black Brunswick fig tree which is exceptionally fruitful. There was nothing else.

Yet one of the impressions made by Great Dixter, as by Sissinghurst, is of long establishment. This is owing, to some extent at least, to the yews, hedges and topiary specimens, which are many. I have

Plate 103

already mentioned somewhere the widespread belief that a mature yew hedge, or a group of clipped yews in one of the forms usual in topiary work, must, if they look well, be several centuries old, can be bought or inherited as part of a garden, but not brought to perfection during the lifetime of the planter. It is not the case, as one can see so well at Sissinghurst (pp. 163–6). And, again, at Dixter, though the yews have exactly that look which suggests that there they have stood, there been carefully clipped every year for centuries whereas in point of fact none was planted before 1910 and some not until 1912. Lutyens made a design which took in the existing farm buildings themselves to be transformed into suitable garden buildings. As at Hidcote, the gardens at Great Dixter were divided into a number of separate enclosures and for the same reason: the fostering, in those who were to enjoy the garden, of 'expectation and surprise'. Christopher Lloyd, the present gardener of the family, refers to this as being 'in the Renaissance tradition', and in so far as that is the case Great Dixter is not an English 'paradise' garden. But, as will appear, the gardener's plantsmanship – Christopher Lloyd is a distinguished academic, as well as a practical, gardener and for some years was a member of the faculty at Wye College, the London University school of agriculture and horticulture – makes this garden into a happy compromise between the two traditions. Lutyens so contrived the enclosures that, one leading into another, the visitor is carried entirely round the house which remains always in sight.

Lutyens worked in the vernacular style of course, but with originality. He made, for example, a new and very pleasant use of Sussex roofing tiles in the design of wall ornaments, and in the construction of laminated columns when it came to the transformation of the farm buildings, as described below.

The building beside the Rose Garden, which appears on the architect's plan as 'loggia' but is less grandly known in the family as the 'hovel' was, when Lutyens started work, a cow shed with a sound enough roof but semi-ruinous walls. The walls were pulled down and the roof held up by the columns described, made of laminae which are, in fact, tiles. This loggia was so designed that it is open on alternate sides, so that one side is always protected from the wind. Whichever is the lee side has an agreeable outlook, one over the Rose Garden, the other over the Topiary Lawn. Typical of the spirit in which Lutyens worked is the fact that the four drinking troughs for cattle, built of old brick, were retained but modern plumbing installed to control the level of the water which is gravity-fed from a pond, all four troughs being interconnected. And typical of the grace of what he added rather than simply retained, are the circular steps south-west of the Yeoman's Hall wing of the house, the part which was brought from Benenden but is of approximately the same date as the original buildings. Lutyens also kept the oast house, that typical feature of the Kent–Sussex landscape. It was in continual use for the drying of hops until 1939; and although now used as a store, the beautifully clinker-built cowls have been retained.

The Topiary Lawn and the Sunk Garden

The Topiary Lawn is the most obviously 'Latin' part of the gardens. It is true that grass would hardly be used in a Continental garden, but the regular placing of the clipped yews is traditional.

Plate 102

In 1923, after the garden was well settled down and planted, that is, after the Lutyens skeleton had been clothed in plants, Nathaniel Lloyd himself commenced garden designer when he decided to make a sunk garden to his own design. The focus is an octagonal pool surrounded by paving which is planted. This in turn is contained within a paved terrace on a slightly higher level, the riser or retaining wall making a 'wall garden'. The higher level, again, is retained within a brick wall at the foot of which is a border of plants. The pond is stocked with water-lilies and with fish.

I have already said that by reason of Christopher Lloyd's plantsmanship Great Dixter is a happy compromise between two traditions. The layout is, even in detail, semi-formal; but the planting is informal. Although there is a long, and among gardeners famous, herbaceous border, most of the plantings are mixed, that is, shrubs, herbaceous plants, and bulbs are all grown together.

And this is not, at Great Dixter, simply a question of economy of labour. Mr Lloyd believes that plants are better displayed if those of diverse habit are grown together.

The principal and semi-floral parts of the gardens are themselves contained within a wide area of rough grass, with some ornamental trees, in which what may be called meadow-gardening, as a branch of 'wild' gardening, is practised. The grass is richly planted with narcissus in variety, crocuses, native orchids, and fritillaries, which give in spring a display of the kind known in medieval gardens as the flowery mead, although then, in all probability, the terms referred to the natural state of the meadows and no special planting was done. The effect is repeated in autumn, with colchicums and the autumn flowering crocuses (*C. speciosus*).

The counties of Sussex and Kent are remarkably rich in fine gardens. At Benenden, east of Great Dixter, is the garden of Mr Collingwood Ingram, one of the greatest of modern English gardeners who has bred fine new garden plants and is famous for the introduction of the flowering cherries of Japan which have added much to the charm of our gardens in early spring. At Wye, near Ashford in Kent, the garden of Withersdane Hall, the hall of residence for women students at Wye College, London University, is one of the most perfect small, or perhaps medium-sized, relatively formal gardens in the country: it is of particular interest in that being made on a soil with a high calcium content, the planting has been restricted by the conditions. But of that subject we shall have more to say when we come to describe and illustrate the garden of Highdown, near Worthing. Meanwhile, the most famous modern garden in this part of England is undoubtedly that of Sissinghurst Castle.

Some time between the year 1540 and 1550, Sir John Baker, popularly known as Bloody Baker for his savage persecution of Protestants, built Sissinghurst Castle in what was, at the time, a relatively new building material, the red brick which mellows to such a beautiful soft rose colour. This brick is a product of the brick-earth clay which, in the county of Kent, nourishes the most beautiful and longest lived cherry orchards in western Europe. The connexion between the local building material and the local plantation crops is always interesting: the same pattern, red-brick buildings and fine cherries and other stone-fruits, is to be found repeated in the Veronese and, of course, for the same geological reasons.

The Sir John Baker who built Sissinghurst Castle, and who was so notorious as a Roman Catholic extremist, was a man of consequence in other respects: he was a Member of Parliament, he had been both Recorder of London and Chancellor of the Exchequer, a Privy Councillor to Henry VIII, and he had been Speaker of the House of Commons.

The castle new-built by Baker was not the first building on the site. The moat, part of which survives, was already there and it is reasonable to assume that it enclosed something. What, in all probability, it enclosed was a twelfth-century manor house which stood in an orchard of apple trees, perhaps some plums, and probably some cherry trees, in which case this was perhaps one of the earliest cherry orchards of any importance in Britain. The records of this earlier demesne are very thin indeed. It is known only that in 1235 the Manor was held by one John de Saxenhurst; that he built a chapel to St John the Baptist on to his house, that in 1270 the Manor passed, by marriage, to the de Berhams, a local family, that the de Berhams held it for nearly two hundred and fifty years and then sold it to Thomas Baker of Cranbrook, grandfather of the new builder, Sir John. Sissinghurst was held in all by seven generations of Bakers until the Sir John Baker who died in 1661 left four daughters as co-heiresses, but no son. Presumably these ladies lived there until 1730 when, perhaps, the last of them died. At all events Sissinghurst then came on the market and was bought by Sir Horace Mann, who had connexions in the county, his brother being owner of Linton near Maidstone.

Why this purchase was ever made is obscure; Mann never lived at Sissinghurst; in 1737 he went to Florence and there stayed for the rest of his life. However, his property brought him some profit, for he leased the Castle to the Government for the accommodation of prisoners of war (the war of 1756–63). Something not far short of three thousand Frenchmen were crammed into Sissinghurst.

Distinguished visitors to Sissinghurst, before and after it was so known, were many: they included Edward I, Queen Mary, who would, no doubt, greatly have approved Sir John Baker's ferocious treatment of his Protestant fellow citizens, and Queen Elizabeth. But perhaps the most interesting of the Castle's residents was the short, plump and pompous little officer of militia who commanded the soldiers guarding the French prisoners from 1760: Edward Gibbon, then twenty-three and yet to become the greatest of English historians.

Sir Horace Mann, then, got nothing but Government rents out of Sissinghurst. He died and his nephew Horatio inherited. We know nothing about him, but evidently he was not a family man for the next heir was another of Horace Mann's nephews, James Cornwallis, Bishop of Lichfield. It remained in the Cornwallis family until the mid-nineteenth century. It then had a period, not quite a hundred years, of decline during which it changed hands on several occasions, being bought by farmers who cared nothing for the now ruined Castle but wanted the rich wealden land. In 1855 a farmhouse, known as the Castle House, was built by the first of these owners, and was used as a residence by him and his successors. Finally, in 1930 it was bought by the Hon. Victoria Sackville-West, direct descendant in the thirteenth generation of Sir John Baker, through Sir John's daughter Cicely and her husband, Sir Thomas Sackville, 1st Earl of Dorset. The new owner and her husband Mr (later Sir) Harold Nicolson had acquired a ruined castle and a wilderness of bramble.

It is not my business to write of the restoration and transformation of the ruin into a habitable dwelling-house of great distinction and without losing the quality of the red-brick Tudor buildings. The garden, which was begun in 1929, is another matter: so completely had the grounds been neglected that, as the vast and dense thickets of bramble were cleared away, more walls, whose existence had been unsuspected by the new owners, were discovered. The first stage of the work, in fact, was really that of liberating the whole area from the brambles and other weeds to discover the shape and nature of the ground the gardeners had to work with.

When that had been done, the Nicolsons shared the work: design was, on the whole, his part; her's was the planting. Neither of them had had much experience nor, of course, were they in any sense trained gardeners; they were self-taught. Mrs Nicolson developed an astonishing degree of proficiency in plantsmanship, a memory for names and an ability to put names to a very wide range of plants of all kinds. This faculty enabled her to choose the best materials in which to express their designs.

As is usual in such cases, the influence of gardening friends was of the first importance. And it happened that among them was the most remarkable and successful English gardener of the times, Lawrence Johnston (see p. 152). The Nicolsons stayed with him at Hidcote and were it not for the fact that the standing and very beautiful walls of the Sissinghurst garden grounds had been in place for centuries before this friendship was formed, one would be tempted to see in the breaking-up of Sissinghurst gardens into a number of enclosed places, each leading to another, a copy of what Johnston Plate 94 achieved at Hidcote with hedges instead of walls. In fact, however, much of the division was there to start with, and must have suggested the creation of more barriers – not walls this time but hedges – on the Hidcote model perhaps, in order to carry out what, it was early decided, should be the theme of the garden, expectation and surprise. Moreover, although the Nicolsons, like Lawrence Johnston, made use of a wide range of plants with that ultimate sophistication of gardening skill which contrives to suggest the random growth of flowering herbs among shrubs, at the foot of walls, under hedges, between flagstones, 'after' nature but with a selection of the most beautiful species which has nothing natural about it, their plantsmanship was different from Johnston's; this was partly a matter of taste, partly of soil and climate. Partly, too, of experience: Harold Nicolson and Victoria Sackville-West were not quite as widely travelled as Johnston and were not plant collectors in the sense that he was; but, for example, while Nicolson was *en poste* in Persia they were enchanted with the ancient garden flora of that country, and on returning to England they brought with them Persian roses which were among those to flourish, in due course, at Sissinghurst.

The Tower Lawn
Plate 92
One enters the garden by the arch of the double-towered gateway from the Tower Courtyard, down broad stone steps on to the Tower Lawn. The lawn is enclosed, then, by walls planted to roses, now

enormous plants, clematis, honeysuckles and other wall plants including a very large myrtle. At Sissinghurst there is no serious competition for one's attention between the general *coup d'oeil* and the detail: until one emerges into the orchard which is part of the garden, the view is always limited by walls or hedges; the enclosure in which one happens to be is swiftly taken in, comprehended, and thereafter one is free to concentrate on the detail of the decoration, detail providing satisfaction for the botanist as well as the gardener; for Victoria Sackville-West had a marked preference for species over hybrids, and a remarkable power to make difficult plants, especially bulb plants from remote places, settle down as if they were at home.

To the left of the Tower Lawn is the White Garden, divided into four equal parts by a cross of paths meeting at a circle at which point is placed a large urn always planted with some unusual scandent or sprawling plant and often with something very surprising indeed: I can recall seeing a Chilean puya – my first – flowering in this urn, one of the few occasions when an erect plant and not one which overflows the urn, was used. For the rest the garden was one of white flowers and silvery foliage, partly shaded, which made the choice of plants one requiring skill and knowledge. *The White Garden*

From the White Garden there is a way into the Yew Walk which separates the Tower Lawn from the orchard. This Yew Walk has always seemed to me a remarkable achievement of sheer good practical gardening: the first time I went round the garden in Mrs Nicolson's company I said that of course they had at least found these yew hedges in place when they bought Sissinghurst, since they were clearly some centuries old. They are, I think, about ten feet tall, certainly well over a yard through, and perfectly dense and regular. At the time of my remark, these hedges, enclosing the walk, were in fact in their twenty-fifth year. Their quality had been achieved by feeding and mulching. And they were by no means the only thing in the gardens which made this impression of antiquity: as all gardeners know, a garden is never perfect, or as near perfect as it can be, until it is mature; in fact, until it is, or at least looks, old. The look of age was accomplished at Sissinghurst within twenty years, a remarkable triumph of art. *The Yew Walk* / Plate 93

The Yew Walk is one way into the Rose Garden which can, however, also be reached from the Tower Lawn and even from the Tower Courtyard. A system of straight paths divides it into eight parts, centred on a rondel. The roses form one of the most interesting collections in England, probably the most interesting outside of one or two nurseries and perhaps even including the greater nurseries for that matter, since the shrubs were acquired from a large number and variety of sources. There are no hybrid tea roses at all. The Nicolsons did not like them, and in any case they would, with their awkwardness and stiffness as shrubs, have been out of place in this garden. The roses are therefore of the 'shrub' type, large, often very large, and shapely plants and all of them belonging to those categories in the planting of which some writers anxious to defend suburban taste have seen a manifestation of snobism. In point of fact, of course, what is manifest is simply taste. Botanical species are much used; also the 'old-fashioned', the Bourbon and similar forms. And, of course, climbers for the walls. *The Rose Garden*

The walks are bordered with other genera; iris are a feature: they were very successful at Sissinghurst and still are. Ingenious methods of supporting without uglifying the floppier kinds of roses were devised, and later widely copied. In June it is possible to spend hours in this rose garden without being tempted out of it: the diversity of forms, colours and even scents seems to be infinite. Lady Nicolson's writings on the garden (as Victoria Sackville-West in the *Observer*) were responsible for the revival of interest in the more graceful and less flamboyant kinds of roses; and in the popularizing of species (*R. acea* is an example) which had, until then, been confined to a few specialists' gardens. Nor was the influence of Sissinghurst confined to getting species roses out of the botanical and into the pleasure garden: it accomplished the same good work for tulips and other genera.

Sissinghurst is notable for lilacs, and there is a planting of them between the Rose Garden and the Cottage Garden. This is literally a cottage garden since it is associated with one of the estate cottages called the South Cottage. But it is a cottage garden in the academic horticultural sense, too, for it is *The Cottage Garden* / Plate 171 planted to a variety of kinds – shrubs, herbaceous plants, bulbs, and corms in close association, in the manner developed by Gertrude Jeckyll out of traditional cottage gardening. There is, as in all the best Jeckyll gardens, a pleasing touch of what perhaps I may call Marie-Antonionette-ism about it. For while the method is that of the cottage gardener, the material is more sophisticated: rare as well as common plants have been used together; the criterion has been beauty and nothing else.

From the Cottage Garden one makes one's way into the Nuttery, a feature of the gardens which has a curious history. It consists of five long and perfectly regular rows of hazel-nut trees which were growing there when the Nicolsons bought Sissinghurst. But they did not know it: so completely was the whole of this regular coppice overgrown with bramble that it was not until clearing had been for some time in hand that the trees were revealed; and not until a pick-axe struck masonry that the wall limiting the Nuttery at the far end was discovered and, subsequently, uncovered.

The Nuttery   The Nuttery provides an excellent example of the mutability of English gardens by comparison with the unchanging gardens of Italy; an enormous number of polyanthus plants were raised from seed, and the whole area under the nut trees was planted with them after thorough clearance of weeds. For two or three years the result was breath-taking, a Persian carpet of soft colour beneath the broken shade of the hazels. So striking was it that one came to associate it with Sissinghurst as a permanent feature. But this, in the nature of things, it could not be; or at least could not continue so successfully to be. It turned out that the soil became primula-sick and the plants declined in vigour; then the lesser celandine, one of the least eradicable of weeds, got into the plantation. English gardening, unlike any other kind, is full of such cases: a brilliant stroke of this kind can rarely be repeated, and inventiveness is always necessary.

At the bottom of the Nuttery is a low wall, one of four containing a formal, paved herb garden, a very pleasant place for scents on a warm day. At this point you are at the level of the old moat which is used as a wild water-garden and, L-shaped, contains the rougher part of the orchard. Here, among old apple and cherry trees themselves very beautiful in both spring and autumn, a form of wild gardening is practised by the planting in the grass of many thousands of daffodils. Separating it from the more formal parts of the garden is a walk of pleached limes, paved, but so generously planted with tulips, in the botanical species, anemones, fritillaries and many other spring-flowering bulbs that they come up between the paving stones and wherever there is a square inch of soil.

It is possible to discover at Sissinghurst the influence of all the principal traditions in English gardening, of at least two famous gardeners, and, if you like, of half a dozen gardening theories. Yet it is unique, like no other garden in England. And this because it is the expression of one of the strongest gardening characters in the history of English horticulture. I can use it to demonstrate none of the points I have tried to make excepting perhaps this one: that a great garden is invariably the work of a single artist – Sir Harold and Lady Nicolson were one in their garden; and that an English garden is unlikely long to outlive the man or woman who made it in the form which he or she gave it.

The chalk garden   The great woodland gardens of Britain, the English 'paradise' gardens, are, to some extent, dependent for their creation and existence upon a certain kind of woodland soil, very rich in organic material and acid in its chemical reaction; a humid air; and relatively heavy mean annual rainfall. For this reason these gardens are to be found in the west, in Devon and Cornwall, in north Wales, in south-west Scotland, and in Ireland. The reason is that the plants suitable for the creation of the exotic, secret, romantic atmosphere in which such gardens excel and which answers a need in the English character, come for the most part from countries which have a milder average climate, a much higher rainfall than Britain's; and where, on the whole, limestone soils are exceptional. Although there are important exceptions, a very large number of North American, South American, southern hemisphere and Asiatic plants are more or less intolerant of soils which are rich in calcium salts, although it is also true that no plant will grow in the total absence of calcium. So true is it that the English gardener yearns for a paradise garden that those who find themselves on limestone soils, and a very large part of England is either chalk or limestone in some harder form, complain of their hard lot and envy those whose soil will accommodate the calcifuge as well as the calcicole plants. Moreover, in many thousands of English gardens attempts are made, rarely with success, to contrive special conditions so that the lime-hating plants can be grown. The better way was shown by Sir Frederick Stern at Highdown near Worthing on the solid chalk of the Sussex coast. This garden can be fitted into no category; it creates a new one, the chalk garden. And since a very large part of Europe is made of chalk or limestone, the achievement of Highdown has a wide significance.

Highdown

Sir Frederick Stern is, moreover, the greatest living example of the way in which a love of plants in detail has developed, among English as among Japanese and Chinese gardeners, into an art which has little to do with science yet which leads to the study of botany. Sir Frederick, a soldier turned gardener, has become a world authority on some of the genera he was led, in his search for chalk garden plant material, to cultivate and study: his *Study of the genus Paeonia*, and his treatise on the genus galanthus are standard works.

The reader had better be told at once that Highdown, a very 'special case', is not a garden in which traditions of design, architecture, the fine arts, literary notions of what a garden should be, have played any part at all. It is a plantsman's garden. I do not wish to infer that it is shapeless, or a muddle of plants, or a museum of plants in the manner of a botanical garden. It is none of these things and as Edwin Smith's photographs show, it has shape, it has views, it has vistas, it comprises a number of *coups d'oeil*. But it is above all a garden in which, under conditions which are common in England and even commoner in continental Europe, a vast range of plant species have been persuaded to flourish, selected from an even vaster range tried, and representing those which are worthy of a place for their beauty and for their readiness to settle down in the chalk.

In one sense Highdown has carried an English gardening style to its extreme. It was always implicit in the ideas of William Robinson that exotics should not only be introduced into the English land-scape garden and woodland garden, but that they should become altogether at home there, even to the extent of naturalizing. In Sir Frederick Stern's own account of Highdown, *A Chalk Garden*, one phrase repeats itself time and time again as plants tried there are described: '. . . it seeds itself about', or some variant of this. It is one of the Highdown principles to let plants have their own way so long as they are giving pleasure to the gardener, delighting his senses and satisfying his curiosity. Thus, for example, the hoe is not used over this very considerable garden; every inch of it is (or for many years was) weeded by hand, so that seedlings of the exotics which, in hundreds, perhaps thousands of species have been introduced to the Sussex chalk, shall be spared to grow and flower, and sometimes to reveal themselves as hybrids which could never have occurred in nature, since the parents have habitats remote from each other. This, of course, is the very essence of the man-made paradise.

The following passage, quoted from *A Chalk Garden*, will give an idea of what Sir Frederick Stern started with:

'Our house, built about 1820, is situated 100 feet above sea-level on Highdown Hill, facing the Channel, which is almost one mile distant in a straight line. Highdown Hill is the nearest of the South Downs to the sea in the district between Worthing and Angmering. In 1909 when we first began to think of gardening, there was no garden at all except two small lawns, one on each side of the house. On the west of the house there were large evergreen oaks which are excellent wind-breaks against the prevailing south-west winds. Beyond these trees there was a grass paddock, and to the north of the paddock a belt of beech-trees protecting a large chalk-pit from the south and south-west winds. . . . In 1909 the pit was used for keeping pigs and chickens, and all the refuse was thrown into one corner. . . .'

The pit was used to make a tennis court and as the pigs and chickens were not very agreeable company for the players, they were removed elsewhere and it was decided to plant flowering shrubs instead. This was the beginning of one of the most remarkable gardens in the world. 'No one was able to advise us on what would grow on this nearly virgin chalk, and many discouraged us from trying anything. One eminent nurseryman when asked what to plant on the chalk cliffs which are about 30 feet high on the north side of the pit, said nothing would grow there. . . .'

But not all the would-be gardener's friends were Job's comforters: thus, Sir Arthur Hill, later Director of Kew Gardens, and one or two others, were encouraging. Hill, in particular gave sound advice and this was rather to find out by experiment what would grow on the naked chalk than to import good topsoil from elsewhere. And to confine the enrichment of the soil to 'mulching' it with beech leaves and farmyard manure in the usual way.

The lesson of planting in the pure unbroken chalk, simply by breaking out a hole and leaving the plants themselves to do the rest, was not encouraging. But an accident, of the kind which teaches useful lessons only to men gifted enough and observant enough to be teachable, went a long way towards solving the problem. At one point of the chalk pit there had been a big fall of chalk and topsoil from the top of the cliff, which had formed a sort of broad and spreading heap of rubble known as 'Musgrave's Corner'. In this the chalk had, in its fall, broken into small and medium sized lumps mixed with such topsoil as there had been, formed by the slow decay of grass roots and old grass, on the clifftop. Shrubs planted in this grew strongly and healthily if they were not of the known lime-hating species. From this it was deduced that although chalk itself was not a hopeless handicap, it must first be broken up. Thereafter, gradually and year after year, this was done over an increasing area: the chalk was broken up to a depth of two feet.

In only one case was the rule of not attempting to grow known calcifuge plants broken. Much later in the garden's career a special bed by the house was made, with peat two feet deep, for the growing of camellias. Most experts would have said, and would say even now, that this would be expensive labour lost, since it would not be long before water saturated with lime flowing into the camellia beds would cause that chlorosis leading to death which afflicts calcifuge plants in the presence of chalk. In fact, however, this has not happened and the camellias have flourished. For the rest, Highdown is a garden of chalk-loving, or at least of chalk-tolerant plants.

Another experiment, in a different spirit, was a failure. Reginald Farrer, the great collector of Asiatic plants, had declared that he had found certain species of rhododendrons, notoriously calcifuge plants, growing on limestone formations. It was decided to obtain and try these on the Highdown chalk. The rhododendrons perished. It does not follow that Farrer was wrong: Dr Tod of the Edinburgh Botanical Garden has shown that these so-called lime-haters will flourish on very alkaline soils in the presence of sufficient magnesium salts. At Birr Castle in County Offaly, the Earl and Countess of Rosse, both notable gardeners, have very flourishing plants of *R. yunnanense* and its hybrids in a soil so limy that it is death to other rhododendrons and to camellias.

The plants　Highdown is in flower for twelve months of the year. One of the great advantages which it has enjoyed has been the Sterns' friendship with notable plant collectors. But even before this, collectors' plants (before they had become generally known to gardeners) formed the basis of the earliest plantations because in 1912 there was a great sale at Veitch's Coombe Wood Nursery, and Veitch had long been the patron of the most successful collectors. At that sale the Sterns bought a number of plants raised from seed collected by E. H. Wilson in China; some of these were named, others were as yet identified only by the collector's number. They were bought as a speculation, for it was at that time unknown whether these Chinese shrubs would flourish on chalk. Most of them did. In 1914 Reginald Farrer made his first collecting expedition to Kansu in Northern China, and Stern took a share in the expenses; it was customary for a number of gardeners and institutions to form a syndicate to finance plant collectors. It was Farrer's seed, excepting that of his rhododendron discoveries, which provided Highdown with many of the most interesting plants still to be seen there. After the First World War, Colonel Stern, as he then was, took shares in other plant collection syndicates, notably in those which financed Frank Kingdon-Ward after 1920. As well as plants collected by Wilson and Kingdon-Ward, Colonel Stern had cuttings and seeds from great gardens where plants of Forrest's collecting were flourishing. The point is that a great part of the plant material at Highdown was new to British horticulture and it is probably true to say that the garden has always been dominated by an unfamiliar flora rather than by the kind of plants which one can buy from any nursery. Only later did the plants first grown at Highdown come slowly into nursery commerce.

Plants from East Asia were by no means the only ones to be grown first at Highdown. Among Colonel Stern's friends were F. K. Balls, who sent back numerous bulbs, corms and herbaceous plants from his expeditions to Greece and Asia Minor, and S. C. Atchley who lived in Greece and kept High-down supplied with anemone and cyclamen corms for trial. Many of these Greek and near eastern plants found the conditions at Highdown congenial, and flourished and spread, more or less naturaliz-ing themselves in the garden. The success of the earlier plantings, and then of the subsequent ones, began to make the garden's reputation, which attracted other gardeners, some of them well known and experienced. Among them was the naturalist, botanist and very great gardener H. J. Elwes, and it was he who suggested to Colonel Stern that paeonies would be at home in the Highdown chalk, if cultivated by the method which had been discovered in the manner described. It was also Elwes who suggested that the genus *Eremurus* should be tried at Highdown. Both suggestions had important consequences for the whole future of gardening in Britain, for the experiments with species carried out at Highdown led to a great enrichment of English gardens, passing, as it did, a large number of hitherto unknown exotic plants into nursery commerce and so into thousands of gardens. W. R. Dykes of *Iris* fame was also a friend of the Stern household, with important results on the use of iris in English gardens. Something must also be said about the Highdown influence on the growing of true lilies in English gardens.

It had generally been supposed, even as late as the 1920's or thereabouts, that lilies would not grow on chalk soils. In 1914 Farrer sent lily seed collected in Kansu back to England, and James Buckman, the Highdown head gardener, raised two kinds which were identified as *Lilium duchartrei* and *L. leucanthum*: that was the beginning. Subsequently a great many other species, and later hybrids, were tried, and although many of them, especially those from America, were not able to grow in the chalk, others succeeded until, in the end, Colonel Stern was able to give general guidance to gardeners on the chalk and other limestone soils as to what they could and could not grow of this genus. But the work was carried further than that: experiments in crossing species, made at Highdown and elsewhere, had shown that if an Asiatic (often lime-tolerant) species be crossed with an American (often calcifuge) species of the same genus, the resultant hybrid offspring will be tolerant of lime. Work was therefore undertaken to breed a race of lime-tolerant garden lilies.

If I had to pick out the genera for which Highdown is most famous, and ignoring the garden's wealth in roses, its success with davidia, the innumerable shrubs and trees, herbaceous perennials and bulb plants which grow together in company to form a paradise of flowers, I do not think it would be diffi-cult: *Galanthus* – the lovely race of snowdrops and snowflakes which, from January almost throughout the year adorn the garden; *Lilium* – both species and the lime-tolerant hybrids, which spring in great clumps among the evergreen and deciduous shrubs; *Paeonia*, both shrubby moutans and herbaceous kinds. There is one tree-paeony (it is a misnomer but the term is too well established to be dropped now), *P. suffriuticosa*, which is of itself sufficient justification for a visit to this garden, a plant some ten feet in diameter and ten feet high and carrying, in due season, many hundreds of enormous and per-fectly formed flowers, white, flushed at the heart with maroon, and of indescribable beauty.

Plate 85

It would be out of the question to name all the interesting plants which are grown at Highdown. Only a catalogue in several volumes would cover the work. But a few other things must be mentioned. *Magnolia* × *highdownensis* originated in a curious way: three seedling magnolias were sent to Sir Frederick by J. C. Williams of Caerhays, a garden very famous for its rhododendrons and its magnolias as well as for camellias (see pp. 213–14). They flourished and turned out to be something new and outstanding, belonging to that group of magnolias which have pendent flowers of very pure form and deep maroon or crimson centres, pure white petals (*M. wilsoni, M. sinensis*). It is not certain whether this is really a hybrid or perhaps a mutant form of a species; it is at all events the best of the group.

Echiums are not familiar to many English gardeners: they are well known to those who have visited the Canary Island, or the gardens of Tresco Abbey, in the proper season. They are spectacular, great spikes up to twenty feet tall, densely set with myriads of soft blue flowers. That these seed themselves and have virtually naturalized on Tresco, with its very mild climate and almost frost-free winters, is not extraordinary. But that they should have done the same at Highdown does seem to me remarkable.

It should, finally, be repeated that because Highdown is a garden of plants, displaying the forms and colours and scents of flowers in astonishing diversity, from small groundlings to tall trees, it does not follow that the shape of the garden itself and the disposal of its great riches in plant material have received no consideration. The garden has not been 'designed' in the architectural sense. But a gardener with such a feeling for plants, such tact with plants, as Sir Frederick Stern, has a feeling for the placing and the grouping of plants, knows which will best accompany which others. The result, although this garden is on chalk and in the semi-arid part of England, is a 'paradise' garden in the sense we have given the word here. In some respects, indeed, it is more successful than any other garden in the country in the displaying of such a scene as nature might have accomplished if all the best of her products in the race of plants had been brought together in support of each other instead of being scattered all over the five continents.

Notes on the Plates

84 HIGHDOWN

A paradise on the chalk.

85 HIGHDOWN

The great achievement of Sir Frederick Stern at Highdown, Sussex, has been growing a vast range of plant species in harmony on a notoriously difficult chalk soil. The tree is *Davidia involucrata* from W. China, popularly known as 'handkerchief tree'.

86 HIGHDOWN

It was discovered that whereas few plants will grow well on unbroken chalk, a surprisingly great number will flourish if the chalk be broken up to a considerable depth. In the soil thus improved exotics of many kinds naturalize themselves to grow into a community in which art imposes just so much order upon nature as will produce an ideal romantic plantscape.

87 HIGHDOWN

When photographing Highdown an attempt was made to avoid the innumerable rare exotics and to show what can be done by skill with more commonplace plants perfectly grown. *Hydrangea villosa*.

88 HIGHDOWN

Not another of the Highdown shrubby hydrangeas, but an ordinary *Viburnum tinus*. Grown as they are in this garden, the commonest shrubs demonstrate the reason for their original popularity.

89 HIGHDOWN

A corner with *Caltha polypetala* in flower. Note the happy combination of three entirely different kinds of foliage. One of the garden's achievements has been to enlarge the range of plants safe to plant on chalk.

90 HIGHDOWN

In the foreground *Paeonia emodi*. Sir Frederick Stern's monograph on the genus *Paeonia* is based on his experience with both shrubby and herbaceous species at Highdown. The flowering tree is *Prunus padus watereri*.

91 HIGHDOWN

Cherry-blossom petals. This chalk garden in a low rainfall part of England has nevertheless all the romantic richness of the great woodland gardens in high rainfall, peat-soil regions.

92 SISSINGHURST CASTLE

The Gatehouse seen from the Cottage. The garden was created within a framework of red Tudor brick walls and buildings of great distinction, to which the plant material has been matched with faultless art.

93 SISSINGHURST CASTLE

The towers of the Gatehouse dominate many parts of the garden, outstanding for its 'species' and 'old-fashioned' roses. This view is from the White Garden.

94 SISSINGHURST CASTLE

The theme of Sissinghurst Castle garden is 'expectation and surprise'. These are accomplished by the division of the garden into many parts, each part glimpsed from its neighbours.

95 SISSINGHURST CASTLE

Part of the Spring Garden. A walk of spring-flowering bulbs beside and between flagstones, with an avenue of pleached limes between fine beech hedges.

96 SISSINGHURST CASTLE

Angelica, clipped yew and poplars. The herb garden at Sissinghurst is one of the most charming of the smaller enclosures.

97 SISSINGHURST CASTLE

The Moat, separating the garden from the open fields of the home-farm.

98 KNIGHTSHAYES COURT

Sir John and Lady Heathcote-Amory have created a great garden in which the formal, the landscape and the romantic paradise traditions of the English garden are brilliantly combined.

99 KNIGHTSHAYES COURT

The use of topiary is restrained and gives an Italianate touch, helped by discreet use of stone ornament, which is very pleasing.

100 KNIGHTSHAYES COURT

From the formal garden immediately about the house, the eye is led through landscaped park embellished by magnificent trees, to the open country. In open glades among the trees are the woodland gardens of exotic flowering shrubs.

101 KNIGHTSHAYES COURT

The water-lily pond is enclosed in a clipped yew hedge. Beyond impends the steep bank of fine trees and flowering shrubs.

102 GREAT DIXTER

A garden created by Nathaniel Lloyd and Sir Edwin Lutyens. The old cattle sheds, transformed, were retained as summer houses. The topiary lawn is one of the features.

103 GREAT DIXTER

Garden entrance before the ancient Saxon Hall house of Great Dixter; a part of the wild garden. The soil with its high calcium-content entails growing shrubs which do not mind lime.

104 GREAT DIXTER

The front. The flagged path runs between areas of rough grass very richly planted with spring-flowering bulbs to form a 'flowery mead' in an ancient tradition.

105 GREAT DIXTER

View over the garden from one of the windows. Yew hedges form the enclosures; the mixed borders contain shrubs and perennials; fruit tree blossom is a feature.

106 GREAT DIXTER

The 'farmhouse': this view is from the 'hovel', the garden pavilion which Lutyens made out of the old cowsheds. The excessive modesty of the family's private name for it is uncalled for.

107 SHEFFIELD PARK

From a drawing by Humphry Repton published in 1741. Transformed early in our own century by A. G. Soames who made the lakes the axis of this lovely garden.

108 SHEFFIELD PARK

There are two principal lakes at Sheffield Park, linked by a cascade. This shows the lower lake from the point of junction.

109 SHEFFIELD PARK

The upper lake from the cascade. The shores of the lakes are planted with taste and skill with a vast range of exotic trees and shrubs whose reflection in the water competes with thousands of water-lilies.

110 SHEFFIELD PARK

Much of the beauty of these gardens derives from the contrasts between a thousand different forms and shades of foliage. Here a fine *Acer* is displayed against the weeping dark green of *Picea breweriana*.

111 NYMANS

The Pinetum. The conifers are underplanted with rhododendron in variety.

112 NYMANS

Nymans is one of the great twentieth-century gardens in which the paradise ideal is fully realized. Very rich in exotics, one of its glories is the mighty *Rhododendron sino-grande*. The young leaves, as they burst from the bud, are dusted silver. At maturity they will be two feet long.

113 NYMANS

From under an *Araucaria* (Monkey Puzzle) whose beauty can only be seen against a background of deciduous trees.

114 NYMANS

In the Heather Garden. In parts of this garden the ground cover sub-shrub is not heather but dwarf Himalayan rhododendrons which have naturalized themselves.

115 NYMANS

Another aspect of this infinitely various garden which is very rich in species of rhododendron, camellia, eucryphia and innumerable other flowering trees and shrubs in a partly woodland, partly semi-formal setting.

116 HIDCOTE MANOR

The pleached hornbeam avenue. In both the art of garden design and in plantsmanship, Hidcote is in many ways the most impressive of the twentieth-century gardens.

117, 118 NYMANS

Clipped yew, in the more formal part of the garden. The fountain is the focal point of the four principal paths. The rule in the twentieth-century gardens is to have a good representation of the formal traditions, rather Italianate, in the parts about the house, gently grading into wild, paradise or woodland garden as one gets farther away from the house. The landscape garden tradition is often respected in the park-like region between formality and wild nature.

119 HIDCOTE MANOR

The main vista at cherry-blossom time.

120 HIDCOTE MANOR

Note the skilful combination of many species into a harmony. The tree paeonies are *P. lutea ludlowii* with yellow flowers; the palm a trachycarpus, hardy throughout Britain.

121 HIDCOTE MANOR

A garden of many enclosures, each leading into the next, each a small masterpiece of the art of the formal, the cottage, the natural traditions. The tree on the left of the steps is one of many species of magnolia in the gardens.

122 HIDCOTE MANOR

Bridge, stream and cherry blossom. Although this garden is very rich in exotic plants they are never used simply for their rarity, but always as elements of a design.

123 HIDCOTE MANOR

In no garden, as you follow the paths and steps from enclosure to enclosure, is the theme of expectation and surprise more perfectly realized; or the formal and natural styles more perfectly reconciled.

124 HIDCOTE MANOR

Another example of the way in which glimpses of what is still to come draw the visitor on – in this case the Theatre Lawn. Every wall, gateway and arch is used to support climbing plants like this clematis.

87

88

89

90

93

94

98

99

104

105

106

107

108

115

114

117

116

*Plantsmanship
and design*

THE LAST GARDEN to be described and illustrated, Highdown in Sussex, cannot, as I have said, properly be criticized from the point of view of design. It is true that the shape of the land, the very clever use of the old chalk-pit, and the maker's taste, have caused a pleasing design to grow, as it were, while the plants themselves were growing. In some of the gardens which come nearest to being paradise gardens, in the sense, by now I hope clear, that I have used the term, there has obviously been a struggle to reconcile plantsmanship and design, with results which have not been altogether happy from the aesthetic point of view, however interesting and attractive to the horticultural botanist.

In the great woodland gardens of Cornwall and Devonshire, of south-west Scotland, and of Ireland, this has not been the case simply because no design has been imposed at all in many cases. It is true that in some of them, the very shape of the land and flow of waters has been changed in a manner almost eighteenth-century: but, on the whole, the gardeners have simply planted exotics into a naturally pleasing piece of country, their taste and skill being manifest in the more or less of success with which this has been done. That success is not simply to be judged by the flourishing condition of the exotic plants; the choice of forms and colours is all-important in ensuring that although the effect produced is 'not in nature', it is that of a 'possible world' and does not outrage nature. Of the newer gardens of this kind, in many ways the most successful is that made by Sir George Campbell at Crarae, to which we shall come in due course: there, the reconciliation of plantsmanship with the local 'nature' has been beautifully accomplished.

Bodnant

The problem of accomplishing this reconciliation has been greatest, perhaps, at the garden next to be described, Bodnant, on the north coast of Wales. On the whole this garden is completely successful and only a garden architect of great integrity and great austerity of taste will feel able to criticize it while actually looking at it. But, considering a visit in retrospect, some very interesting faults emerge which I would rather discuss here than while describing the garden. They are faults which are, quite obviously, by-products of the strife between brilliant plantsmanship and the exigencies of taste. They are not many and they are not, perhaps, of the first importance; without them Bodnant would be just about perfect as an horticultural work of art in the 'paradise' garden style. Two of these faults are worth discussion because they will help to make the point I am after here.

Bodnant is one of the two or three most famous rhododendron gardens in Britain, and in it grow many hundreds of species and hybrids. In the woodland parts of the garden their use has been faultless. But in that part of the garden which compromises between the formality of the terraces and the Pin Mill garden, and the wild woodland garden, boskages densely planted with rhododendron have been made threaded by narrow walks. The plantsman has here quite overcome the gardener; the desire to display the great versatility of the genus and to have as many representatives of it as possible, and to have them in number, produces, at the time of flowering in a good year (e.g. the spring of 1963), an effect which is certainly spectacular, certainly a great *tour de force* of horticultural skill, but which is aesthetically less satisfying. The effect of so much massed colour is to stun the eye, to deprive the scene of clear detail, and in the end even to bore the observer. In such plantings the choice is between massing the colours, as in the case of the Punch Bowl garden at Windsor as it used to be; and mixing the colours which, on the whole, is even worse. I think that the real solution is not to plant like this at all, to exercise deliberate restraint, to refer back, when considering the planting, to the austere standards of the eighteenth-century picture garden and to confine oneself to placing discreet bursts of suitable colour in a green landscape.

Before coming to the second of the Bodnant faults which I wish to discuss, another example of the difficulty of reconciling plantsmanship and design, on a much smaller scale, may be mentioned. As I have already pointed out, in the garden of the Garden House at Buckland Monachorum, Mr L. S. Fortescue has created one of the most remarkable and one of the most beautiful gardens in England. He has had a regard for form, for the excellent rule of 'expectation and surprise', for the pleasure of vistas and of enclosures. But he is a great plantsman, one of the greatest, and he has not entirely resisted the temptation to stress the note of massed colour in some parts of the garden. For the most part, the colour does not overwhelm the green; but there are places where plants themselves, very beautiful and interesting plants as far as that goes, have been allowed to count for more than their contribution to the total effect.

The most obvious case of plantsmanship, and one might almost say plant worship, which has led to a fault at Bodnant is on the terrace where (see below) *Magnolia delavayi* has been used as a wall plant. It would have been interesting enough to have one or two representatives of this handsome evergreen with gigantic leaves, in the woodland garden; but no doubt when it was planted it was thought too tender for any situation but a wall. The desire of the plantsman to have this species in the garden completely overcame the taste of the gardener, for not only has it been necessary to prune this tree in a most unnatural way, but the wall has not provided the right kind of protection and in very cold winters the trees are defoliated. The walls in question would have been better planted to some less uncommon, hardier and more beautiful species, some plant which would not have thrown the whole excellent design of the terrace in question quite out of proportion merely for the sake of having a rather unusual species of no very great merit.

There is, in some gardens where the important thing has been design, the shape of the whole, a fault which is the reverse of this one. At Chilham Castle in Kent, at Powerscourt in Ireland, and in far too many continental European versions of the English garden, there is a marked want of plantsmanship. Effects are obtained, but they are obtained with dull and uninteresting plants. Now the proper progression of appreciation in a garden is from the whole to the parts, from the vistas and the *coup d'oeil*, down to the detail. If the detail is not interesting then something is lost; it is as if the whole mass effect of a building were very good, but the carving and moulding turned out to be poor and dull upon close examination. It is true that, as Russel Page once said to me, a true garden can better be made with a golden elder and a load of gravel, by an artist, than with half the plant species of Asia by a mere plantsman. But if the artist in question know enough about plants, he can choose instead of golden elder something which, in form, in texture and, if it flower, in its inflorescences, will be pleasant and interesting in itself, as well as right *qua* mere 'plant material'.

Having allowed myself to criticize Bodnant and even the Garden House garden at Buckland Monachorum, I should, in fairness, add that my points were only worth making because these gardens are, on two different scales, so outstandingly fine. The faults of a mediocre painter are taken for granted; in a Raphael a fault sticks out and demands explanation.

Perhaps there is no garden in Britain which comes nearer to the ideal I have repeatedly referred to than Bodnant. Once inside this great garden, in which every device of every good school of English gardening has been used, you are inside the English gardener's dream. It is a garden in which 'the most direct and energetic efforts of nature at physical loveliness' have been brought together from the four corners of the world, not into a mere collection but combined into a work of art, after nature yet exceeding her happiest combinations. The men who made this garden had absorbed the earlier traditions, the traditions of formal gardening, Italianate gardening, picture gardening, so that in the laying out of the walks and plantations, and in the use of country in such a manner as would enable them to exploit the immense wealth in plant material available to them, they had the benefit of what had almost become an instinct for right design. If a visitor, anxious to know what the 'English garden' has become at last, had time for but a single garden, this is the one, out of many hundreds, I would send him to.

The garden of Bodnant is at Tal-y-cafn, near enough to the warm western sea to have a relatively mild climate. The site commands views of mountains and river, across the valley of the Conway, and, as in so many of the best gardens, it slopes steeply, the fall of the land being to the south-west. As well as having a mild climate and fertile soil, Bodnant has much water in running streams and the river itself, one of the greatest advantages which a garden maker can dispose of.

Apart from the fact that the site had fine stands of indigenous trees planted late in the eighteenth century, the garden is a twentieth-century accomplishment, for the first real laying out of the grounds was undertaken by Henry Pochin, great-grandfather of the Lord Aberconway who now lives at Bodnant, who supervises the garden for the National Trust, and whose father, the second baron, presented the garden to the National Trust in 1949.

Bodnant is in two parts. The higher gardens, a series of terraces flanked by sloping, informal lawns protected by trees; and a lower part, the Dell or Wild Garden whose serpentine axis is the river Hiraethlyn which flows into the Conway. This part of the gardens includes a Pinetum. Although this general division was contrived by Henry Pochin, and executed by Milner, a landscape gardener of merit who flourished in the last decades of the nineteenth century and who was likewise responsible for the Pinetum, the garden as we have it is very largely the work of two men: the second Lord Aberconway and his head gardener, Mr F. C. Puddle. It is true that Henry Pochin's daughter, the first Lady Aberconway, took a great interest in the development of the gardens and planted many flowering shrubs and a vast quantity of bulbs, as well as creating a number of the then very fashionable herbaceous borders; but the execution first of her own ideas, later of his, was entrusted to her son, Henry Duncan, the second baron, while he was still in his early twenties. As a result of this early start he was able to work upon the transformation of the garden to realize a vision of his own for over half a century. This is important and it is unusual. It too often happens that a man turns gardener too late in life to see the full realization of a vision which, if he dies, will never be realized, for though his heir be a gardener it does not follow that he will envisage the same kind of garden. Any work of art cannot but be the work of a single individual: art is not produced by committees. And it rather rarely happens that a gardener lives long enough to see his conception through to completion. Moreover, it so happened that Henry Duncan had both taste and imagination, as well as the necessary learning, when it came to the laying out of a garden; and a love of plants which is, in a gardener, tantamount to knowledge of his materials in any other kind of craftsman.

The focus of the higher garden as Henry Pochin left it was a vast lawn which sloped down from the house towards the valley and on either side of which were groups of trees, notably two fine cedars, one on each side, about half-way down the slope. In 1905 Lord Aberconway undertook the work of transforming this lawn into a series of terrace gardens in what is rather loosely called the 'Italian' style. This work took nine years to complete. The highest of these terraces – the terrace gardens are on the west side of the house – is a rose garden and from it one has a magnificent view, down the other four terraces,

Plate 128

canalized by the flanking trees, and leading naturally away across the Conway valley to a group of mountains. The mountains are, in the background, Snowdon, to the left and in front of it, Carnedd Llewelyn, and to the right of that Foel Fras, the Drum and Tal-y-fan. What, among other things, Lord Aberconway achieved when he created this terrace garden, was to bring these mountains into the garden: it has always been a principal object of both English and Chinese landscape gardeners to do this, but success of the order achieved at Bodnant is rare.

The terraces

The Rose Terrace itself is geometrical, a small formal garden, as are several of the other terraces. Bodnant is, notably, one of the three or four twentieth-century gardens in which the combination and wedding of the two great traditional master-styles has succeeded in a manner which would have delighted the eye of the great Loudon, and which demonstrates the compatibility of the formal and natural styles where the gardener has talent and, almost equally important, elbow room. The formally planted roses are the nucleus of this higher terrace, but other plant material has not been excluded: apart from under-plantings of herbaceous subjects, the house wall is planted to *Camellia williamsi*, a hybrid of robust constitution bred at Caerhays in Cornwall.

Gilding the lily

The stone steps from the Rose Terrace begin as one flight, but divide to curve round both sides of a fountain and pool, to make two flights: the fountain is French baroque and by way of gilding the lily has been embellished with two wistarias, both of them white, not the commoner lavender, *W. venusta* and the white variety of *W. sinensis*. The practice of training climbing and lax or scandent shrubs over the artefacts of a garden is peculiar to the English; it softens, some would say spoils, the line of stone ornaments, but also it gives to the garden, in a relatively few years, an air of maturity, even antiquity, which continental gardens with their austere hardness of line seldom achieve even when they are, in fact, ancient. Where the two flights of steps debouch on to the second or Croquet Terrace they do so through a gracefully curved wall which provides shelter for a number of flowering shrubs, on one side *Eucryphia nymansensis* and the rare dwarf lilac *Syringa palibiniana* to cover the nakedness of the eucryphias' trunks; a Chinese daphne (*D. tangutica*), the New Zealand eucryphia (*E. lucida*) and a *Magnolia campbelli*. Thus in spring the principal colour scheme of this planting is rose-pink, when the magnolia produces its enormous flowers and the daphne followed by the lilac comes into bloom. In the autumn, however, the dominant note is pure white, when the eucryphias come into bloom and are covered with their cupped flowers.

On the other side of the fountain the plants are equally distinguished: a third eucryphia, *E. intermedia*, the extraordinary *Pieris forrestii* whose young leaves through spring and summer are crimson, and whose flowers are great racemes of what look for all the world like large bouquets of lily-of-the-valley; magnolia, escallonia and hoheria. The principal plants of this Croquet Terrace bear witness to the way in which plant collectors have ransacked the world to stock the great English gardens: the countries repre-sented by natives on this single terrace are Yunnan, Szechuan, Peru, Chile, New Zealand, Japan.

The water-lilies

Two flights of stone steps lead down again from the Croquet Terrace to the Lily Terrace. The epony-mous 'lilies' of this third terrace are in fact water-lilies, for the principal feature of the terrace is a formal pond, an oblong with a semi-circular bay, in which are planted a whole range of hybrid water-lilies which flower from early in June to late in September, and cover the spectrum from pale yellow and creamy white to deep blood red. At the height of the water-lily season the spectacle here is astonishing; on a day of strong sunshine which brings these aquatics swiftly into full bloom, there may be as many as a thousand great flowers open at one time, and even on a day less brilliant there will usually be several hundred. In 1875 when this part of the garden was still lawn, Henry Pochin planted two cedars at this point, a cedar of Lebanon and, to balance it, the North African cedar with glaucous blue foliage (*C. atlantica glauca*). When designing this terrace Lord Aberconway kept these trees and made the line between them the axis of the pond, so that they now flank it. They have, in less than ninety years, reached a great size: the age of trees, judged by size, is always enormously over-estimated; if there was no record of these two cedars, no doubt several centuries would be attributed to them.

In the making of this as of all the terraces it was necessary to build buttressed retaining walls to hold up the soil which was thrown up to level the slope. Thus on this, as on the higher terrace, there is a wall which gives so much shelter that many tender subjects can be grown in its lee. Consequently this terrace, like the Croquet Terrace, contains an interesting and beautiful collection of exotics. The eucryphia at this level is the southern Chilean *E. cordifolia*, a small, spirelike tree with tough, dark foliage which, in early autumn, becomes completely covered with large creamy cup-shaped white flowers with golden centres. In some Irish gardens this species has reached an astonishing size, but even here it is a strikingly beautiful plant. There is also the giant-leaved *Magnolia delavayi*, the rare and tender *Buddleia colvilei* with its long racemes of large crimson flowers, and the tender *Camellia reticulata*, a species whose flowers sometimes attain a diameter of six or seven inches. Among these larger shrubs are planted rhododendrons of the '*maddenii*' series which have very large white flowers richly scenting the air with a fragrance of spiced honey. These, again, are generally considered tender and not to be grown where sharp frost is to be expected. As wall plants they are not altogether a success, however.

Two curved flights of steps, following the curve of a wall enclosing a long oval, lead from the Lily Terrace down to the lower Rose Terrace. The steps themselves are ornamented by a pergola planted to climbing roses and the Chilean creeper *Solanum crispum* which produces an abundance of very pleasing blue flowers throughout the spring and summer. This solanum is not the type, but a form or variety produced at the National Botanical Garden of Ireland, Glasnevin in Dublin. The curved walls are planted to magnolia, the familiar evergreen *grandiflora* in the giant-flowered form, and to that strangely beautiful Andean shrub, *Crinodendron lanceolatum*, an evergreen bearing thousands of waxy, pale crimson flowers shaped like Chinese lanterns. The Rose Terrace itself is formal, consisting of four large symmetrical beds and paved, as rose terraces perhaps always should be, with bricks, laid in a pleasant pattern. In one corner there is a tall specimen of *Eucalyptus gunnii*, and there are mass plantings of the South African dieramas, and of the green-flowered hellebores. A Chinese clematis (*C. tangutica*), which bears small yellow lantern-shaped flowers, covers the railings above the descent to the next terrace of the series.

This lowest terrace is called the Canal Terrace, and it consists of a series of rectangles one within the other, the central one being the 'canal', a long narrow stretch of water kept clear excepting for plantings of water-lilies at each end. This water is enclosed in a rectangular lawn, and the lawn in a rectangular border planted to herbaceous plants with grey or silver foliage, and blue or lavender flowers. The borders, in their turn, are enclosed on one side by a wall built with recesses in which tender plants can be safely grown; and on the other side by clipped yew. The Canal Terrace is terminated at its northern end by an open-air stage of lawn contained in a broad curve of clipped yew and with wings of more clipped yew in what is called the classical Italian style, a style which was, in fact, copied from eighteenth-century Italian gardens although in different plant materials. There is a stone seat on the stage, a copy of one designed for another garden by William Kent.

Italianate formality

At the south end of the same Canal Terrace is a still more striking use of architecture in the garden, but this time in masonry instead of in turf and yew. This is the Pin Mill, a very charming little building. Despite its name it was not in fact built as a pin mill at all, but as what it now is, a garden house, but at Woodchester in Gloucestershire in the garden of an Elizabethan manor house and in the year 1730. It was doubtless some financial disaster to the owners which led to the building on of a small factory or workshop to the back of this garden house, so that it could be used as a mill for the manufacture of pins. This enterprise failing, the buildings were degraded one more step and became a small tannery. By the year 1938 the garden house was slowly decaying into its squalid surroundings of industrial slum, where the late Lord Aberconway found it. He saw its quality despite its setting, bought it, and removed the roof, the carved and dressed mason's work, and the principal timbers which were all sound, to Bodnant, re-erecting the Pin Mill on a new brick foundation. The Pin Mill contains some good Fontainebleau tapestry dating from about 1565.

The Pin Mill

The North Garden

Before continuing down the slope beyond the lowest terrace and the Pin Mill, it will be best to return to the Croquet Terrace and make a detour into the North Garden. It is a sort of enclave to the right, that is, to the north, of the Rose and Croquet Terraces as one descends them towards the valley. Such enclaves, consisting usually of lawn surrounded by borders of flowering shrubs, surrounded in their turn by completely enclosing trees, is a very characteristic feature of the English garden; it is a secret place, welcoming a single visitor, but excluding, by means of a strong 'atmosphere', what I can only call a 'hushedness', those who come in parties, and chatter. The exotics are mostly of the rhododendron, azalea, eucryphia and magnolia genera, but there is a noteworthy tulip tree and what must be one of the largest Judas trees in Britain. Who, I wonder, was the author of the 'legend' that this tree (*Cercis siliquastrum*) received its vernacular name because Judas is supposed to have hanged himself from one of this species? The legend is repeated by writer after writer, but it has no ancient foundation whatever and the tree, when first introduced into England probably from Italy rather than Palestine, was called Tree of Judaea, which has clearly become corrupted to the present form. The Bodnant specimen has flowers of an unusually deep purple; nor is that the only colour-distinction to be found in this garden. On the pathway which leads back to the series of terraces on to the lower end of the Croquet Terrace in fact, is a large massed planting of *Rhododendron augustinii*. The so-called 'blue' flowers of this fine species are as a rule a sort of bluish purple, but the Bodnant form is true blue and this planting, when in flower, is one of the most beautiful spectacles I have seen in any English garden.

The lower garden

There is a sloping path behind the Pin Mill which leads down into the garden below the Canal Terrace. The first feature of this lower garden is the camellia bank; there is no point in trying to list the species and varieties grown there; there is a very wide range, all well-grown to a considerable size equalled, in my experience, only in one or two Cornish gardens and about Sintra in Portugal. Below this and still going down hill, you come to a series of large borders separated by straight paths, all of them parallel with the Canal Terrace above, and the borders planted to a collection, a sort of formal wood, of magnolia species. Among them the taller trees of this genus are low-growing rhododendrons, camellias and some other flowering shrubs, and the planting is enclosed in tall beech trees and spreading yews as a background for still more rhododendrons, mostly species but with some of the better hybrids. Bodnant has probably supplied more hybrid rhododendrons for distribution to other gardens, and for nursery commerce, than any other garden in the world.

The Rock Garden and the Dell Garden

Still farther down and to the south lies the Rock Garden, beyond that the river Hiraethlyn, and the Dell Garden. The Rock Garden also has its water, a tumbling stream which falls into the river. Its natural course has been altered by damming it so as to form a series of pools and waterfalls. The principal plants of the Rock Garden are, as a background, the large-leaved rhododendrons such as *R. falconeri*, and among the stones primulas, mostly of the Japanese (candelabra) sorts, the ground-creeping rhododendron (*forrestii repens*) with its waxy scarlet flowers, and many small-leaved dwarf rhododendrons from the high Himalaya, the dominant flower colours being lavender-blue and pale golden yellow. But among these are many of the Himalayan meconopses, 'poppies' flowering sky-blue, lavender, purple, salmon red and yellow, and notably the very beautiful *M. napaulensis* with its hairy silver leaves.

Plate 127

There are two ways to see the Dell which is planted, in the strict Robinsonian tradition, on both banks of the Hiraethlyn. Either by going down into it; or by looking down on it from a path which overlooks, in fact overhangs, it and which ultimately leads to a part of the garden known as the Shrub Borders. It is better to go down into the Dell, however, in order fully to experience an aesthetic 'shock' produced by the planting of some of the most remarkable plants known to botany. Apart from their native habitat in Asia, the rhododendrons of the *Grande* series grow to perfection in only two places: the south-west Scottish and Irish, north-west English and Welsh high-rainfall region; and the 'fog-belt' of maritime California north of San Francisco. In Bodnant Dell there are *R. sino-grande*, *R. macabeanum* and *R. falconeri*, among others. They are primitive plants which have remained unchanged for about fifty million years. The architectural effects which can be produced with them in the rather few gardens where they will grow properly are extraordinary, and can be achieved in no other way. The leaves of, for example, *R. sino-grande*, may be two, even three feet long and a foot wide, of perfect form and thick, leathery substance. The colossal heads of flowers are creamy-yellow. In a planting of this kind one is not only in an alien world, a very strange world, geographically, but temporally.

But quite apart from this, the Dell represents the English garden as Robinson probably envisaged but never accomplished it, in perfection. A measure of order has been introduced, for example, by mowing the lawns from which rise magnificent specimens of a wide range of exotic conifers, silver firs, wellingtonias, cryptomerias and others, which brings the whole of this garden nearer to that dream-world, that 'paradise' which the English garden aims to accomplish. The Dell is nature improved by the bringing together of plant species remote in their habitats, and by introducing a measure of tidiness. There are paths through the Dell on both sides of the river and either will lead you to the mill-race.

The mill-race was made in the sixteenth century, probably to turn the wheel of a flour mill. Later and into the nineteenth century it was used to drive the fans of a blast furnace on the banks of the Conway. In our own time it has driven the Bodnant sawmill after a short period of restoration to its original purpose of grinding corn. The garden, or at least the plantings, does not stop here. The hillside which dominates the mill-race is planted to a collection of conifers including Douglas fir and *Pinus radiata*, interplanted with the loveliest of our native flowering trees, the gean, or wild cherry. Under these trees are azaleas and hybrid rhododendrons flowering in a range of colours which covers the whole spectrum. The path on the far side of the river Hiraethlyn continues still farther and commands a view of the mill-pond waterfall above which is a rustic bridge from which you look down on to a planting of 'Penjerrick' rhododendrons and near which is a rarity among trees, a specimen of *Juniperus coxii* which the Chinese value above rubies for the making of coffins, so that it has become extremely rare in the wild. Above the mill-pond Henry Pochin built himself a mausoleum. There is a path beyond this and it leads to an especially contrived viewpoint with a seat from which the Dell can be seen in both directions. Behind this the whole hillside is planted with magnolia species, arbutus, and the Chilean fire-tree embothrium, each specimen of which becomes a sort of living scarlet flame when in flower. Beyond this, again, is one of the most successful planting of autumn-colour species in the whole country; there is no need to particularize them, but among the better known are eucryphias, red oaks and species and varieties of sorbus; the colour scheme in September and October is from pale primrose through the whole range of yellows and golds, through crimson, to scarlet and purple.

The principal shrub borders are reached from this point by a climbing path. Shrubs which flower very early in spring are here underplanted with spring bulbs, heaths, hellebores and other species to form a carpet of subtle colours. Just off the main path is a circular garden enclosed in clipped yew, and devoted to the rarer and more softly coloured oriental primulas, and to the blue and rose-coloured meconopses. This little paradise also commands a high view down on to the Dell.

The path upwards from the shrub borders leads by way of an open hillside planted to beech and *The Round Garden* sycamore and kept mown as a fine lawn. At the foot of the hill is a formal oval pond enclosed in an oval of rhododendrons which flower rose-pink and lavender-blue. There are plantings of the sweet-scented white flowered rhododendrons, in clumps beyond the oval, so that in season the air is honey sweet with their fragrance. From here another rising path leads to the Round Garden, the nucleus of which is a large circular bed which, from the technical horticultural point of view, as well as aesthetically, is of particular interest, since in it, growing to form a dense mass, and all equally prosperous, are the dwarf rhododendrons which are supposed to flourish only in acid soils, and a collection of daphnes which are supposed to need lime in order to prosper. The bed is divided by diagonal flagstone paths, and at its centre is an eighteenth-century 'scalloped' dolphin-fountain.

The final feature of this garden, leading the visitor back to his point of departure, is to be seen at *The Laburnum Arch* its best in the last two weeks of May and the first two weeks of June. This is the Laburnum Arch: it consists of pleached laburnums trained over to form an arch from both sides and which, in the flowering season, is hung with a myriad of long golden racemes of flower.

Even in Bodnant, however, with frosts every winter and, occasionally, severe frost when, four or five times in a century, Britain suffers a continental winter, some limitation is imposed on the choice of plants. This is much less the case in certain great woodland gardens even more favourably placed in the matter of climate. All these gardens are, as it were, variations on the theme of the Hiraethlyn Glen at Bodnant, though in some cases much larger in extent. They include the greatest Cornish and Devonshire gardens, such as Penjerrick, Trewithan, above all Caerhays; Knightshayes, the garden made by Sir John and Lady Heathcoat-Amory near Tiverton, having about it a touch of traditional formality in at least part of its extent, is less a pure paradise garden. The gardens of Ireland are, at their best, paradise gardens, plantings of magnificent exotics into woodland scenes; so, superlatively, are the gardens of south-west Scotland. For the extreme south-west I propose to take the outstanding example, Caerhays; for Scotland, three woodland gardens which are not the three best known by name to the public in general (Inverewe, Brodick and Lochinch), but which are interesting as gardens made in the lifetime of any reader over fifty and are, at the same time, outstandingly successful in their class.

The movement towards the creation of romantic paradise gardens in England received its most remarkable expression in the extreme west, for climatic and geological reasons which have already been given. In the mild climate and peaty woodland soils of Cornwall, south-west Scotland, parts of Wales, all regions of relatively high rainfall, hundreds of the Asiatic, Andean and Australasian species of plants introduced to Britain between the sixteenth and twentieth centuries, found conditions in which they could flourish. Outstandingly successful and exciting gardens of the kind we are here concerned with were made in Ireland, perhaps Mount Usher, in County Wicklow, the work of four generations of the Walpole family, being the most remarkable. In Cornwall such gardens as Trengwainton and Penjerrick are fine examples, and Glendurgan with its magnificent vistas down to the Helston river. But superlative among the English examples is Caerhays Castle, partly because of its situation and partly because the family which owned and owns it produced one of the greatest English gardeners.

The maker of Caerhays was John Charles Williams. In 1854 Michael Williams, Sheriff of Glamorganshire in 1839 and Member of Parliament for West Cornwall from 1853 to 1858, bought Caerhays Castle and all the land in the parish excepting the glebe. Although his son and heir John Michael Williams took an interest in the garden, he was, as a banker, financier and Sheriff of Cornwall, too busy to give much time to it. Fortunately he was not too busy to marry Elizabeth Maria Davey of Bochym near the Lizard. John Charles was their second son. In due course he went to Rugby which he disliked, then toured Europe with a tutor, later went up to Cambridge, travelled again including to Australia, became interested in geology, returned to England and, his father having died and his brother inherited Caerhays where his mother still lived, he married and bought himself a house, Werrington Park near Launceston. From 1918 to 1936 he was Lord-Lieutenant of Cornwall, having been High Sheriff and, for many years, a County Councillor. From 1892 to 1895 he was Member for the Truro and Helston division of Cornwall. But he did not stand for election a second time; he detested London; he did not want his children to be brought up there; and, as Bishop Hunkin of Truro wrote in the *Journal* of the RHS in January 1943: 'his friends said that in London he could not see his water-lilies opening. . . .'

Caerhays Castle stands close to the sea with its own sandy beach, its own bay where the sea, as so often off the Cornish coast, can be bluer than the Mediterranean ever is. The land rises either gently or steeply all about it. All this land is gardened and it is possible to walk all day and perhaps several
days in the garden and yet not to see everything. As to the nature of the garden it is what one would expect of a man who had such a love of and interest in plants that he would check his horse when out riding to ask a road-man not to cut down a wild orchid or even one of the common ferns of the Cornish lanes. The worst enemy of this garden is wind; part of it is protected by a natural wood on the

hillside; for the rest, a great laurel hedge, a remarkable feature, breaks the wind force across a considerable area of plantation, and elsewhere more laurels and huge clumps of bamboo do the like for other sections.

From the Lodge at the side of the road which runs beside the sea, there is a gently rising drive half a mile long up towards the house. It is richly planted with cherries, with Asiatic and American magnolias, with many species of mountain rhododendrons, with hydrangeas which in that acid soil are a fantastically deep blue. The whole is on so large a scale that nothing had to be done pinchingly, every species is represented not by one specimen or two, but by many, a coppice, a wood in which lilies from all over the world are the wild flowers. The impact is indescribable. It is as if a great romantic poet and a great gardener had had the plant resources of the whole world placed at their disposal and a commission to make a garden of Eden to satisfy the yearnings of English horticultural romanticism.

The principal plantations consist of shrubs and trees in an immense variety and diversity through which broad walks or rides lead to many small points of rest or view, often protected by plantings of laurel. As Bishop Hunkin describes it: '. . . the sights that suddenly meet the eye are unforgettable. The visitor bursts in upon not one or two but a whole group of great rhododendrons, trees rather than bushes, blazing with large trusses of magnificent flowers, white or pink or red. . . .'

Many of the trees and shrubs planted at Caerhays were new to gardens, being from seed sent home by Wilson and by Forrest. Enormous under-plantings of daffodil and crocus were made; a notable plant breeder in several species, J. C. Williams produced many new daffodils, many new rhododendrons. His rhododendron breeding began in 1885 and must have been greatly encouraged by the fact that rhododendrons of even quite difficult species readily seed themselves at Caerhays and are, in fact, virtually naturalized there. Williams had first choice of plants raised from Wilson's seed by Veitch; he financed Forrest's expeditions to Yunnan. *Rhododendron fargesii, sutchuense, orbiculare, auriculatum, sinogrande* and many others flowered for the first time in Europe (or anywhere else but on their native mountains), at Caerhays. Among them was *R. williamsianum* which was named for him. Of Forrest's collectings, forty-seven species flowered for the first time at Caerhays. Bishop Hunkin, in his biographical note on Williams from which I have already quoted, says: 'No one knows the number of rhododendron species eventually planted at Caerhays; it must run into many hundreds if not into thousands. [It can hardly have been 'thousands'; there are between 800 and 900 species known to science. E.H.] Mr Williams made very careful notes of them; he had a marvellous power of concentrating upon a difficult and complicated subject and becoming master of it. . . . He himself was not content until he knew not only the height at which collected plants grew as well as their position, but also the geology of the district. . . . He was keen on experimenting but once satisfied that a situation was wrong he took the line that there was always some other plant that would do there and would look well. . . .'

Rhododendron breeding

It is perfectly possible to see as many as eighty, and perhaps a hundred species of rhododendron, from sub-shrubs a few inches tall to plants the size of trees, in flower, each represented not by one but by scores of specimens, on the same day. Of the Caerhays hybrids now planted in gardens all over the world, at least twelve are incomparably good in their class. And Williams was generous with these and with all his plants. In 1927 a new house for Chinese rhododendrons was being built at Kew. C. P. Raffill of Kew came to visit at Caerhays: he was sent off, when his visit ended, with a railway truck full of specimen rhododendrons for the new greenhouse.

Plate 132

If I have given the impression that Caerhays is simply the most remarkable rhododendron garden in the world, I have not intended to do so. It is at least equally remarkable for magnolias and camellias; and the non-botanical visitor is probably more likely to be struck by, for example, the stands of tree-ferns or some other and more obviously exotic plant, than with any of these. Camellia planting was begun a little later, as far as one can tell, than rhododendron planting. Again, the species were planted but whereas there are probably about 800 species of rhododendron in cultivation, there are very few

Magnolias and camellias

species of camellia. Like the rhododendrons they were planted in mass. *Camellia saluensis*, seed of which was sent home by Forrest, was first grown at Caerhays. It became of the first horticultural importance because Williams crossed it with the better-known and extremely hardy *C. japonica* which had long been in cultivation though mistakenly and widely regarded as a tender shrub, to produce the *C. × williamsi* race of camellias which are now the best we have for general garden planting. Other crosses were made to produce fine plants which have not, however, made such an impression on gardening in general. Perhaps the most remarkable camellia to be seen in the whole gardens is a specimen of the *C. reticulata* which was developed from the wild form by Chinese monks and was found growing only in Chinese monastery gardens. It is often in flower at about Easter-time, and the fully double flowers, of a very rich pink, are almost the size of soup plates. This, at least, is the most spectacular of this genus; more attractive, to my own taste at all events, are the old specimens of *saluensis* and *sasanqua*, very beautiful evergreens with myriads of small, single, white or blush-pink flowers.

I do not know whether Caerhays has every known species of magnolia, but there certainly cannot be a collection to equal it. I should make it clear that they are not planted as a collection; they were used as what so many of them are, forest trees, to form woodland in which rhododendrons, camellias and other shrubs, and below them iris, daffodil and a hundred other groundlings could grow. It is quite impossible to convey in words anything of the impression made by these trees in flower. In all magnolias the flowers are large; in some they are enormous. The form is always good, often of a peculiarly pure line and suave substance. Most are white, some are rose; notable among the latter are *campbelli* which makes a huge tree and may carry several thousand flowers nearly a foot in diameter; and *sprengeri diva*, at one time uniquely grown at Caerhays.

I have concentrated on these three genera because J. C. Williams himself probably gave them more of his attention and did more work on them than any others. But it would be quite wrong to give the impression that they occupy the whole of the gardens at Caerhays. It would be possible, by filling this whole volume with tabulated lists of shrubs, herbaceous perennials, bulbs and corms and rhyzomes, to catalogue the plants in these gardens; and from anything but the botanist's point of view, it would be pointless. The gardens are rich in tree heaths, in primulas, exotic oaks and beeches, in maples, in enkianthus, in . . . but what is the use? I am in precisely the same difficulty as that French gardener who came over to see the Cornish gardens and whose case is recounted by Bishop Hunkin: the Frenchman's host had noticed that as, day after day, his guest came back from a visit to some garden he sat down to write notes on it; but on the day he returned from Caerhays he wrote nothing. He was asked why, and he gave this despairing answer: 'Because it is impossible. They will no longer believe me.'

What, in terms of a garden, has been accomplished with this immense wealth of material? There are some primitive paintings to be seen in Italy in which the painter, a priest, has composed a picture in which the loveliest of nature's creatures, plant or animals, are combined in a paradise, all living peacefully together. Such paintings are reflections of man's realization of what might be possible, aesthetically, if the most beautiful living things from all the world were to be gathered into a single community. This is what has been done, at Caerhays, with plants; and it has been done with such art, an art whose effects time has enhanced, that the art never obtrudes upon the attention. There is order, there is proportion and there is balance; but the whole seems to be the outcome of a natural miracle rather than of a gardener.

But for woodland gardens in which horticultural aesthetics have played no part, in which form, design, shape have been left entirely to nature and the gardening has been confined to plantsmanship at a very high level of skill, two Scottish gardens are of particular interest.

Glenarn Glenarn is a garden of fourteen acres at Rhu on the Gareloch in south-west Scotland. Into a typical piece of loch-country hillside, steep, rocky, peaty, with two streams falling over the naked granite and a wealth of mosses and ferns, have been planted some thousands of rhododendron trees, shrubs and sub-shrubs representing not less than 650 species or blue-blooded hybrids. The climate is very mild; there is not much sunshine and there is a mean rainfall of seventy inches. In short, this corner of Scotland reproduces, almost perfectly, the climate of the hill country of northern India in which the first great collections of rhododendron species were made, notably by Sir Joseph Hooker. That pundit, in his introduction to the great folio of paintings and descriptions of the plants which he collected in Sikhim, gave a table of the climate of the country in which he had worked: it might be a record of the weather in south-west Scotland over a period of years.

The reader should imagine himself walking in a Scottish wood of native hardwood trees and familiar conifers. He is climbing a path which has been cut into the side of a steep and narrow valley; at the bottom of the path he was on a level with the stream which runs through that valley, a stream of tur-bulent, peat-brown water rippling and chuckling over stones. But as he climbs, path and the stream diverge in the vertical plane, and he finds himself looking more and more steeply down to the noisy little water. At one or two points tributaries make their way into the main stream, and these are crossed by means of small bridges made of a slab of stone or a few stout planks. There is water everywhere, in the air, in the soft and spongy soil, manifest too in the luxuriant growth of sphagnum and other mosses, of ferns, of the grey lichen which beards every twig and branch. So far, nothing out of the way. But the undergrowth of this wood consists of shrubs, between 600 and 650 species each represented by anything from one to a dozen specimens, of kinds native to Sikhim, to Bhutan, to the mountains of Burma and China. A big rock beside the path which winds as it rises, will be clad in the deep green, heart-shaped foliage of *Rhododendron williamsianum*, and that mound of foliage decorated with a myriad rose-pink bell-flowers. A vista of familiar tree-trunks defining a little glade is startlingly illuminated by the enormous golden-yellow flowers of a tree with a gnarled and twisted trunk, huge leathery leaves, and inflorescences the size of footballs: it is *Rhododendron macabeanum*, and it towers and spreads like an oak. Looking up and forward to follow the line of the path, the visitor catches a glimpse of what he takes for a moment to be clear open sky between the heads of trees. It is a huge clump of *Rhododendron augustinii*, the foliage entirely concealed under the cloud of blue flowers. Still climbing, he becomes aware of a fragrance in the air, of a scent of vanilla which hangs in the moist atmosphere and grows stronger and sweeter until, rounding a curve in the path, he is among tall, leggy bushes each bearing, at the extremity of numerous slender branches, great loose trusses of large white flowers which look for all the world like lilies; here the scent is almost overpowering: the plants are *Rhododendron lindleyi*, or *johnstonianum*, or *bullatum*, or the aptly named *fragrantissimum*, or perhaps a coppice of all and more together. The rocky edge at the other side of the path is open to the sky and receives some warmth and light directly from the sun; over it grows a dense, twiggy, repent plant with tiny bright green leaves turning in places to a coppery green, and, all over this finely textured mat of foliage, small wine-red bell-flowers, each carried erect on a golden stem, myriads of them all turned one way and moving a little in the mild breeze: *Rhododendron radicans*, or perhaps, if the plant be a little taller and more open, *campylogynum*. Higher still, and the visitor comes upon a group of tall, narrow shrubs with pale lance-like leaves almost hidden by thousands of white, frilled flowers marked in their throats with rose-red, flowers of a moving delicacy of form, colour and texture, stirring a little as if to play with the filtered, greenish light: *Rhododendron davidsonianum*. He turns from these to look down the valley. There is no riot of colour, no vulgar masses of pink or purple or yellow: the infinite range of greens and browns is simply lit, here and there, with touches of yellow, of cream, of blue, of scarlet, of blood-red, or orange or crimson – all rhododendrons.

He emerges at last on a small plateau where, at once, the wind is felt and there is, at last, sound other than birdsong, the rustle of leaves. The plateau is of fine turf and it is enclosed by trees and banked, on the higher side, by tier upon tier of foliage above which tower giant-leaved trees which at once trans-form the native scene into something exotic and romantic. Above each rosette of huge, dark-green, oval leaves, some perhaps two feet long and most more than a foot, are borne great heads of translucent

Sikhim in Scotland

Plate 133

cream flowers seemingly made of some shining kind of wax, touched in the throat with burgundy red, and borne in so high and stately a fashion that the visitor must throw back his head to look up at them: *Rhododendron falconeri*, or perhaps it should be *sino-grande* or, if the flowers be rather yellow than cream, *macabeanum*.

For all the protean diversity of rhododendrons, they are not all that the visitor attends to. Underfoot are the groundings of the Himalayan alpine meadows and gorges, the tall candelabra primulas, the blue, and white and salmon poppy-flowers of mecanopses, and, from time to time, something alto-gether strange, the Chilean philesia whose yew-like foliage drapes a great outcrop of granite, and is draped with myriad tubular flowers wrought in pale crimson wax; or an azara from the Andes whose minute golden flowers fill the air with the scent of spices. But it is to the endlessly diverse forms, colours, stature, habit of the rhododendrons that the attention returns time and again: some, plants less tall than a man, are covered with flowers of so dark a red that the buds look black; the flowers may be bells, tubes, trumpets, funnels; the leaves like lance-heads, or pure ovals, or heart-shaped, or even almost circular as in *Rhododendron orbiculare* with its rose-pink flowers. The stature may be such that one must crouch and peer to admire the plant in detail; or, on the other hand, stand well back and crane upwards, as to the mighty and ancient *Rhododendron falconeri* whose timber might almost yield a bed-room suite, and which was grown from a seed sent home by Sir Joseph Hooker one hundred and twenty-five years ago. Its flowers, each a cream bell of thick and fleshy substance, each one of a truss of ten or twenty, are numbered in thousands and when they fall the ground underfoot is ankle-deep in them.

Crarae — Such, in an account necessarily impressionist and romantic, is Glenarn on Gareloch, a gardened wood. Although Crarae, the garden created by Sir George Campbell beside Loch Fyne, is of the same kind, yet the impression is not the same. At Glenarn it is the trees which make the atmosphere, the atmo-sphere of a wood, closed in, secret, shaded. There are as many or more trees at Crarae, and in any case it is a larger garden, probably about forty acres and certainly not less than thirty. But here the river is more important, the whole is more open, the visitor does not have the feeling of being inside the scene, but above it, dominating it; there is more light, less secrecy, the movement of air is more felt and the sound and changing lights of the water – the stream here is a much bigger and more spectacular one – are dominant.

The shape of the land, the rise of the hill and the fall of the river water over numerous cascades, owe nothing whatever to art. Sir George Campbell has gardened into the natural scene; he did not have to make the skeleton of his garden, it was there and no art could have bettered it. The Chinese considered that the man who found, removed, and set up an eroded stone of a shape in which they could find significance or some spiritual benefit, had the merit of the artist; why not, then, the man who sees what can be done with a piece of landscape, just as well as the man who makes it? Basically, Crarae is the two sides of the river. You ascend one bank, and you descend the other. The valley is precipitous, and all down its sides, to the water, are places, provided by outcrops, where with a boldness which he declares to have been owing to ignorance, Sir George has set here a tree, there a shrub. He has been assisted by nature herself, for some of his exotics have themselves seeded down the slopes, and, for example, *Drimys aromatica*, an Andean shrub with richly aromatic dark green foliage on garnet-red stems, has sprung up where he did not plant it, to bear its yellow flowers in the sun and scatter more seed. Other South American species flourish here as beside some river in the foothills of the Andes: the Chilean eucryphias, for example, glorious in late summer with their pure white saucer-shaped flowers, and beside them their New Zealand congeners. Striking use has been made of exotic trees, for this gardener is also a dendrologist: *Cunninghamia* grows beside larch, and the handsomest of the firs, *Abies nobilis* and *Abies forrestii*, beside the Scots pine. The former, in spring, has crimson growth buds in startling contrast with its formal, dark-green foliage; the latter, when stirred by wind, displays flashing silvery lights from the undersides of the leaves. Leptospermums, the so-called tea-trees of

New Zealand, with tiny coppery red or light green leaves and clouds of white or crimson flowers, flourish in this Scottish landscape. But here, as in Glenarn, the dominant species are the Asiatic rhododendrons in enormous variety. There is no point in describing, once again, their forms and colours. They have been used with art so that they seem to be native where they grow among the rocks, on little plateaux, in the grassy hillsides which lie above the river. There is a 'series' of rhododendrons (the species of this genus are so numerous and various that they have been grouped in 'series'), with tubular, waxy, pendent flowers, the tube lobed and spread at the mouth, of which the type species is *R. cinnabarinum*. It is very well represented at Crarae, in both the species, and in their best varieties, and in their hybrids. One group of *R. cinnabarinum roylei*, with red flowers in vast numbers, and which was grown from seed, has created a new category of rhododendrons, for when it was inspected by Mr H. H. Davidian, the rhododendron specialist at the Royal Botanic Garden, Edinburgh, the greatest living expert on the genus, he pronounced, with all due solemnity, 'Sir, this is not *cinnabarinum roylei*; it is cinnabarinum roylei *magnificum*!' This phenomenon, that is, the appearance, in plants grown from seed, of a new and superior form, is not unusual in the great Scottish rhododendron gardens. The new forms soon become known, for the Scottish gardeners of the south-west compete with each other to show the finest or rarest blooms at the Glasgow horticultural shows, and they manifest a degree of *expertise* altogether unusual among amateur gardeners. Small morphological differences, small diversities of habit or stature or flower size, are instantly noted and made use of. These gardeners all have a good working knowledge of botany and, if they are artists first, are scientists too.

These, then, are two of the woodland-and-water gardens of south-west Scotland, less famous but not less interesting than Inverewe, farther up the west coast, and Brodick on Arran. But there is a newer one which owes far more to both art and science, in the same region; the gardens of Achamore House on the island of Gigha. It has been made, in less than twenty years, by Sir James Horlick who bought the whole island in 1944, rebuilt the manor house, and began, with nothing but a small forest of native trees which gave some protection from the Atlantic gales, to make a garden. It is comparable with Bodnant rather than with Crarae or Glenarn, in that the design and plantings in the immediate neighbourhood of the house are semi-formal. There is a rock garden of daphnes, dwarf rhododendrons, hebes and many bulbous subjects; a broad terrace of fine lawn, with a slope down to more lawn, the slope planted with tens of thousands of daffodils. There are smooth edged gravel walks among shrubberies and shrub borders; there are rectangular plantations behind the house. But this formality is gradually shaded off, as it were, into the woodland garden of some fifty acres, and this is a garden which is like no other I have ever seen, for its design has been dominated by a single consideration: wind. The island of Gigha, which is about sixteen square miles in area, lies fully exposed to the Atlantic gales and, moreover, the prevailing wind is the west wind so that there is very little respite from it. The form of the land, with very low hills and shallow valleys, made it just possible for an earlier proprietor to get trees established; that is, by the time they were tall enough to be exposed, they were sufficiently established to stand this exposure. And what Sir James Horlick has done is to cut out glades in the woods, enclaves completely surrounded by trees and accessible only by a small opening for the pathways, in which to grow his rhododendrons. One is a little reminded of Hidcote, but this newer garden has not the finish, the art, of Lawrence Johnston's masterpiece. One passes from enclosure to enclosure among the trees, coming first upon a planting of giant-leaved Himalayan rhododendrons, next perhaps to a coppice made of one of the gardener's own hybrid rhododendrons (he has been a great breeder of new plants), and again to another group of some botanical species. 'Expectation and surprise,' again. The best way to see this garden is to wander slowly, alone, and preferably lost, for several days, from glade to glade.

Although here as in the other south-west Scottish gardens, rhododendrons dominate the scene, Gigha has other things to show. In semi-wild plantings Sir James has made much use of the deciduous rhododendrons most of us know as azaleas. The most glorious of the Australasian daisy-bushes,

Achamore House

Olearia semidentata has been widely used, and has become absorbed into the general flora. Eucryphias grow very large and handsome, both the Chilean and the Australasian. Embothrium, the flame tree of the Andes, has been used to make a little avenue in the semi-formal part of the garden which connects the house plantings to the wild. Asiatic primulas have naturalized themselves, for the ground is very wet and in places even boggy. The same conditions favour the Himalayan mecanopses.

Gigha, Crarae and Glenarn, then, represent, in their several ways, the extreme form of the 'English' paradise garden, a style in which the Scots have excelled their neighbours, the attempt to work exotic plants into the native landscape in such a way that while the effect is 'natural', it is of a nature which might have been, rather than one which is. The familiar woodland scene is transformed as in a dream; the dream is paradise regained.

But such gardens are in the first place not to every man's taste, and in the second place not possible for every man even if they were. By the artists in gardening they are apt to be dismissed as being without form, simply collections of plants grown for the sake of growing the very exotic. That they are something more than that I hope has been shown, but it is true that they depend for their success, indeed for their very being, on a certain kind of water-saturated peaty soil, and soft winter weather and very high rainfall.

The extreme case The extreme case of the English garden dependent for its existence on a very special climate, the garden of Tresco Abbey in the Scilly Isles, will serve to display the nearest-to-perfect realization of the dream of paradise. And although Tresco Abbey Gardens would not be accepted by the horticultural aesthete as a good example of design, it is not nearly as open to criticism on the ground of formlessness as some of the true woodland gardens. The principal and central parts of these gardens are firmly drawn. They are surrounded by woodland gardens in which flourish an extraordinary collection of exotic trees; there, uniquely in Britain, the lovely scarlet gum of Australia can be seen in flower; proteas can be gathered for the house at Christmas time; and natives of the Canary Islands, twenty degrees of latitude farther south, have set up flourishing colonies. The case of Tresco Abbey Gardens is extreme in that the peculiar climate of the site made it possible to plant not only such exotics as English gardeners had long been introducing into the English landscape and woodland garden, but an immensely wider range of exotics. The temptation to plant some of every species of ornamental plant which will grow in the given climate is dangerous to the integrity and therefore to the overall beauty of any garden; the garden in question tends to become a botanical collection and not a garden at all; too literally a 'garden of plants'. This danger on the whole has been avoided at Tresco not only by the taste of four generations of Dorrien Smiths, but by two other factors; the large scale on which the gardeners were working and the fact that, owing to the climate, it has been possible to use exotics for background and basic plantings, that is, to replace some of those native trees and shrubs which, in an English garden on the mainland must form the backcloth against which exotics are displayed, with trees and shrubs which are themselves of sub-tropical provenance, great botanical interest, and a beauty altogether rich and strange.

The English sub-tropics The Isles of Scilly lie in the angle formed by the intersection of the 50th degree of N. latitude and the 6th degree of W. longitude. They are thus the most southerly of the British Isles excepting the Channel Isles which are within the influence of the continental climate, less mild than that of the Atlantic. The island of Tresco is very slightly north of the extreme point of the Lizard, but it has the climatic advantage of being completely surrounded by warm sea on the easterly edge of the warm North Atlantic Drift. It is nearly enough true to say that the island does not experience frost: this is not literally true. From time to time the temperature in winter may fall a shade below freezing point and an occasional snow-shower is experienced. In the savage winter of 1963 the thermometer fell to 28°F. (−2·2°C.) and there were falls of snow. But the average January minimum is 45°F. (12·2°C.). And the rule is that the winter temperature does not fall below 40°F. and is usually well up to 50°, while, on the other hand, very high summer temperatures are equally rare: the temperature range is, in fact 40° to

60°F. The temperature range of the Canary Isles, just over 20 degrees of latitude farther south, is 50° to 70°F. (mean figures in both cases). But whereas the mean annual rainfall of the Canary Isles is under ten inches, that of the Scilly Isles is about thirty inches, a good deal lower than at Penzance on the mainland and lower than is desirable for the really lush type of gardens such as those of south-west Scotland, but perfectly adequate for an enormous range of plants. Sunshine hours in Tresco are as high as anywhere in the British Isles.

In order to make clear the extraordinary climatic advantages enjoyed by Tresco, with its great garden of sub-tropical exotics, its Australian and South African trees and shrubs exceeding in size their congeners to be seen in the wild, it may be worth drawing attention to the fact that the island is, in point of latitude, level with Prague, about 4° north of the most northerly point of Japan, 2° north of the U.S.-Canadian frontier, and 10° north of New York, nearly all of which places far to the south of it suffer sub-zero winter temperatures every year.

In 1834 Augustus Smith became lessee of the whole archipelago from the Duchy of Cornwall. Not only were the islands wretchedly poor but there was, at this time, nothing bigger than a gorse bush growing on Tresco. We have nothing to do here with Smith's work in raising the standard of living for all the islanders; it was admirably conceived and very successful. Meanwhile he built himself a house near the site of the ruins of an ancient abbey and set about the planting of trees and the building of a wall between the old abbey and the new house, to contain a garden.

Augustus Smith

Although Tresco is free from the winter cold and summer heat which make gardening difficult, it has one great climatic disadvantage: gales. The gales which scream about the island from the west have to be experienced to be believed, and they are, at times, terrifying. The trees had therefore to be planted on the lee side of the hill which provided some shelter from the prevailing winds: they were oak, elm, sycamore and poplar and the original object of planting them was as cover for game. While the garden wall provided some shelter it could not, of course, be high enough to protect the garden against gales, and for that purpose Smith began to plant shelter-belt woods to seaward, using *Pinus insignis*, *Cupressus macrocarpa* and the evergreen oak *Quercus ilex*. Of these the pines have proved the most valuable although even these are often torn up by gales, doing great damage in the woodlands. As the shelter-belts grew the Lord Proprietor of the Scillies, the title by which Mr Smith was known, took more of the hillside into his garden until twelve acres were being gardened not counting the woodland plantings.

Tresco Abbey Gardens are among those which were not designed of a piece, but grew: when more land was to be taken in, designs of how it should be done were put on paper, but at no time in its history has the garden been designed as a whole. Yet it is an integer, it has the air of a work of art. From the very first Augustus Smith took advantage of the climate, and of the slightly acid soil, to plant species which would not grow on the mainland. He obtained plants from Kew Gardens, and seeds from the whole southern hemisphere, some from correspondents and others brought to him by the masters of ships, with whom he was friendly. The general layout of the garden, as well as the plantings, was also Augustus Smith's, and this has been retained so that the shape of the garden as visitors now see it is much as it already was a hundred years ago.

Perhaps a garden architect might have provided a better frame for the display of Tresco's wealth of plants. But this garden grew richer as successes justified ambitions. By the year 1850 the gardens had, despite the fact that the wind-breaks can hardly have grown very tall, made much progress. Augustus Smith had a friend and regular correspondent in Lady Sophia Towers and his letters to her have been preserved because she had them printed for family circulation after his death, or at all events a selection of them covering twenty-five years of the garden's early history. One of the earliest introductions, from South Africa, were mesembryanthemums which are still a feature of the ground-cover in the gardens and have become naturalized all over the island and other Scilly islands, notably St Mary's. Since Smith was bringing so many plants from the southern hemisphere his garden was unique in being bright with colour in mid-winter as well as spring and summer. Thus, from a letter to Lady Sophia dated 24

The original plan

December 1851: 'My garden was left in high colour, the clianthus just bursting into flower and the *Acacia lophantha* also covered with yellow blossoms.'

Clianthus puniceus, a spectacular climbing evergreen legume from New Zealand with large crimson-scarlet flowers, has since been much planted in south-western gardens but was more or less exterminated in the winter of 1963; the acacia Smith names has since been reclassified as an *Albizzia*; it is Australian. As time went on Smith introduced plants from the whole sub-tropical zone. Pelargoniums as well as the mesembryanthemums from South Africa, a large range of Canary Island natives of which the spectacular echiums have since naturalized themselves, palms of several kinds, aloes, fuchsias, hebes, correas, genistas, dracaenas, puyas, cinerarias . . . but it is impossible to give anything approaching a complete list nor would there be any point in doing so. By the end of the 1850's not only were visitors capable of appreciating Smith's extraordinary garden coming to see it, but also what he calls, in his letters, excursionists.

'The gardens are looking very well and are made a mighty fuss about by visitors, it appears, being a little out of the ordinary rut and their contents rather peculiar. They are now invaded by excursionists which would be a bore did they not seem to enjoy themselves and appreciate the place and its peculiarities; some fifty here this week from all parts of the kingdom, of which a few were really learned in plants, to Chivers' great satisfaction; the Scotch, he says, are the most intelligent as shown by their questions and observations: the Cornish the least so, and who, when he points out some botanical rarity, answer "Well, that's not so good as a cabbage" . . .' *(14 September 1861)*

Augustus Smith died in 1872, and since he had never married he was succeeded by a nephew, Thomas Algernon Dorrien Smith who was a lieutenant in the 10th Hussars. He married Edith, the daughter of Lady Sophia Towers. Fortunately Algernon Dorrien Smith not only took to gardening with as much enthusiasm as his uncle had shown, but with more science and more art as well. He was also remarkable as a practical promoter of the Scilly Islands' prosperity. It was he who started the business of growing daffodils for market, taking advantage of the island climate to get these flowers to London much earlier than anyone else could hope to do it. This industry has been the mainstay of Scilly Island finances until very recently, when new techniques of growing daffodils under glass in the east have neutralized the climatic advantage enjoyed by the Scillonians. Horticulturally the most interesting fact about the start of this flower-growing industry is that the two most valuable varieties to be planted in numbers, 'Scilly White' and 'Soleil d'Or' were found naturalized and growing 'wild' about the old Abbey ruins. Another consequence of Algernon Dorrien Smith's practical bent was a great improvement in the shelter-belt plantings. In an article by the then Bishop of Truro published in the *Journal* of the RHS, June 1874, the author tells us: 'Meanwhile the plants in the garden had been growing and a number which Augustus had never seen in flower came into blossom in the seventies and eighties. The great enemy still was wind. One day after a severe storm Thomas Algernon, sailing up the channel, noticed a tree standing up among a number of others which had blown down. He took a bearing on it and found it to be *Pinus radiata*. This gave him an idea and he started planting a shelter-belt of this tree on the South Western Hill.'

This planting has been continued ever since, and although many even of these pines are blown out of the ground in the worst gales, they still hold on better than any other species. The original planting was, incidentally, also the initiation of Algernon's heir, Arthur Dorrien Smith, into that care of the garden which was to be his own: as a small boy he helped in the work of planting the sapling pines.

Flower paintings   It was during Algernon's reign at Tresco Abbey that his aunt, Mrs Le Marchant, made those paintings of plants and flowers in the Abbey Garden which give us a distinguished pictorial record of the species which flourished there from 1873 to 1883. The whole series of her paintings is preserved in the library of Tresco Abbey. Mrs Le Marchant's subjects included many acacias, pittosporums, hakeas, leptospermums, eucalypts, aloes, fuchsias, correas and other genera which were simply ungrowable in the open anywhere else in north (and often south) Europe, as well as many which have since proved to be possible in very favoured mainland gardens. From accounts published in the *Gardener's Chronicle* and other garden journals of the time, it is possible to discover what made the greatest impression on knowledgeable visitors; the most interesting information one gleans from these, at least to me, is that none of them take any notice of the garden as a whole. They take it for granted and pay all their deliberate attention to detail, to individual plants. And even now this is certain to happen if only because the visitor is confronted at every step with plants whose forms and colours are strange and which therefore concentrate his attention. Yet in fact all these rarities and novelties have somehow combined together to form an integral picture, and when one becomes tired by the excitement of seeing the new and strange, then the satisfying quality of the whole garden becomes apparent. At certain seasons – I am writing of the present but it must have been so in the latter part of the last century – certain species dominate the garden: in June, for example, the lavender-blue towers of the scores, perhaps hundreds of echiums are predominant. These are Canary Island natives and like other plants from the same source they flourish in Scilly as they do at home, if not more so; for example, Canary Island cinerarias have become a weed of Tresco Abbey Gardens.

Plate 140

Mrs Le Marchant was not the only member of the family to make pictorial records of the garden. In 1902 Miss Gwen Dorrien Smith began what became a collection of flower-paintings made in the garden, and including enough subjects to show the glories of the garden in every month of the year, from the astonishing metrosideros in January to the sempervivums of December. It is interesting to see how, as a result of the work done in the garden by later generations, the outstanding plants for each month are in some cases still the same, in others very different: for me, during a mid-winter visit, the most exciting plants in flower were the proteas from South Africa and the banksias from Australia.

The heir to all these marvels was Arthur, the son of Thomas Algernon, and his interest in the gardens and participation in the work of improving them began in boyhood. As a soldier he took part in the South African War, and it is typical of his whole life as a gardener that even while he was on active service on the Veldt, while he kept one eye on the alert for Boers, the other was looking for plants. As a result a number of interesting and beautiful species were collected and sent home to be planted at Tresco Abbey. Arthur Dorrien Smith's activities as a plant collector did not cease with the end of the war, during which he came of age and was awarded the DSO. In 1907 he was a member of the New Zealand Southern Islands Expedition – he was then thirty-two – and contributed a paper on it to the *Kew Bulletin*. The expedition explored the Snare, Auckland and Campbell Islands, Dorrien Smith doing the plant-hunting. Again, in 1910, a paper by him appeared in the same *Bulletin* (No. 4), entitled 'An attempt to introduce *Olearia semidentata* into the British Isles'. Arthur Dorrien Smith had found this very lovely 'daisy-bush' in a Chatham Island peat bog. The introduction was successful. Nor was it the only one of its family: in June 1962 I was on Tresco and saw, in the marshy woodland just outside the east entrance to the gardens, where a stream flows among ordinary native shrubs and trees underplanted with the white arum-lily (*Zantedeschia aethiopica*) and the graceful *Osmunda regalis*, a great bush of *Olearia angustifolia*, an even more beautiful species than *semidentata*, in full flower. This species and the related *O. chathamica* were discovered by Arthur Dorrien Smith and first flowered in Britain in Canon Boscawen's famous garden at Ludgvan Rectory. He made other discoveries, contributing papers about his plant-hunting in West Australia and the Chatham Islands to the *Journal* of the RHS.

Arthur Dorrien Smith

In 1918 he succeeded to the Lord Proprietorship of the Scillies and ownership of the Tresco Abbey Gardens, when Thomas Algernon died. He was then Major Dorrien Smith, and as if to mark his succession the spectacular *Metrosideros collina* which he had introduced from New Zealand, flowered that year for the first time.

Kew Bulletin No. 5 (1920) has an account written by the Director of Kew, Arthur (later Sir Arthur) Hill, of Tresco Abbey Gardens as they then were. It will be useful to draw upon this for his division of the garden into three parts, and his notes on the soil and climate, are still valid. Hill described the

The three parts of the garden

Plate 134

walled part of the garden as 'The Garden Proper'; it has, he wrote, a light soil of sand and peat with outcrops of granitic rock; it is well sheltered, in summer it becomes hot and dry so that such genera as mesembryanthemums and pelargoniums flourish as on their native heath. The same can be said of every other species which likes these conditions, from the Mediterranean, from Mexico, from Australasia and South Africa. The second of Hill's divisions is 'The Higher Ground'. Here the natural flora is chiefly gorse and heather; among this the shelter-belt trees had been planted, *Pinus insignis* and *Cupressus macrocarpa* and among these trees, in clearings more or less open to the sky, he found many exotic species planted and flourishing, including melaleuca, hakea, acacias, auracarias and the lovely Table Mountain silver-tree, *Leucadendron argenteum*. Forty years later I spent many hours simply loitering and wandering in these woods; in mid-winter many different species of acacia are in flower, the 'mimosa' of the florists. The leptospermums have gone native and one comes suddenly upon small groves of these light and delicate little trees covered with white or pink flowers. Loveliest of all is *Eucalyptus ficifolia* with its flowers like translucent orange-scarlet flames. Finally, Hill distinguished a third division, 'The Northern Slope' on the central hill (Abbey Hill) which was planted to rhododendrons, including the mighty *R. arboreum* and such fragrant flowering species as *R. veitchianum*. I believe that one might also consider the drive up to the great house as a division, the fourth. It is between a rising slope on one side and a falling slope on the other. The rhododendrons of the Northern Slope garden tower on the right; from time to time, as one takes ten times as long as is necessary to walk from the gates to the courtyard of the house, one becomes conscious of some delicious fragrance filling the air. Traced to its source it proves to be emanating from a group of some rare and tender rhododendron of the *fragrantissimum* group. The drive, moreover, is, as it were, the main walk of an aboretum of exotic trees. That all this should still be so, that the gardens are as fine as ever, is an astonishing tribute to the Dorrien Smiths' sense of responsibility and energy. Not only must the present reigning member of the family, Commander T. Dorrien Smith, struggle like other landed men against a rate of taxation which his grandfather would not have dreamed possible; but in 1929, the whole garden was devastated and wrecked by a tempest of unprecedented violence.

The tempest of 1929

It occurred in December; beginning on the Monday of this terrible week, by the Wednesday the wind was blowing at 93 m.p.h. from the south-east; Major and Mrs Dorrien Smith were on the mainland at the time, and telegrams began to arrive describing the damage as it occurred. On the Friday the wind had shifted into the south-west, as if determined to get at the garden from every quarter, and its speed had risen to 110 m.p.h. At no time from the Monday to the Sunday did the wind velocity fall below 70 m.p.h., and on the Sunday it was again blowing at over ninety. In an account of this storm contributed by the Bishop of Truro, the Right Rev. J. W. Hunkin, DD, to the *Journal* of the RHS, we are told: 'Altogether about 600 trees on the island were blown down. When Major and Mrs Dorrien Smith finally reached home in a torrent of rain they could hardly find their way. Paths were blocked and obliterated; trees had come crashing down on bushes and beds, and the ground was thickly strewn with branches and debris. Even the ilex lost their leaves. The Major said to Mrs Dorrien Smith, "Well, this is the end of the garden in my time. I hope the children will see it again".'

In the event the garden recovered much more quickly than seemed possible at the time. It was only six years before the most obvious, in fact all but such fundamental damage as loss of wind-protection, had been made good.

The garden today

It would be only too easy, in giving an account of the garden as it is now, to make that account the description of a long walk, a tour of the whole gardens, punctuated by the names of plants like exclamations; there are between three and four thousand distinct species and varieties in the gardens and such an account would be like a Latin horticultural litany. Much more to the point would be to convey, to communicate, something of the total effect, the kind of impact which these gardens have on the beholder; one cannot convey the significance of a painting by describing in detail each brush stroke and, in scientific terms, the composition of each pigment which the artist has used. The impression made on me during a total of twenty days spent in the gardens or mostly in the gardens, was very powerful and rather strange. Each day I returned, sometimes by way of the drive and so, turning left at the archway into the courtyard of the Abbey, into the garden proper; sometimes to the woodlands which surround the walled garden and the house, I hurried to get within the barrier – I do not mean a visible barrier of walls and hedges – the invisible barrier which separates this garden from the rest of the world. It is true that all successful gardens, or rather all successful English gardens (for the purpose of French and Italian gardens is quite different), give something of this feeling of having reached a refuge which one had dreamed must be there, must be somewhere. The garden acted on me like a drug to which one grows addicted; I was supposed to be seeing all the Scilly Islands, to be out in a boat looking at seals, to be camping for a day on Bryher or one of the uninhabited islands, to be watching for rare birds. But all I wanted to do after breakfast at the hotel, and for that matter after dinner and a long day, was to get back inside the gardens.

At first I found that I hurried, running from one detail to the next, from the astonishing forms and strange metallic colours of the puyas, to the natural nursery provided by the crevices in the trunks of the great Canary Island palms for seedlings of hebe, pittosporum and metrosideros; from the subtly coloured mesembryanthemums sprawled in beauty over the rocks, to the proteas of the top terrace to see if even in summer there might be a few flowers. But in time, although I never for a moment lost interest in such detail in the enjoyment of which one could spend many months, I began to see the garden as a whole. I had a favourite sitting place in a little summer-house by a small fish-pond surrounded by annual mesembryanthemums and freesias, on the middle terrace. From it you look down over a strange, beautiful and, above all, romantic panorama of gently waving palms, towers of broad-leaved and coniferous trees from all parts of the world, colour which, in any lesser garden, would be over-whelming, and so towards the sea which, in these islands, is much bluer than the Mediterranean ever was. The key word here is romantic. You are in an idealized paradise; you are in the Coral Island of boyhood reading. Tresco Abbey Garden, more than any other garden I have ever seen, realizes the dream which must have been always in William Robinson's mind when he conceived and fostered his idea of a garden.

Plates 139–144

For what, in fact, has been done in this great work of gardening art? By bringing together into one blessed place, and by harmonizing the elements into an integral whole, the loveliest of the earth's plants from every continent, and by so planting them as to make use of the shape of the land to exclude the rest of the world, the Dorrien Smiths of four generations have realized the Eden in the heart of every romantic, have created a landscape of the imagination, 'natural' in the sense only that it is not formal, but such as nature could never accomplish; the fortunate climate of their Cassiterides, but likewise that peculiarly English feeling for the poetry of plants and their own natural taste, has enabled the Dorrien Smiths to do, with soil and rock and water, with trees, shrubs and herbs, what a romantic landscape painter might do who set out to create a landscape on canvas, paying absolutely no regard to climate and geography of the plants he put into his picture. Such a painter might even, indeed, invent strange plants of his own conception instead of sticking to scientific botany; even that seems, almost, to have been done at Tresco, for it is hard to believe, when confronted with the great bank of Chilean puyas, that these fantastic spires of weird forms and 'unnatural' metallic colours are products of nature.

And because all this is so, Tresco Abbey Gardens are, in another sense also, the extreme case of the English garden. Vast though they be by the standards of ordinary gardening, they are not vast enough for more than a single inhabitant at one time; or for two, very intimate. I found it necessary to exercise especial restraint in order to look amiably at other visitors to the gardens, people who had quite as much right as I had to be there, in order not to allow myself to feel that their presence was an outrage. It was as if they had come marching and chattering into a very private daydream; a daydream which, by a miracle, had become realized in three dimensions and all the forms, all the colours, in the world.

Notes on the Plates

125 BODNANT

Probably the most nearly perfect of the twentieth-century gardens in which all the traditions of the English garden are brought together. Looking towards the Dell from the level of the cypress pool.

126 BODNANT

Snowdonia in the background of this view from one of the terraces of the semi-formal part of the gardens.

127 BODNANT

The paradise of nature perfected. The woodlands in the Dell are underplanted with one of the greatest collections of Chinese, Himalayan and hybrid rhododendrons in the world.

128 BODNANT

The principal vista down the terraces with the lily pool in the middle ground and the mountains of the Snowdon range in the background.

129 BODNANT

Discreet use of statuary pays tribute to the eighteenth-century tradition.

130 BODNANT

Formal corner of clipped yew and statuary facing down the long canal pool towards the Pin Mill.

131 CAERHAYS CASTLE

In this great woodland garden in Cornwall, thousands of exotics are planted into the wild. Wild garlic in the foreground.

132 CAERHAYS CASTLE

The garden is remarkable for the way in which rhododendrons, camellia and magnolia compose the 'natural' woodland scene.

133 CAERHAYS CASTLE

Rhododendron williamsianum, named for the maker of the garden. The flowers of this dwarf shrub are shell-pink.

134 TRESCO ABBEY

Symbolic of the achievement of a natural paradise of exotics from all over the sub-tropics is the tameness of the fieldfares.

135 TRESCO ABBEY

In the stony banks beside the winding paths, house-leeks (*Sempervivum*) from the Canary Islands and other sub-tropical countries seem native where they grow.

136 TRESCO ABBEY

One of the long terrace walks which run at right angles to the main rising vista of the gardens. The borders include such plants as Cape heaths and proteas from South Africa and an immense collection of Australasian plants.

137 TRESCO ABBEY

The Wild Garden theme as expressed in a corner of the gardens where native and exotic plants grow together in community.

138 TRESCO ABBEY

The curious plant in the foreground is a *Dasylirion*. The pelargonium – a genus which flourishes out of doors in the island – is 'White Unique'. Monkey Puzzle trees of the genus *Auracaria* in the background.

139 TRESCO ABBEY

Low palms on each side of the lily pond are *Cordyline banksii*, and the tall ones *Phoenix canariensis*. The picture also includes a *Metrosideros*, *Bursaria*, *Hebe* and others.

140 TRESCO ABBEY

Two Canary Island species, *Echium pininana* and *Phoenix canariensis*.

141 TRESCO ABBEY

The *Echinocacti* of Mexico make possible some curious effects at Tresco where they flourish in the open garden.

142 TRESCO ABBEY

Three *Dasylirion* looking very exotic in an English garden. Background trees are *Banksia integrifolia*, *Grisselinia lucida*, *Myrkina faya* and a Paulonia.

143 TRESCO ABBEY

The tall spike is a dead inflorescence of *Furcraea bedinghausii* between two live plants of the same. On right, *Chaemerops humilis*; *Phoenix canariensis* in the background.

144 TRESCO ABBEY

Water-lilies and an *Erigeron*; one of the small pools at Tresco.

145 TRESCO ABBEY

This *Erigeron* which has colonized a low wall in Tresco Abbey gardens has behaved like many half-hardy plants there and established itself as a native.

146 TRESCO ABBEY

Among the exotics are the *Dicksonias* and other tree-ferns of Australasia.

138

139

140

141

142

143

144

145

YET IT WOULD NOT DO to conclude this study of England and Scotland's great gardens, presented here in a few examples chosen partly as representative of one or more of the traditions of English gardening, partly to please the author's own taste, with the gardens of Tresco Abbey. In the last section of this book we have taken a glance at what, socially and economically, are the most important gardens in Britain, the little ones of the villages and suburbs and cities. The design of these owes much more, probably, to the traditions of semi-formal gardening than to those of romantic woodland gardening. It is obviously bound to be so, for the scale of these millions of small gardens is quite unsuitable for anything else. But there is another and equally important point to be considered: the future of great gardens in Britain. That many of the older ones and some not so old have come into the hands of the National Trust means that they will be preserved. But will any more great gardens be made, will the traditions and rules established over several centuries for the making of gardens on the grand scale, be quite lost? Not necessarily so: in the first place, public gardens and parks made by municipalities are on the grand scale as to size; and the men in charge of them, often trained at Kew or at Wisley, are themselves in the great traditions and strive constantly to improve the plant material as well as the form of the gardens and parks which they maintain. There may be fewer and fewer private citizens able or willing to make gardens of ten, twenty, fifty or more acres; but there is no reason why the municipalities should not take their place. The second way in which the traditions of grand gardening may be continued is in the surroundings of housing estates and in the gardens about great residential blocks. The co-operative effort of many poor men may, if it prove possible, do as much as the private efforts of a single rich one.

But in both the cases here envisaged the possible garden would not be of the pure woodland, the romantic kind: it must, of necessity, be of the semi-formal or even formal type, for it would be urban or semi-urban in surroundings, and it would have to make many practical concessions to the way of life of people living as citizens, not as rustics, and living, moreover, in crowded communities. The best of the modern garden designers are well aware of this, and have already found some solutions to many of the problems with which the facts of modern, urban, industrial life confront them.

And there is this, too, to be said: it is very well known that the English are a people of two cultures: if, on the one hand, they are romantic in their tastes, they are also, and long have been, under the influence of the Mediterranean, for ever moderating the line and detail of their work by reference to Italian or French taste. Some of the earliest great gardens in England were laid out by Le Notre and the main lines of the great Frenchman's work still here and there survive. Bicton Park in Devonshire is a case in point and the same great gardens include an 'Italian' garden of distinction. But it is not in gardens actually laid out by Frenchmen or Italians that the ambivalence of the English soul is apparent, so much as in the inclusion of Italian gardens within such English gardens as are large enough, and most of all in the use of Italianate detail to decorate an otherwise English garden. In our final example, however, this 'classical' influence is more broadly apparent. The Dartington Hall gardens are woodland, romantic, 'paradise' gardens, but there is a stateliness in the line and use of levels, an art-consciousness in the use of ornament, a discretion in the choice of plants, which are, as it were, 'Mediterranean' or at all events show the influence of the Latin tradition in English culture.

Dartington Hall

The English Garden properly so called has its most recent manifestation in the gardens created by Leonard and Dorothy Elmhirst on the river Dart in South Devon. As the most modern, in point of time of the great gardens, it is of particular interest, for it was made in the light of all the traditions, all the knowledge which had been accumulated during the long slow growth of the art of horticulture which we have been describing.

Mr and Mrs Elmhirst acquired the house and grounds in 1925 and in 1926 they moved into part of it. The great courtyard was so far from being what now it is that it was found very difficult even to envisage it as a whole; it had been divided up, by stone walls, fences of chicken-wire, and other obstructions, into many small rectangles in which chickens and pigs were or had been kept. There were barns and other out-buildings occupying part of it, and well-established if straggling hedges of quickthorn and other hedge plants. Another, and perhaps the most striking feature of the present garden, the Tiltyard, was not what it is now: it was partly filled up, and contained what had been a formal rose garden of paths and beds; for the rest it was a sort of vast hole in the ground full of living and dead rubbish, a chasm of weed trees, shrubs and brambles. The great rising bank with its noble flight of granite steps, its planting of heath and magnolia, its sweeping simplicity of line topped by trees, was simply a dense and, at first sight quite hopeless, jungle of undergrowth.

Something must be said first about the people who have had the making of the garden as we shall endeavour, with words and pictures, to describe it. From the beginning, in the middle twenties, the Elmhirsts have exercised, with a very sure taste, the right of decision or veto over the plans and ideas of the professional garden designers, gardeners and nurserymen whose services they have employed. Neither of them were gardeners to start with; they learnt to be as they made their garden and worked in it themselves. They welcomed not only the help of professionals but of gardening friends, some of them well-known and successful gardeners, whose advice was sought. One of the most striking features of the gardens as they now are is what one might call a negative one: there are no poor plants in it; or, stated positively, only the most distinguished varieties and species have been planted. Botanical species have usually been preferred to garden hybrids. For this the Elmhirsts themselves have been largely responsible, both have a great feeling for trees and shrubs, and although professionals have designed the plantings, the material planted has been chosen by the Elmhirsts. Secondly, and here again the controlling taste is evident, there are no niggling, bitty plantings, no single specimens; whatever has been planted has been planted in masses or groups, and this is important for the garden is on quite a large scale – thirty-five acres – and only such plantings would be in proportion. For the Elmhirsts form was all important, the form they could cause to emerge from the chaos they found by revealing the shape and falls of the land itself; and the form which could be given by mass-plantings. Dartington, as will appear, is full of colour; but it is restrained colour and the garden is not a flower garden although full of flowers. All these fundamental features are attributable to the Elmhirsts themselves.

But while they could judge and even, in their imagination design, they needed practical and experienced help in realizing their vision; even in having what their vision really was made clear to themselves. In their beginning at Dartington neither of them had any English gardening friends or contacts and they were themselves unknown. It was, therefore, natural that they should look for help to the United States where they were known and where they knew who to go to. As a result, they consulted Mrs Beatrix Farrand, a well-known landscape gardener of Washington DC, who thereafter spent, until 1939, a small part of every year at Dartington and under whose direction some of the most difficult of the basic work was carried out.

Broadly speaking, Mrs Farrand's contribution was to clear the courtyard and make it what it now is; to create lawns round the house where only paddock and meadows had formerly existed; to lay out and plant the parts of the garden in the immediate neighbourhood of the house; to lay out and plant the Rhododendron Walk which is by no means confined to rhododendrons, for Mrs Farrand also planted a considerable number and variety of magnolias. It should be said that the Elmhirsts and their helpers, amateur and professional, had one enormous advantage to start with; the grounds they were working on were and are full of magnificent native trees and some exotic trees. Oak, beech, Turkey oak, Spanish chestnuts, elms and various conifers reach an immense size while retaining their health despite the fact that they are growing in a soil which would not, I believe, meet with the forester's unqualified approval. The way in which these trees were used as bones of the shrub garden is admirable; the care taken of them by Leonard Elmhirst, so that trees of great age suffering from the insults of time are preserved, is beyond praise.

Beatrix Farrand at Dartington Hall

Mrs Farrand's work on the garden continued until 1939 when with the outbreak of war all work of the ornamental kind had to stop, the land was devoted to the production of food, and much of the garden started to 'go back' for want of labour. During this time nothing was done to forward the design, but as soon as the war was over Percy Cane was called into consultation, and while the work which Mrs Farrand had done was restored to order – happily shrubs and flowering trees grow without much attention and Mrs Farrand had, for her background plantings, relied on varieties of native plants, for example hollies, of which there is a great variety at Dartington – new work was undertaken.

Mr Cane's principal contributions to the shape of the garden were first the opening of vistas, second the clearing of the great bank and the Tiltyard to make the present theatre-like feature of fine lawns (it was in fact first conceived of as an open-air theatre), and finally the opening of vistas, notably the High Meadow vista, and the vista of the Glade, one of the most pleasing and successful of its kind in Britain. Mr Cane designed and supervised the making of the great stairway and the stone look-out or belvedere to the left of the top step, and he suggested the mass plantings which fill in the outlines of his concept. Here again, however, it was the Elmhirsts who had the choosing of the plants. It was in making their choice of these that amateur helpers, friends with large gardens, were of more importance, perhaps, than professional garden designers. Visiting nurseries and receiving the advice of such nurserymen as Mr Hillier of Winchester was, of course, and as usual, one way of learning about plant material. But it was under the guidance, by way of example this, of William Arnold Foster that the then new flowering cherries introduced by Mr 'Cherry' Collingwood Ingram were planted; that Judas trees (*Cercis siliquastrum*) were introduced to the garden; and that a planting of *Malus hupehensis*, one of the loveliest features of the garden in autumn, was made.

Percy Cane's work

As we have seen in some of the gardens already discussed, the head gardener was, in the past, usually a person whose influence in the making of the garden was quite important and sometimes paramount: this is typical, of course, of the native empiricism of the English in the arts and sciences. Dartington Hall gardens were an exception to this rule, for in the first two decades of their making while there were men who bore the title of head gardener they were not important to the shaping of the garden; in the late twenties and early thirties the head gardener was Stewart Lynch who was a first-class plant propagator and as such ran, for the estate, two plant nurseries which were profitable commercial enterprises and, at the same time, supplied some of the material required in the planting of the Dartington gardens. But not until the appointment of Mr Johnson in 1947 did these gardens have a practical man who had the kind of love to give the garden, which is so important in making great gardens. W. J. Johnson, superintendent of the gardens until his death in 1963, began his gardening career as a lad on the estates of the late Earl of Liverpool at Hartsholme Hall in Lincolnshire. There, under Albert Wiph, the German head gardener and a man of ability, he received his training. Thence he entered the service of Lord Monson working at Hamsterly Hall in County Durham and at Burton Hall near Lincoln. Thus his apprenticeship and early work as a gardener were in great gardens and very much in the traditions of the nineteenth century. After service in the machine gun corps during the first world war, he went, on demobilization, to a well-known nursery, Pennell and Sons, with the deliberate intention of learning more about shrubs and trees. It happened that these were his chief interest in gardening which was a piece of good fortune since the future of English gardening lay, for economic as well as aesthetic reasons, with that kind of plant material. There he remained for eight years after which he became head gardener to Sir V. Warrender, in Rutland. He went from there to Lincolnshire again to be, for eight years, head gardener to the Earl of Yarborough. It was in 1943 that he came to Dartington Hall where he could find ample satisfaction for his interest in shrubs and trees and a climate far more propitious for gardening than any in which he had yet worked. There, among his other work, he established one of the best training courses for boys proposing to become professional gardeners, in the country. He was responsible for carrying out those plans by which the Elmhirsts have made the gardens.

As to the gardens as they now are: the principal features are, as it were, derived from what is basic, permanent or at least semi-permanent. Thus the immense trees, planted by the old owners of Dartington, the Champernownes, having been cleared of undergrowth, have been used to draw the lines of the vistas and to link the garden with the countryside of the surrounding hills and valleys; the old buildings, the good which remained after the accumulation of architectural rubbish had been cleared away, have been used, as in the great Chinese gardens, as points of focus and of reference; the Tiltyard, first created by John Holand, Duke of Exeter, in the fourteenth century, has been brilliantly used, its original form restored.

The Courtyard The major gate of the complex of buildings leads into the Courtyard, restored to its fourteenth-century proportions. In the centre, which is surrounded by paths in pleasant and unobtrusive patterns made of stone flags, limestone sets, and shingle pebbles, is a wide lawn planted, as Mrs Elmhirst points out in her descriptive pamphlet on the gardens, to provide a firm green base for the Great Hall. The big trees which were kept when the courtyard was cleared of its clutter, are two Scots pines and a single magnificent specimen of the deciduous Florida cypress *Taxodium distichum*, bright larch-green in spring, pale bronze before the leaf-fall. In 1945 a planting of seven *Prunus yedoensis* was made to flower the Courtyard in April. The soft grey of the old stone walls has been enhanced in beauty by a careful choice of climbers, some roses, wistaria whose soft colouring is exactly what is required in this setting, *Solanum jasminoides album*, holboellia, and winter jasmine. A few shrubs have been planted to break the line here and there, *Choisya ternata*, some viburnums, teucrium, camellias. The general effect of spaciousness and peace is enhanced by the discretion of these plantings.

Plate 148 The Tiltyard is approached from the Courtyard by a gravel path which has, on one side, the right, a long and narrow herbaceous border backed by a wall, and known as the Sunny Border; and, on the left, a wide lawn falling away and focused upon one of the finest trees in the west, an immense and shapely Turkey oak. Other fine lawn trees are oak, beech and cedar. However, on the way to this part of the garden you pass one of the most remarkable plants in Britain: an enormous specimen of *Acacia dealbata*, the florists' mimosa, has been so trained as to cover, over a vast area, the wall of what is, in fact, the fourteenth-century kitchen quarters of the Hall. This flowers in January and is an indescribable sight in a good year. Its maintenance has been impeccable and in cold spells the roots and base are protected. This is, however, an exotic which is more or less hardy in South Devonshire gardens, though we know no specimen to equal it east of Old Conna in County Wicklow, Ireland.

The wall behind the herbaceous border is planted to clematis (*montana* in variety) and roses, also the tender *Mandevillea suaveolens* which can be grown out of doors in South Devon. The border itself is planted to avoid that 'riot of colour' effect, first noted in the 'Lawrencian' garden, which so often shocks the eye in this kind of gardening: verbascum, rue, fennel, the shrubby and silvery-leaved *Potentilla vilmoriniana*, rosemary and some delphiniums are the principal plants. At the lower end of the path and border and at a lower level is the row of very large Irish yews known as the Twelve Apostles.

At the far end of the Sunny Border to you go up a few stone steps to a paved terrace, and if you there turn left through a gap in a yew hedge you have a clear view over the heart of the gardens, the Tiltyard. This feature is unique: it has been dealt with by covering the whole area, base and terraces which provided the spectators with seats, with lawn. Above the terraces is a row of Spanish chestnuts planted *c.* 1560, lower four enormous London planes, and on the lower terrace but one a century-old Monterey pine. From the point-of-view of the Tiltyard more steps lead up to an ancient stone cider mill on which, in 1949, two granite swans were carved by Willi Soukop. You are then in the Dell where the predominant plant is *Azalea mollis*, and other azaleas, including Ghent, Kurumes and Exbury hybrids. *Acer palmatum*, flowering cherries and a naturalization of daffodils have also been used.

The Tiltyard

Plate 150

Something should be said here, for the benefit of plantsmen, about the soil of Dartington Hall gardens, if only because it has not been allowed entirely to govern the choice of plants. There are both light and heavy soils within the area, and despite the presence of the leaf mould of many centuries, these soils are not acid; they apparently vary from something just on the acid side of neutral to something on the alkaline side. They overlie a kind of rotten slate locally known as shillet which, in certain conditions, gives excessively sharp drainage, while where it lies level it may cause water-logging. It is almost impenetrable to roots of anything less than forest trees, which has the curious advantage of keeping shrub roots on the surface where soil acidity can be controlled, though with much labour and difficulty. The point we wish to make is that the soils of Dartington are not such as are considered suitable for the lime-hating ericaceous plants, or for camellias, or for many other plants which are nevertheless flourishing in it. We have experience of a neighbouring garden where this is also true; where, for example, rhododendrons do well, pieris, acacias, daboecias and so forth flourish, yet where the leaf mould, upon analysis, is neutral; or even slightly alkaline. The reason is not clear; on the whole we are inclined to think that it is owing to the limestone being present in an insoluble or inactive form. The difficulty is that authorities are not in agreement on the subject of why calcifuge plants are so; some hold that lime in the soil inhibits the intake of iron salts; others that though the iron is taken up it cannot be used by plants whose own acidity is too low. At all events, gardening skill also has a lot to do with the success of calcifuge plants at Dartington: rhododendrons, for example, are not so much planted as set upon the surface of leaf mould and constantly mulched with peat and compost so that a topsoil is built round them, into which they root. The success is the more notable in that such difficult species as *Rhododendron falconeri* and *R. macabeanum* make fine specimens. Experience at Dartington has shown that rhododendron species differ very considerably in their tolerance of lime; in fact a useful monograph could be written on these differences. By way of example, *R. decorum* flourishes in parts of the garden which are death to other species.

The soil

But it is not soil conditions alone that have governed the choice of rhododendrons. Taste has rejected the flamboyant hybrids, and climate, together with much shade from trees, has made possible the planting of species or fine hybrids in the Edgeworthii series, for example, *R.* × 'Lady Alice Fitzwilliam', *R. fragrantissimum* and *R.* × 'Princess Alice'. These appear to be tolerant of soil alkalinity nearly up to the neutral point. There is a fine Dartington Hall form of *R. augustinii* with flowers which are almost true blue; *R. williamsianum* flourishes and, in the series of large-leaved rhododendrons, *R. macabeanum* and *R. falconeri*, whereas *R. sino-grande* does not seem happy.

This is attained by way of steps dominated by a trio of immense and beautiful trees, a Lucombe oak, an ilex (*Quercus ilex*) and a mighty beech tree which towers above the other two. As the Woodland is on the side of a hill, its three main paths are on three different levels. The lowest level is Rhododendron

The Woodland Garden

Walk, but it might almost as well be called Magnolia Walk, for *M. campbelli* and *M. veitchii*, both pink-flowered species, have been planted at this level. The *campbelli* was planted in 1928 and first flowered in 1958, the usual thirty years' interval. There too is the evergreen magnolia with enormous leaves, *M. delavayii*, whose flowers seem to open principally and perhaps only at night.

Elsewhere, the garden is very rich in magnolias, and among the species are to be found *soulangeana* in variety, *brozzonii, hypoleuca, denudata, kobus, cordata, stellata, lennei* and others.

In the planting of Rhododendron Walk the colour range was given careful forethought: it is limited to ivory and blue, with a very small touch of rose-pink here and there. There is a group of *Magnolia stellata* at the end of this Walk. The Rhododendron Walk turns at the end and leads round and up into Camellia Walk. To me the most attractive of the many camellias planted is *C. sasanqua*; its flowers, white or pale rose-pink, are small, single, very simple, like wild roses; it has none of the opulence but ten times the grace of the *C. japonica* varieties. Botanical species camellias are elsewhere in the gardens, and Camellia Walk is mainly planted to *C. japonica* varieties. But here are also *C. × furvan, C. × gauntletii* and *C. × williamsii* specimens. This Walk is an encouraging spectacle for the gardener with new plantings in mind; it is not yet thirty years old yet the camellias are up to fifteen feet tall and immensely bulky, and look as if they had been there for a century. The Walk borders are underplanted with *Cyclamen neapolitanum* naturalized.

A second turn and rise at the end of Camellia Walk leads into Spring Walk by way of a group of *Viburnum tomentosum mariesii*. From this Walk the most striking spectacle, away through the trees and other shrubs, is that of massed hydrangeas, very tall and flourishing, and for the most part blue. Hydrangeas at Dartington have provided an interesting garden experience: the soil tends to give pink, not blue flowers (it is well known, of course, that flower colour in this genus is never stable); but with constant mulching mainly with peat, the colour on the older plants becomes blue. No chemical means have been used to effect the change.

Expectation and surprise

More stone steps lead to the viewpoint called High Meadow. The focus of the vista which Mr Cane opened from this point is the Hall itself, a very long vista. The detail of the spot itself rests the eye after contemplation of this long perspective, notably in May and again in autumn: in May for the white cloud of crab-apple flower (*Malus hupehensis*); and in autumn for the leaf colour – scarlet, gold, purple – of the Stewartias and a group of *Cercidiphyllum*. In midsummer the flowers of a *Magnolia watsonii* drench the air with their scent. Even from here, however, the real height of the hillside is not apparent; like all good English gardens, Dartington is a succession of surprises, of secrets suddenly revealed. From High Meadow you move out between two colossal beeches into what is called the Upper Drive and across to The Glade, and it is from here that the fall of the land down to the Tiltyard and the Hall is suddenly revealed and you realize that you have been climbing all the way. The descent, by way of the Glade itself, is one of the most successful features of the garden: particularly well-demonstrated, in some details of the plantings here, is the use of foliage to introduce colour in mass with, for example, the red and purple-leaved rhus varieties. Likewise, the use of a single exceptional tree or large shrub to throw a mass of others into relief by its difference, notably eucryphias and the great *Davidia vilmoriniana*.

It is a rule of good English gardening that although a path or walk be contrived principally for the purpose of displaying the plants which frame it and the view which they also serve to frame, it should have an object, and, as it were, a destination. The Glade at Dartington ends in an ancient terrace lined with the Spanish chestnuts we have already mentioned, trees which are not less than four centuries old and in the preservation of which all the skill which forestry can muster has been employed. Here on this

Plate 149

terrace is placed a *Reclining Woman* by Henry Moore. The work was completed in 1947 and the artist himself chose the site for it.

'I tried', he wrote at the time, 'to make a figure which could rightly be called a memorial figure. I wanted the figure to have a quiet stillness and a sense of permanence as though it could stay there for ever; to have strength and seriousness in its effect and yet be serene and happy and resolved, as though it had come to terms with the world, and could get over the largest cares and losses.'

Mrs Elmhirst herself has best described the spectacle from any point in the neighbourhood of Moore's *Reclining Woman*: '... across the jousting ground, in a formal setting, stands the Great Hall. From the lowest level the ground builds up in tiers, rising from the Twelve Apostles to the wall of the Sunny Border, then, higher, to the bowling green and the old stone arches, and finally to the level of the Hall itself. Here and there a tree breaks the horizontal lines, like the Monterey on the terraces and the Scots pine above the bowling green, while on the left, mounting high, the old oaks and beeches provide protection from the north and west. A view of a different kind can be seen from the Bastion, just above the long flight of steps' . . . (see below) '. . . From here the ground falls away to the parkland and over the hills towards the sea. The land in the distance seems to take the form of soft green waves, silently rolling in. . . .'

Plate 151

The long flight of steps referred to in the above passage climb what is known as the Heath Bank. This was, in the making, one of the most troublesome parts of the garden; it was, through very long neglect, a jungle of scrub and bramble and small, unwanted trees. Percy Cane was responsible for the design of which the Heath Bank is the realization. The steps, cut in Cornish granite, are very wide and shallow, and on each side of them have been planted masses of heaths in the softer colours. Technically, the work gave trouble because heaths had to be found which would flourish in a soil not altogether suitable for many members of this family of plants. Among them the white-belled *Erica lusitanica* begins to flower in November, and the red *E. mediterranea* does well. The rest are lower, spreading species and varieties which have covered the ground to provide shade for the roots of magnolias.

The Heath Bank

The view from the base of the Heath Bank is of wide parkland framed by a planting, on the right, of trees chosen for autumn colour, maples, the red oak, parottias, euonymus and others. Immediately below the Tiltyard is a paved semicircle and beyond that a stone seat at which point there are alternative routes back to the point of departure. One path is distinguished by Willi Soukop's amusing bronze donkey; the other, by way of steps commanding a planting of magnolias in variety, and past a summer house, to a lawn separating this part of the gardens from the tennis courts and also from the rose border, planted with species, hybrid musks, bourbons and again more botanical species. Thence across more lawn and back to the Turkey oak. The best summing-up is, again, Mrs Elmhirst's: '. . . from the great Turkey oak the old Hall looms up again. Like the quiet consummation of a classical play it builds up and gathers into itself the main themes of the story, and the old stone buildings compose the final picture to be held in the memory.'

I began by saying that the gardens at Dartington Hall resume the principal traditions of English gardening. There is an element of formality in the parts nearest to the Hall itself which derives from the French influence; there is, in the use of evergreens, masonry and sculpture, just a touch of Italian; in the wide sweeps of lawn and beyond lawn of meadow, and the use of native trees, we have the eighteenth-century landscape garden; in the contrivance of serpentine walks, surprising turns and rises, halts and viewpoints, there is the 'Chinese' (or, as I should prefer to call it, the poetical romantic) tradition; in the discreet use of perennial herbs with much forethought given to the colour effects which will be achieved when these are in flower, we see the influence of Gertrude Jeckyll; in the lavish and yet carefully considered planting of exotic flowering trees and shrubs so to mingle with the natives as to be absorbed into the native scene while giving it a richness and diversity it could not possibly have without these aliens, it expresses the influence most important of all, of William Robinson. In the manner in which these several styles have been combined to create an integral garden, each where it is appropriate to the lie of the land and what was already on it when the work began, there is at least something of the great Loudon's so sensible tolerance. Finally, in the fact, so apparent in the 'personality', the singular integrity of this garden, that the makers of the garden have imposed themselves, using styles and traditions and botanical knowledge and artistic taste as tools, and refusing to allow these

Synthesis of traditions

instruments of the art to use them as tools which is what happens to so many Continental European gardens, the most important English tradition of them all is respected. In any important sense, Dartington Hall gardens are a compromise: they are modern in spirit. We used a deliberately and provokingly excessive claim to express the principle of the English garden carried to the extreme: it is a garden which is not meant to have people in it and which exists, as it were, *gratia hortis*. Dartington exists for its own sake, but is not complete without people in it . . . as it is permanently open to whoever wants to go in, it always does have people in it. To that extent it is a Latin garden but visually it owes everything to the English traditions listed above.

Another of the points we have tried to make in this book is that plantsmanship, and gardening as one of the visual arts, are only with difficulty reconciled and that a plantsman's garden is too often simply a collection and not a garden at all. But the reconciliation has been accomplished at Dartington. The visiting gardener will find rarities: but they have never been planted to *épater*, or in the spirit which animates the plant collector and spoils his garden. By way of example, if *Ilex camelliaefolia* has been planted rather than the common holly, it is because the composition calls for a broader-leaved, more substantial evergreen. Nothing is in the garden merely for the sake of having it there; in very few gardens have the rare and the commonplace been so successfully combined.

Although, then, Dartington Hall gardens represent a successful synthesis of the principal English gardening traditions, they are a paradise, in our especial sense of the word, only in certain parts; and this for obvious reasons; the spirit of the Dartington Hall community of people is very 'social'; the place is, after all, an *academe*, indeed, it is one of the few places to which the word can properly be applied. Its gardens therefore are bound to be open, to be unsecret, to be a setting for man in the style of the Italian or French garden, however English in design, in planting and above all in plantsmanship. And we have chosen to conclude the study of great gardens with these because they have a special significance for the future: for this is the kind of garden with which it is possible that today's and tomorrow's institutions, industrial, administrative, educational, even residential, could well surround themselves. It provides recreation not for one man or one family, like the great English gardens of yesterday, but for a working community of people who, despite jeers which one sometimes hears at Dartington's 'monasticism', are very much *dans le siècle*. It is, in short, in gardens like those of Dartington Hall that the traditions of the great English garden will, if at all, find their continuance.

'English' gardens abroad

It should be remembered, however, that the word 'English' in the above context and in the title of this book is not used geographically so much as aesthetically: it identifies a certain kind of garden, devised in England but which can perfectly well be made in a great many other countries. Since it is often said, and with some truth, that one of the influences which make the English garden what it has become is the peculiarly mild climate of the British Isles, it will be worth examining this statement, that English gardens can be and are made elsewhere than in Britain, in some detail.

First, as to places where the climate is obviously suitable for the creation of paradise gardens, the whole style and traditions of English gardening have been taken over with enthusiasm in Australia, and in New Zealand; particularly in S.W. Australia and in Tasmania is it possible, from the point of view of soil and climate, not only to make English gardens, but to do so more easily than in Britain. In the northern hemisphere the case is not quite so simple. In Europe the choice of plant material is very restricted by the fact that so much of the Continent is made of limestone; but although this entails losing the use of the calcifuge plants, it is still true that the English garden style can be practised, for after all it is successfully expressed in such gardens as Highdown, which we have dealt with and which is on the chalk. In North America limestone soils are much less common and calcifuge plants can be grown almost everywhere throughout that vast region. Of this matter of soil however it should be said, in general, that it need never be regarded as important when the question of the English style is being considered, simply because that style can be expressed in either lime-tolerant or lime-hating plants, although it is true that the best of the great paradise gardens are on acid soils; and that Dartington Hall, our 'type' of the future great garden, is at least on a neutral soil where calcifuge plants will grow and even flourish. And finally, on this subject, certain technical advances which it would not be convenient to deal with here seem likely to make it possible to grow the lime-hating plants in soils of high calcium content, within a few years.

British nurseries for the supply of ornamental plants, especially of ornamental trees and flowering shrubs, are more numerous and much richer in species and varieties than those of Continental Europe or North America. No doubt they would welcome the export business which a further spread in the fashion for English gardens might lead to. And although the labour-and-wages revolution in the western world's economy immediately after the second world war seemed very likely to condemn the great garden to extinction not only in Britain but elsewhere, it is at least possible that the later, in fact the very recent, advances in horticultural mechanization may help to save the art of making them. The number of hands formerly needed to work a great garden and especially in the propagating department, was very great. Ten, twenty, as many as seventy gardeners might be employed. But the simplification of styles in the romantic paradise gardens, and the use of power-driven cultivators, mowers, hedge-trimmers, trucks and barrows have together reduced the labour requirement to about one tenth of what it used to be. Greenhouse automation has been particularly helpful in this respect: in a modern propagating-house, heating, watering and ventilation are regulated by electronic devices; and the electronically controlled 'mist-propagation' system has almost eliminated the need for skill and at the same time greatly raised the yield of new plants at the propagating benches.

When, however, we come to the matter of climate in relation to geography, the case is different. First, there is a very great number of plants commonly grown in English gardens which are not hardy in harsher climates. When dealing with the question of hardiness we have, of course, to consider winter climate first. The coldest month of the year in the northern hemisphere is January. The mean temperature for that month is above 4·4°C. for the whole of west Britain, and above 5°C. in the extreme south-west. The whole island has a January mean temperature above 3·5°C. with the exception of East Anglia and a part of east central Scotland. Now these conditions obtain on the Continent, in the Atlantic provinces of France, Portugal and Spain and on the west and south coasts of Italy and of Greece; and along the south coast of France. And in the mild winter belt of Portugal, France and Italy there are, in fact, a number of English gardens of the paradise type; the perfect climate for them is to be found in Portugal rather than in the other two countries, the high humidity of an 'Atlantic' climate having much to do with this.

Inland in western Europe, at low or moderate altitudes, the January mean temperature is below the freezing point but not extremely cold. Here the conditions exclude a large range of evergreens, but the fact remains that English gardens, only less rich in plant material, are quite feasible and are, in fact, to be found. In Eastern Europe the winters become so severe that the plant material which can be used in the making of great gardens is much more restricted.

'English' conditions in North America are, for reasons which we need not enter into, shifted south, as it were, by almost twenty degrees of latitude. Only south of latitude 35° N. are the winters as mild as they are in south and west Britain, and along part of the west coast, of both Canada and United States, from about Vancouver Island south to the northern half of California; southern California is, of course, warmer than southern Britain in the winter. It is generally considered that the state of Oregon can grow most of the plants which flourish in Britain, but even there winters are harder. Nevertheless, over a very vast area of North America, especially the coastal regions and in regions of high rainfall, 'English' gardens are possible and are, in fact, to be found.

Winter cold is not by any means the only climatic consideration of importance, however. The paradise garden does not flourish in the absence of summer rainfall or where the summer temperatures and sunshine hours are very high, unless irrigation is practised (as it increasingly is, of course), and where the shade of trees can be provided. In the seventh and eighth centuries of our era the gardeners of the

Climate and geography

great centres of Arab civilization developed a form of water-and-shade gardening far more suitable for the hot and arid parts of both Eurasia and America. The conclusion here must be that in most of north-western Europe and perhaps a third of North America, English gardens can be made; and, indeed, have been made.

The genius of the gardener

So much for the kind of soil and the kind of climate, and the kind of plants required for the creation of paradise gardens. Quite as important, no doubt, is the nature and temperament of the gardener. The horticultural genius of the Americans, of the Germans, of the Dutch, Italians and French, differs from that of the English; perhaps each people has one of its own. But there does seem to be some recognition of the peculiar excellence of the English kind of garden, since so many men and women of other lands look to England for a model. The 'ideal' English gardener is neither a plant-collector nor an architect; neither a mere naturalist nor a horticultural geometrician. He combines a feeling for design after Nature with a love and knowledge of plants; his object, in both his planting designs and his care of individual plants, and even in the restrained use of garden buildings, is a Nature perfected. Above all, he is one who earns the epitaph which was written for John Rose, gardener to King Charles II –

> On earth he truly lived, old Adam's heir
> In tilling it with sweating, pains and care;
> And, by God's blessing, such increase did find,
> As served to please his Gracious Master's mind;
> Till from those Royal Gardens he did rise
> Transplanted to the Upper Paradise.

Notes on the Plates

147 DARTINGTON HALL

One of the points of view contrived to command the many fine views. These gardens, made round the Old Hall on which centres the academic life of this community of teachers and pupils of the arts, are the most recent of the great English gardens and have a special significance for the future.

148 DARTINGTON HALL

A glimpse of the Tiltyard between the fine trees which distinguish every part of the gardens.

149 DARTINGTON HALL

Henry Moore's *Reclining Woman*, and one of the many vistas in which a little formality is set into a natural woodland or parkland scene. 'I tried', writes Henry Moore, 'to make a figure which could rightly be called a memorial figure. I wanted the figure to have a quiet stillness and a sense of permanence as though it could stay there for ever; to have strength and seriousness in its effect and yet be serene and happy and resolved, as though it had come to terms with the world, and could get over the largest cares and losses.'

150 DARTINGTON HALL

A corner of the Tiltyard, showing the terraced banks of 'seats' from which spectators watched the jousting. This great 'theatre' is now all fine sward.

151 DARTINGTON HALL

The Irish yews known as The Twelve Apostles. In the foreground, the evergreen *Clematis armandii*. All Irish yews are said to come from a single parent tree at Annes Grove, County Cork, Eire.

152 DARTINGTON HALL

The humid climate of south Devonshire favours the growth of the magnificent rhododendrons, magnolias and camellias which have attained a great size in two decades.

153, 154 BRIDGE END GARDENS, SAFFRON WALDEN

One solution to the problem of continuing the great English gardens, both old and perhaps new ones, is municipalization. Bridge End Gardens, Saffron Waldon, in the county of Essex, formerly the private garden of the Gibson family, is now a municipal garden. There is no reason why the finest traditions of the English garden should not be expressed in municipal gardens. Fine examples of civic gardening and municipal gardening are to be seen in the Rock Gardens at Harrogate, the municipal gardens of Bristol and Torquay, Falmouth and Penzance, and in the gardening of the London parks.

155 CLANDON PARK, SURREY

Grotto and statuary, conjuring memories of an eighteenth-century mania.

154

IT IS PERHAPS a mortifying consideration that the great gardens we have dealt with and the many more which we have not dealt with are now of no importance whatsoever, socially and economically, by comparison with the many millions of small gardens which embellish Britain's cities and villages, occupy the leisure of about ten million amateurs, make a not inconsiderable, but declining, contribution to the nation's food supply, and a very considerable one to her amenities; and which, finally, have called into being a great industry manufacturing machinery and tools, and another manufacturing horticultural chemicals, by-products of gardening which themselves, by their exporting, contribute largely to the national income. We should be very sorry indeed to lose our great gardens: but the fact remains that they are now either preserved as museum pieces by the National Trust; or kept up with great difficulty by private owners so absorbed in the beauty of gardens that they restrict their lives in other ways in order to have money for their gardens. To emphazise the point, we will make a comparable but even more outrageous statement: the masterworks of art in the national and in private collections are of no importance whatsoever – again socially and economically – by comparison with the tens of millions of photographs made annually by millions of amateurs.

Why, then, devote a book to great gardens and give to the little ones only a few pages in a tailpiece? Because, of course, it was in the great gardens that the national horticultural style was formed; that the immense wealth of our plant material was collected; that the technology of English horticulture was developed; and, even, that the small-garden style itself, having been borrowed by such great gardeners as Gertrude Jeckyll, was refined, dignified with aesthetic standing by recognition, and had its rules abstracted and stated.

But we are far from arguing that the millions of Britain's small gardeners, not to mention the more millions of European and American gardeners using English styles, plants and techniques, owe absolutely everything to the great gardens which owe little to them. It is well known that the English accomplish their best works by putting the cart before the horse; that is to say, they are empiricists, who get the rules of art and science out of works already made, rather than making works by rules arrived at first: the empirical garden science and art of countless, nameless little gardeners contributed enormously to the making of great gardens and to the laying down of the rules by which they are made.

We seem to know very little indeed about small gardens before the sixteenth century. The petty burgesses of the fifteenth, and even of the fourteenth, certainly had gardens and so perhaps did some of the rural poor. England lagged behind continental Europe in gardening until the seventeenth century. But at least in the south-east, and remembering that she was always relatively rich, life for ordinary people cannot have been very different (indeed, Chaucer makes that clear) from that lived in, say, the Ile-de-France. The gardens of the petty burgesses of Paris in the late fourteenth and early fifteenth centuries, from the impression gained of them in the relatively rich source material used by social historians, from, for example, the *Journal d'un bourgeois de Paris* or the *Ménagier de Paris*, were devoted to the production of green and root vegetables, culinary herbs, apples, pears and damsons, and a very few flowers, notably violets and roses.

In the sixteenth century we get a clearer picture; for we have Thomas Tusser's *Hundred Points of Good Husbandrie* from which a good deal can be inferred if we bear in mind the fact that even today the average amateur rarely does, in practice, as well as the books he applies to say he can. Tusser is not the only source for the period. From him and others we can gather what was grown in small gardens, and how. But more important, we can find the origin of the cottage garden style, that famous sweet confusion of the useful and ornamental. The fact is that the first flowers to be grown in small gardens only happened to be ornamental; they were grown for use as herbs of one sort or another. Such, for example, were violets, primroses, marigolds and roses: they were in the gardens of the sixteenth century as medicinal, strewing or culinary herbs, and not to provide ornaments among the peas and the Good King Henry.

The knot garden

The fashionable style in the great gardens of Tudor times was the knot garden, a style which Miles Hadfield thinks came to us from Italy by way of Holland. More or less elaborate formal patterns, or even stylized pictures, usually heraldic, were composed with clipped dwarf evergreens such as box, and either coloured sand or pebbles, or sometimes with flowers. The style is not extinct: about fifteen or twenty years ago the Earl and Countess of Rosse made a very charming knot garden at Birr Castle in Ireland, a garden in any case remarkable for its box both dwarf and giant; and this knot garden is still maintained. It is likely that by the end of the sixteenth, and certainly early in the seventeenth century the more prosperous owners of small gardens had borrowed this style; if so, this was perhaps the first instance of ornamental gardening, gardening which cost, instead of saving, money, at that level of society. The only written evidence for it that I know is that Lawson in his *Countrie Housewife's Garden*, published early in the seventeenth century, printed a number of plans for knot gardens.

Cottage gardens of the nineteenth century

But if, from time to time, writers paid some attention to the small garden, the fact remains that not until the rise to a measure of prosperity of a large lower middle class did the kind of garden which is now socially and economically by far the most important, receive thought from the horticultural pundits, the first of them being Loudon, as we have already noted. But at this point it is necessary to make a clear distinction between two lines of evolution: that of the cottager's garden; and that of the garden which, whether in town or country, we may perhaps call suburban. For the origin of the first is to be found in necessity, indeed in poverty; whereas the small garden of the prosperous class of small burgesses is, on the contrary, a product of increasing wealth. What Flora Thompson has to say of the cottager's garden in the mid-nineteenth century (see below) was no doubt true of an earlier epoch, although probably that kind of garden was not, in the eighteenth century, as desperately important to the very survival of the families of the rural poor, as it had become by the time she describes: in the last third of the nineteenth century the farm-labourer's wage throughout Britain was between 8s. and 12s. a week. How did people survive on this pittance? Well, for one thing, as Flora Thompson says in her masterpiece, the *Larkrise to Candleford* trilogy:

'. . . all vegetables, including potatoes, were home grown and grown in abundance. The men took great pride in their gardens and allotments and there was always competition among them as to who should have the earliest and choicest of each kind. Fat green peas, broad beans as big as a halfpenny, cauliflowers a child could make an armchair of, runner-beans and cabbage and kale, all in their season. . . . They ate plenty of green food, all home-grown and freshly pulled. . . . A few slices of bread and home-made lard, flavoured with rosemary, and plenty of green food, "went down good" as they used to say . . .'

Here, at once, is a case in point: the rosemary was in these little gardens to give a relish to the lard made from the cottager's pig; it happened also to be ornamental; it was there for use but it supplied an amenity.

'The energy they brought to their gardening after a hard day's work in the fields was marvellous. They grudged no effort and seemed never to tire. Often, on moonlight nights in spring, the solitary fork of someone who had not been able to tear himself away would be heard and the scent of his twitch fire smoke would float in at the windows. It was pleasant too, in summer twilight, perhaps in the hot weather when water was scarce, to hear the *swish* of water on parched earth in the garden-water which had been fetched from the brook a quarter of a mile distant . . .'

The gardens of the rural poor as Flora Thompson describes them were strictly utilitarian; like any good vegetable garden they gave their owners some aesthetic pleasure; but there was as a rule neither time, money nor, perhaps, inclination for flowers excepting where the wife planted a few or persuaded her husband to do so. But there existed, in the hamlets and villages of Britain at this time, an older and better tradition, a relic of the relative prosperity of a class which had been depressed into wage-slavery only within the last two generations. The garden of the aged couple who lived at Lark Rise, and who represented the last vestige of that better time, was very different. It was large:

'. . . tailing off at the bottom into the little field where Dick grew his corn crop. Nearer the cottage were the fruit-trees, then the yew hedge, close and solid as a wall, which sheltered the beehives and enclosed the flower-garden. Sally had such flowers, and so many of them, and nearly all of them sweet-scented! Wallflowers and tulips, lavender and sweet-william, and pinks, and old world roses with enchanting names – Seven Sisters, Maiden's Blush, moss rose, monthly rose, cabbage rose, blood rose and most thrilling of all to the children, the big bush of the York and Lancaster rose, in the blooms of which the rival roses mingled in a pied white and red. It seemed as though all the roses in Lark Rise had gathered together in that one garden. Most of the gardens had one poor starveling bush, or none. . . .'

It was this kind of garden, owing very little and perhaps nothing to the great gardens excepting very remotely in, for example, the clipped yew hedge which the poor substituted for the box and other evergreens of an earlier century, and which the great gardens borrowed from the cottagers, which provided a tradition of small gardens for the future, when the lot of the poor was to improve again; and from which Gertrude Jeckyll took those hints which formed her style and which even William Robinson was persuaded to respect.

Thus one of the component traditions and styles of the modern small gardens of Britain had its origin in that class whose members would never be able to afford more than a few score square yards. The tradition was of enormous social and economic importance in its influence. When the people of Britain were dispossessed of their land by the enclosures and the developments of high farming, the alternative to letting them starve or paying them decent wages, was to let them each have, at least, a little piece of land, preferably about the house, but if not then in the 'allotments' which Flora Thompson refers to. It was from this that arose the habit, the feeling, that every house should stand in a garden, should have at least a 'bit of a garden'. And this, again, has led to the outraging of the countryside, to the suburban sprawl, to the ruin of coastal and valley scenery almost everywhere, and to the problem of how to house a population which refuses to live vertically, in flats, and insists on having a house in a garden.

So much for the small gardens which were founded in economic necessity. What of the other line of development? The urban lower middle class, with a rising instead of a falling share of the national income, was demanding more of life; the thousands of square miles of suburban housing develop-ment in which every commercial and industrial town of Britain became enveloped, were theirs. Every

Suburban gardens

house had its garden and while, certainly, some fruit, salad crops and vegetables might be grown in these gardens, they were, in the main, for amenity, that is to say, they were planted with ornamentals. The whole class responsible for these little gardens lived its life in emulation of the class above it, to which its members aspired; in their gardens as in other respects they tried to imitate their social 'betters'. Thus, whereas the gardens of the rural poor helped to support their owners, those of the suburban burgesses, on the contrary, made a call on the family income.

At the epoch of this development it happened that much of what was being done in the great and medium-sized gardens could be imitated on a smaller scale without troubles of proportion: the bedding-out of half-hardy annuals in formal beds cut out of lawns, all very geometrical and symmetrical; the use of a restricted range of shrubby genera, with the emphasis on the new hybrid roses, on syringa and philadelphus and some improved cultivars of such natives as hawthorn, was perfectly possible in the small suburban garden. That this was a matter of class is very clear from one rather curious phenomenon: the man who, although he lived in the country, say upon the outskirts of a country town, but felt himself to be, in income and in social habits, a member of the urban small burgess class, had not a cottage garden but a garden which in style and plant material was a suburban garden; vestiges of such gardens identifiable by their shrubs are still to be seen, now long since embedded within the sprawling towns by later, peripheral housing developments. The devising of light lawn-mowers, and of cheaper greenhouses, were the first steps in that mechanization of the small garden which is now, with electrical automation, nearly complete. The owners of these hundreds of thousands of small gardens, hard-working people with large families to support, could give only a few hours at weekends to working in their gardens. But there arose a numerous class of jobbing gardeners with a tolerable standard of skill despite all that has been said against them; they looked after a number of gardens, giving a few hours here, a couple of days there, and being paid by the hour. Plants for bedding-out were bought from the small local nurseries which were called into being by the new demand in surprising number. Later, retail shops dealing in garden sundries carried stocks of such plants; and there were even thousands of plant-hawkers who pushed their handcarts laden with pansies, marigolds and petunias through thousands of miles of suburban streets, selling as they went. The urban conditions, including atmospheric soot from millions of open coal fires which in autumn and winter frequently became suspended and concentrated in dense smogs, set limits to the range of evergreens which would be used for hedges and foliage-clumps in these gardens; in those towns free from such pollution, box and yew might be planted and clipped by amateur topiarists in imitation of the great country house gardens. But for the most part the native privet, which proved resistant to a poisonous air as the people themselves, and the Japanese aucuba, the so-called laurel which was able to flourish in conditions of very poor light, were planted, and became so excessively popular that the reaction against them in our times has been such that it is now difficult to do proper justice to their merits.

The herbaceous border

Plate 156

The next fashion from great gardens which was almost universally adopted in small ones so long as the supply of jobbing gardeners lasted, was that of the herbaceous border. I have wondered whether this very English contribution to horticultural vogue was not itself developed from the pleasant confusion of the cottage garden, and sophisticated by conscious design and the enrichment of our fund of plant material; but if so then the cottage in question was that of the epoch before the one described by Flora Thompson. The herbaceous border as adopted by the small gardener was an advance: it not only brightened the whole picture of suburbia's front and back gardens, but it brought a wider range of plants into general use. It also saved labour, for once the border was established, and although we now regard such borders as very extravagant of labour, there was nothing like as much work as was necessary to maintain a garden in which bedding-out of annuals was the rule. Not until our own time did this kind of border become impossible to maintain; and even that is not so much because such maintenance does call for much work, as because the whole class of owners of small gardens has now many more ways of using leisure; in more ways than one, the motor car has been the enemy of the well-kept semi-formal garden; it will be interesting to see whether, as motoring becomes increasingly unpleasant and dangerous, the country's millions of small gardens will show the benefit of more attention. The jobbing gardener began to disappear as the motor car began to be universal. But early in the century he was still present in sufficient number, his wage was low and so was income tax; thus hundreds of thousands of herbaceous borders could be stocked with ever more spectacular hardy perennials tried and improved in the great gardens and in commercial nurseries; and could be kept in decent and seemly order.

The range of plants in these small gardens, while still limited, was wider: herbaceous perennials, roses and lilacs but rather few other shrubs, the inevitable lawn, and a strictly formal and even rectangular design – these were the fashion, partly because it did not seem possible to make use of a more romantic, less formal design in a rectangular plot front and back of a house, especially when the house was semi-detached as so many hundreds of thousands were. There might be some small trees, other than fruit trees in the kitchen garden, but there was little or no reflection of the enormous range of flowering shrubs already to be found in the great gardens. Even the use of the spectacular, new hardy hybrid rhododendrons was limited by considerations of soil acidity. It is true to say that a suburban gardener of 1910 or for that matter 1920, visiting a great garden, would have seen far more plants utterly unknown to him, arranged in a manner altogether unfamiliar, than would today's suburban gardener doing likewise. The gap is narrower because clever designers have found ways of shrinking great garden patterns to go into a small space.

Two extraordinarily successful institutions have been the agents accomplishing the transference of great garden styles and plants to the gardens of that common man whose age, we are told, this is: the horticultural press and the Royal Horticultural Society. How significant that one of the best mass-circulation women's journals of France employs the editor of the *Gardener's Chronicle* to write its garden page; and that American and German nurserymen eagerly seek the Society's plant awards. The RHS began, as we have seen, as a learned society like any other; but no other learned society has ever recruited sixty thousand Fellows. At the frequent shows, but above all at the great annual Chelsea show, the amateur with a small garden could and can see not only the new plants but numerous model gardens from which he can learn how the romantic and yet practical design, the labour-saving planting, the better plants of the great gardens can be used in a small space. When the disappearance of the jobbing gardener, the rise in wages and in taxes, the increasingly wide choice of leisure occupations, drove not only 'bedding-out' but even the herbaceous border out of fashion, it was not solely the inventors and manufacturers of machine-tools, fertilizers and pest-controls who came to the rescue of the small garden: for the models for the mixed shrub-and-perennial garden were already in being in many great gardens, to be copied and modified to create a new small-garden style to suit the times. In the case of a surprising number of shrubs of all the principal ornamental genera, dwarf representatives were found, collected, propagated, hybridized. The Robinsonian technique of naturalizing bulb plants under trees and shrubs came into its own on a miniature scale. A numerous class of well-informed journalists, themselves practical gardeners, kept a larger and larger public informed of new plants, styles, techniques, materials and discoveries. Our own time is seeing a very marked and rapid decline in the kitchen garden; as more people can afford to buy their vegetables, very often preserved rather than fresh, and as the cost of raising one's own gets higher; as, too, wages continue to rise and with them the standard of living of the masses, ornamental gardening becomes of more, instead of less, importance even in the class which formerly depended on its kitchen gardens for survival.

From the beginnings made in great gardens there has been another and quite different small-garden development: that of the advanced and very highly skilled specialization of amateurs with small space and little money but much ability. You could not in a small garden do everything the rich did in their big ones: but you could do one thing as well or better. Perhaps the most remarkable development

Rock gardens

in this field of specialization is that of the alpine gardener, with his rock garden or his alpine house. Alpine plants, exquisite in their smallness, had a strong aesthetic appeal; but, perhaps the most difficult of all plants to cultivate, they also offered a challenge. Rock gardens and alpine houses became very numerous and many advances in this kind of horticulture have been due to the small gardener. The cultivation of tropical orchids was at first confined to the rich gardener who could afford the prices asked by collectors and who could employ skilled professional gardeners: but that, too, has become the hobby, and one demanding great skill, patience and intelligence, of the small gardener. These changes and movements have not eliminated the traditional cottage garden to which the whole style of English gardening owes so much: the style persists, it has even benefited considerably by becoming a little self-conscious, and it has been enriched by new plant material. In thousands of villages all over the country exquisite examples of this art are to be found. Because of the decline in vegetable gardening described above, these gardens are now richer in flowers than ever they were.

Plant material A rise in the quality and distinction of the plants commonly grown has been a curious by-product of two wars and the impoverishment of the class of landed gentry. It was natural enough that many of the flowering shrubs introduced from Asia, South America and Australasia should at first have been regarded as tender and confined in cultivation to the conservatories of the rich or to the great gardens of the mild south-western counties. The fascination exercised by the beauty of these plants on a flower-loving race led to the trial of many in the less mild parts of the country; the enforced neglect of conservatories and hot-houses during the two world wars revealed, what botanists had perhaps known all the time, that many of these exotics were less tender than had been supposed. A good case in point is that of the camellia; long grown as a tender plant under glass, excepting in the great Cornish gardens, it has, in at least one species and one group of fine hybrids, proved to be ruggedly hardy. And many small gardeners will now plant a camellia whose grandfathers would have planted privet or aucuba. Nor has this influence of the great gardens in improving the quality of the plant material in common use, been confined to the small private garden. A new generation of superintendent gardeners of public parks is busy replacing old and rather uninteresting shrub material with the much finer material tried and proved in the great private gardens and propagated in the principal nurseries.

It is obvious that the traditions of the English garden, formed of such diverse materials in the great private gardens, and adapted and modified in the small ones, will henceforth, and as a rule, be in other hands. It is not true that there are now no men rich enough to create gardens like Gravetye, Nymans, or Caerhays; there are more rich men than ever there were; mechanization of garden work and automation in the greenhouses make up for shortage of labour; as for skill, it is still as plentiful as ever. But the rich man of the second half of the twentieth century is not the same kind of animal at all as the rich man of the second half of the nineteenth. The small, private gardens in their millions, and the big public ones in their thousands, must now take over responsibility for the continuance of this noblest and most ancient of the applied arts. To a large extent, indeed, they have already done so. From the tendencies which can be observed in the early 'sixties we may expect small gardens to be increasingly 'Americanized' in the sense of becoming outdoor playrooms and lounges rather than miniature collections of plants; yet the English love of plants and of flowers may check this tendency also, and out of this may come a new kind of small garden; new, yet linked quite clearly to the ancient style of formal pleasaunce which goes back to ancient Egypt.

The tradition of the paradise garden as we have called it will, on the other hand, and again if present trends provide a reliable guide, be very safe in the hands of the new generation of public gardeners who have taken to plantsmanship, naturalizing and romantic design, with such enthusiasm. The only loss may be that of the enthusiasm for the rare and difficult exotic: it is certainly the case that fewer and fewer nurseries can, in the absence of demand, continue to carry that vast range of plants still to be found, for example, at Hillier's of Winchester. It is possible that in richness of plant material we have passed the zenith. But in all other respects the future of the English garden is bright.

Notes on the Plates

156 COTTAGE GARDEN AT HORSMONDON, KENT
The future of the English garden lies with municipalities as to the great ones, and otherwise in the hands of the small private gardener in both town and country.

157 THE INFLUENCE OF FASHION
The huge 'market' of small gardeners, several million of them, stimulates the breeding and propagation of new garden hybrids, with roses as the most important. The best novelties, like the rose 'Peace', benefit, like women's clothes, from the influence of fashion.

158 ROBINSON'S GARDEN STYLE
The garden style created and popularized by William Robinson on the basis of the cottage garden, can be expressed *in petto* as well as on the grand scale. Miss Jessie Daw in her garden at Little Barrington, Gloucestershire.

159 TOPIARY IN THE SMALL GARDEN
An example at Ebrington, Gloucestershire.

160 EARISWELL, SUFFOLK
By specializing, the small gardeners of England, stimulated by thousands of annual 'Shows', excel in one or two kinds of flower.

161 LOWER BRAILES, GLOUCESTERSHIRE
Even in the small private garden some expression can be given to garden style which makes a paradise of flowering shrubs and evergreen trees.

162 CLIMBING ROSES
The rose is the most important flower in English horticulture. While the great and medium gardens have restored the shrub and species roses to favour, cottagers still prefer the old climbers and new hybrids. This example is from near Hadleigh, Suffolk.

163 COUNTRY STYLE IN THE SUBURBS
English suburban gardens are socially and economically the most important of all. In such suburbs as Hampstead both great and small gardens achieve an illusion of country by following country-house and cottage styles.

164 WALL GARDENING IN THE TOWN
Wall gardening with Alpines and rock plants is practised in town gardens where space is very limited and vertical surfaces cannot be wasted. This example is from a small house in Gloucester.

165 BUDLAKE, DEVON
Fabulous beasts in clipped box or yew can enliven a small as well as a great garden, maintaining yet another of the ancient garden styles.

166 SAPPERTON, GLOUCESTERSHIRE
Not even such traditional magnificences as pea-fowl need be excluded from the garden if the gardener prefers them to the plants they destroy!

167 EXOTICS IN A COTTAGE GARDEN
The cottage gardens of the little Scilly Isles towns, such as this one in St Mary's, benefit, like Tresco Abbey, from the climate, and are rich in tender exotics, some of which, like agapanthus and mesembryanthemum, fuchsia and hebe, have become naturalized.

168 THE LION AND THE UNICORN
Reminiscence, in a tiny London garden, of the fabulous beasts of the great Jacobean gardens.

169 AN URBAN BOWER
Back of a terrace house in Clareville Gardens, London, turned into a bower of foliage and flowers by the use of vertical surfaces. Even exotic plants which will tolerate atmospheric pollution benefit by urban shelter and warmth.

170 A NINETEENTH-CENTURY TOWN GARDEN
Rectangularity of layout was still *de rigueur* when Walter Howell Deverell (1827–54) painted this lady feeding a bird in the doorway of her conservatory. *Photo by permission of the Trustees of the Tate Gallery.*

171 SISSINGHURST CASTLE
A reminder, to conclude, that, through the influence of William Robinson and Gertrude Jeckyll, the cottage garden found expression in the great gardens.

157

158

159

160

161

162

163

164

170

Notable Gardens in Britain

UNDER THE NATIONAL GARDENS SCHEME, and also under private owners, well over a thousand gardens in England, Wales and Scotland are open to visitors on one or more days in every year. Nobody can know them all; the following shorter list has been made with only one consideration in mind: every garden in it contains something of particular interest to gardeners and of relevance to the theme of this book. The beauty or historic interest of the house, fine views, and many other features which attract visitors, have been ignored. The garden visitor's best plan is to obtain from the National Gardens Scheme, 57 Lower Belgrave St, London s.w.1, or Scotland's Garden Scheme, 26 Castle Terrace, Edinburgh, 1, their full lists of gardens which are open to view.

BEDFORDSHIRE
Woodbury Hall, Everton
Luton Hoo

BERKSHIRE
Frogmore Gardens, Windsor Castle *by
 gracious permission of Her Majesty the Queen*
Buscot Park, Faringdon
Winkfield Manor, Ascot
Englefield House, nr Theale
Wasing Place, Aldermaston
Oakfield, Mortimer
White Horse, Finchampstead
Folly Farm, Sulhamstead
The Old Rectory, Sulhamstead
Culham Court, nr Henley-on-Thames
Pusey House, nr Faringdon
The Lane House, Mortimer

BUCKINGHAMSHIRE
Ascott, Wing
Dorneywood, nr Burnham
Cliveden, nr Taplow

Luxmoore's Garden, Eton
The Abbey, Aston Abbots

CAMBRIDGESHIRE
Tetworth Hall

CHESHIRE
Birtles Hall, Chelford
Tree Tops, Heswall
The Quarry, Prenton
Arley Hall, nr Northwich
Ashton Heys, Ashton
Crowthorn, Willaston
Foreign Hey, nr Adlington

CORNWALL
Penjerrick, Budock
Glendurgan, Mawnan Smith
Trerose, Mawnan

CUMBERLAND
Muncaster Castle, Ravenglass

DERBYSHIRE
Lea Rhododendron Gardens
Hazelbrow, nr Duffield
Melbourne Hall
The Old Rectory, Fenny Bentley

DEVON
The Garden House, Buckland Monachorum
Chevithorne Barton, nr Tiverton
Knightshayes Court, nr Tiverton
Dartington Hall, nr Totnes
Luscombe Castle, Dawlish
Lee Ford, Budleigh Salterton

DORSET
Hyde Crook, nr Dorchester
Yaffle Hill, Broadstone
Minterne, Cerne Abbas
Waterston Manor, Piddlehinton
Athelhampton Hall, nr Puddletown
Icen House, nr Wareham
Lulworth Manor
Marley House, Winfrith Newburgh

COUNTY DURHAM
Neasham Abbey
Quarriston, Heighington
Raby Castle, Staindrop
Neasham Hall

ESSEX
Lilystone Hall, Stock
Gun Hill Place, Dedham
Hill Pasture, Broxted
Abbots Hall, Great Wigborough
Colne Place, Earls Colne
Sawyers, Brentwood

GLOUCESTERSHIRE
Abbotswood, nr Stow-in-the-Wold
Batsford Park, nr Moreton-in-the-Marsh
Old Down Gardens, Tockington
Westonbirt School, nr Tetbury
Hardwicke Court, nr Gloucester
Vine House, Henbury
Hidcote Manor Gardens, nr Chipping Camden
Sezincote, nr Moreton-in-the-Marsh
The Manor, Bourton-on-the-Water

HAMPSHIRE
Wyck, Alton
Priors Barton, Winchester
Castle Green, Woodgreen
Exbury, nr Southampton
Coles, Privett

Ravenscourt, Lymington
Pylewell Park, nr Lymington
Hartfield House, Headley
Chilland, Martyr Worthy
Jermyns House, Ampfield
Bramdean House, nr Alresford
Jenkyn Place, Bentley
Hall Place, West Meon
Broadlands, Romsey
Pennington Chase, Lymington

HEREFORDSHIRE
Hill Court, Ross-on-Wye
Broadfield Court, Bodenham

HERTFORDSHIRE
St Paul's Walden Bury, Whitwell
Bayfordbury, nr Hertford
Knebworth House
Arkley Manor

HUNTINGDONSHIRE
The Hermitage, Hemingford Abbots

KENT
Crittenden House, Matfield
Sissinghurst Castle, Cranbrook
Oaken Wood, Wateringbury
Hole Park, Rolvenden
The Grange, Benenden
Stonewell Park, Chiddingstone
Belmont Park, Throwley
Southmead, Weald
Withersdane Hall, Wye
Husheath Manor, nr Goudhurst
Doddington Place, nr Sittingbourne
Mount Ephraim, nr Faversham
Chilham Castle
Dower House, Knowlton
The White House, Sandwich Bay
Mereworth Castle, nr Maidstone

LEICESTERSHIRE
Sedgemere, Market Bosworth
Long Close, Woodhouse Eaves
Brooksby Hall Farm Institute, Melton Mowbray
Prestwold Hall, nr Loughborough

LONDON AND MIDDLESEX
Beechwood, Highgate
The Elms, Highgate Village
The Manor House, Ham
Sudbrook Cottage, Ham Common

NORFOLK
Sheringham Hall

NORFOLK
Mergate Hall, Braconash
Lamas Hall, nr Buxton
Saxlingham Old Hall
Swanington Manor, Norwich
Bolwick Hall, Marsham

NORTHAMPTONSHIRE
Grey Court, King's Sutton
Cottesbrooke Hall, nr Northampton
Flore House
The Manor House, King's Sutton
Lamport Hall, Northampton

NOTTINGHAMSHIRE
Nottinghamshire Farm Institute, Brackenhurst
Langar Hall, nr Nottingham
Flintham Hall, nr Newark

OXFORDSHIRE
Rousham Park, nr Oxford
Blenheim Palace, Woodstock

RUTLAND
Old Hall, Langham

SHROPSHIRE
Monk Hopton, nr Bridgnorth
Burford House Gardens, nr Tenbury Wells
Ludstone Hall, Claverley
Henley Hall, nr Ludlow
Quatford Wood House, nr Bridgnorth
Powis Castle Gardens, Welshpool

SOMERSET
Wayford Manor, nr Crewkerne
Underway, West Porlock
Ammerdown Park, Radstock
Dillington House, nr Ilminster
East Lambrook Manor, nr S. Petherton

STAFFORDSHIRE
Willoughbridge, Pipe Gate

SUFFOLK
Cousins Hill, nr Needham Market
Heveningham Hall, nr Halesworth
Pentlow Hall, Cavendish

SURREY
Hascombe Court, nr Godalming
Coverwood, Ewhurst
Westbourn, Wentworth
Dunsborough Park, Ripley
Grayswood Hill, Haslemere

Pyrford Court, nr Woking
Farall Nurseries, nr Haslemere
Eastlands, Weybridge
Sunningdale Nurseries, Windlesham
Pinewood House, nr Woking
High Hackhurst, Abinger Hammer
Road Farm, Churt
The Old Rectory, W. Horsley

SUSSEX
Great Dixter, Northiam
Nymans, Handcross
Gravetye Manor Hotel, W. Hoathly
Highdown, Goring-by-Sea
Mockbeggars, Fittleworth
West Dean Park Arboretum, nr Chichester
Rawdon House, Worthing

WARWICKSHIRE
Wootton Court, nr Warwick
Arden Croft, Edgbaston

WESTMORLAND
White Craggs, nr Ambleside

WILTSHIRE
Broadleas, nr Devizes
Bulbridge House, Wilton
Stourhead Pleasure Grounds, Stourton
Corsham Court, nr Chippenham
Nunton House, nr Salisbury

WORCESTERSHIRE
The Orchard House, Broadway

YORKSHIRE
Clifton Castle, Thornton Watlass
Swinton, nr Masham
Sleightholme Dale, Fadmoor

CAERNARVONSHIRE
Hafodty, Bettws Garmon
Haulfryn, Abersoch

GLAMORGAN
Nottage Court, nr Porthcawl
Nant Fawr, Lisvane, nr Cardiff
Newcastle House Gardens, Bridgend

MERIONETH
Glan-y-Mawddach, nr Barmouth
Plas Brondanw, Llanfrothen

PEMBROKESHIRE
Slebech Park

ABERDEENSHIRE
Williamston, Insch

ARGYLLSHIRE
Achamore House, Isle of Gigha
Carradale House, Carradale
Crarae Lodge, Inveraray
Dunlossit, Port Askaig, Isle of Islay

BANFFSHIRE
Cullen House Gardens, Cullen

DUNBARTONSHIRE
Glenarn, Rhu

PERTHSHIRE
Keir, Dunblane

The following National Trust gardens are all worth visiting. Details of opening times may be obtained from The National Trust, 42 Queen Anne's Gate, London S.W.1, or The National Trust for Scotland, 5 Charlotte Square, Edinburgh, 2.

BERKSHIRE
Ascott, Wing

CHESHIRE
Tatton Park, nr Knutsford

CORNWALL
Cotehele, nr Calstock
Helford River, Glendurgan
Lanhydrock, nr Bodmin
Trelissick, nr Truro
Trengwainton, nr Penzance

DERBYSHIRE
Hardwick Hall, nr Mansfield

DEVON
Killerton Gardens
Salcombe, Overbecks

GLOUCESTERSHIRE
Snowshill Manor, nr Broadway

HAMPSHIRE
West Green House, Hartley Wintney

KENT
St John's Jerusalem, nr Dartford

NORFOLK
Blickling Hall

SOMERSET
Montacute, nr Yeovil
Tintinhull House, nr Yeovil

SUFFOLK
Ickworth, nr Bury St Edmunds

SURREY
Polesden Lacey, Dorking

SUSSEX
Sheffield Park

WARWICKSHIRE
Packwood House, nr Hockley Heath
Upton House, nr Edgehill

DENBIGHSHIRE
Bodnant Gardens, nr Talycafn
Powis Castle, nr Welshpool

ABERDEENSHIRE
Leith Hall
Pitmedden Garden, nr Udny

AYRSHIRE
Culzean Castle

BUTE
Brodick Castle, Isle of Arran

FIFE
Falkland Palace

KINCARDINESHIRE
Crathes Castle

KIRKCUDBRIGHTSHIRE
Threave School of Practical Gardening,
   Castle Douglas

MIDLOTHIAN
Inveresk Lodge

WESTER ROSS
Inverewe, Poolewe

NORTHERN IRELAND
Castleward, County Down
Mount Stewart Gardens, County Down
Rowallane, County Down

The gardens of Tresco Abbey in the Isles of Scilly are open to visitors all the year round.

Bibliographical Notes

To offer anything like a complete bibliography of English gardening would be immensely extravagant of both labour and space; but, moreover, it would be beside the point of this book and most unlikely to be of use to more than a minute fraction of the book's readers. Those who, for some special reason or purpose, require such a bibliographical list, will find, however, that if they combine the excellent bibliographies to be found in the three works named in the next paragraph, they will have something approaching a complete bibliography of the subject if they will add one or two of the books named below and published since Mr Hadfield's 'History' was published. For the rest, however, it was felt that what might be of use or at least of interest would be a list of works which give, first, the general history of gardening in Britain in broad outline, with some detail for relief, and told in good narrative style; second, works which would enable the reader to get nearer to, on more intimate terms with, each major gardening movement in that history; to get, in fact, the 'feel' of each epoch from a contemporary source. It is in that spirit that the following briefly annotated bibliography has been compiled.

History of gardening

The history of gardening in Britain needs to be seen against a background of the world-history of the art. A fairly good idea of that can be obtained, and with pleasure in the reading, from *The Story of the Garden* by Eleanour Sinclair Rohde (London, 1932). The first good, general history of gardening in Britain, and with an admirable chronological bibliography, is *A History of Gardening in Britain* by the Hon. Alicia Amherst (London, 1895, and other editions). Up until 1960 this was the standard work. It is, however, now replaced by *Gardening in Britain* by Miles Hadfield (London, 1960), a model of what a social-cum-art history ought to be.

Early period to end of sixteenth century

The source works for the very earliest period of gardening in Britain, or rather 'documents' for there are no 'works' properly so-called, are scarce, scattered and difficult and may safely be left to the industrious specialist. The earliest book worth reading by the non-specialist interested in the subject is *Of Gardens* by Francis Bacon. P. Hentzner, in *Travels in England in the reign of Queen Elizabeth*, has from time to time something to say about gardens. But the most enlightening book for this period, in its manner as well as its matter, is Thomas Tusser's *A Hundred Points of Good Husbandrie* (1557) or his

281

Five Hundred points of good husbandry united to as many of good huswifery. (An edition, edited by W. Payne and S. J. Herrtage, was published by the Early English Dialect Society in 1878.)

The Gardener's Labyrinth by Didymus Mountain (alias Thomas Hill) is useful to the student of the sixteenth century, but I have not seen a copy outside the British Museum. Barnaby Googe's *Foure Bookes of Husbandrie* is of social but no horticultural interest in our context, for it is an uncritical translation of Conrad Heresbach and certainly does not give one any idea of what English gardening was like when it was published in 1577, although perhaps it may give an idea of what English gardeners were trying to do: it ignores climate completely. Two books which are pleasant in giving the feel and colour of this early period in English gardening are Sir Hugh Platt's *The Jewell House of Art and Nature* (London, 1594), and Gervase Markham's *The Country Housewife's Garden* (1613). This author wrote a number of other gardening books, including his own edition of Googe's translation of Heresbach and *The Countryman's Recreation, or the art of Planting, Grafting and Gardening* (1640).

Those who wish to go back further and to penetrate the really dark ages of the subject may find it worth while to read the long and scholarly introduction to *The Herefordshire Pomona*, published between 1876 and 1885; it is by Robert Hogg and names some interesting sources of early information on pomology.

The seventeenth century

The seventeenth century is rich in garden books. For the same purpose, of getting the feel and colour of the gardening of the time, we would suggest John Parkinson's *Paradisi in sole, Paradisus terrestris, or a garden of all sorts of pleasant flowers*, 1629 (a facsimile edition was produced in London in 1904); *The garden book of Sir Thomas Hamner*, completed in 1659 but first published in London in 1933; and John Evelyn's *Sylva, or a discourse of forest trees* (1658). John Rose's *The English Vineyard Vindicated* (1666) is a specialist's book yet it gives much insight into the gardening mind and practice of the times. A good guide into the Herbals of this and earlier epochs is E. S. Rohde's *The Old English Herbals.* Finally, for this century, *The Compleat Gard'ner*: this is John Evelyn's translation of De la Quintinye's work, 'abridged and improved' by London and Wise, the nurserymen and published in 1699; and William Temple's *On the garden of Epicurus and Gardening* in the year 1685.

The eighteenth century

For the eighteenth century the important thing no doubt is to understand the great landscape garden designers. The following will be useful to that end: *New Principles of Gardening, or the laying out and planting of parterres*, Batty Langley (London, 1728); *The Work of William Kent*, Margaret Jourdain (London, 1948); *Observations on the Theory and Practice of Landscape Gardening*, Humphry Repton (London, 1794). Serious students of this subject reading this and other works of Repton should also refer to Uvedale Price's *An Essay on the Picturesque* (London, 1794) and the same author's published letters to Repton; *Unconnected thoughts on Gardening* (in Essays on Man and Manners), William Shenstone (1764); *On Modern Gardening*, Horace Walpole (1785); *Italian Landscape in 18th-century England*, E. W. Manwaring (New York, 1925).

There are scores of other books. An admirable guide into the whole subject is *A History of Garden Design* by Derek Clifford (London, 1962). With this and with books on the landscape and picturesque gardens generally should be read Osvald Sirèn's *Gardens of China* (New York, 1949) and his *China and the Gardens of Europe of the 18th century* (New York, 1950), and *A Dissertation on Oriental Gardening* by Sir William Chambers (London, 1772).

The nineteenth century

Standing at the turn of the eighteenth and nineteenth centuries and linking two epochs and two different spirits in gardening, is James Claudius Loudon. His first published works were *Observations on laying out the public squares of London* (London, 1803) and *A short treatise on some improvements lately made in hothouses* (Edinburgh, 1805). But his most important works came rather later. In 1812, *Hints on the formation of gardens and pleasure grounds*; 1822, and later editions, *An Encyclopaedia of Gardening*; 1836, *An Encyclopaedia of Plants*; *The Suburban Gardener* (London, 1838). The works of Mrs Loudon are hardly less important for the gardening of the early nineteenth century, notably her *Ladies' Companion to the Flower Garden* (London, 1841) and *The Amateur Gardener's Calendar* (London, 1857).

A clear and entertaining impression of the mind and spirit of the gardeners of this period will be found in G. Taylor's *Some Nineteenth-Century Gardeners* (London, 1951). For more particular and intimate impressions of the period, the following can be recommended: John Lindley's *An Outline of the first principles of Horticulture* (London, 1832); William Cobbet's *The American Gardener* (London, 1821) and his *The English Gardener* (London, 1829); the works, covering the period 1821–61, of Sir William Jackson Hooker give the best idea of botanical progress during the century; for the progress of gardening among the generality of small, amateur gardeners, a good plan is to glance through the works of G. W. Johnson, published between 1829 (*A History of English Gardening*) and 1862 (*Science and Practice of Gardening*). Joseph Paxton's published works were about plants rather than gardening: they include *The Magazine of Botany* which started in 1834 and runs to sixteen volumes; and a *Pocket Botanical Dictionary* (1840). They are of purely historical interest. A clear idea of the progress of plantsmanship and of the great increment of wealth in garden plants can be obtained from the *Hortus Veitchii* of J. H. Veitch. For an understanding of how this wealth was accumulated, the following books will be found as fascinating as they are instructive: J. D. Hooker's *Sketch of the Life and Labours of Sir W. J. Hooker* (Oxford, 1903); Robert Fortune's *Three Years Wandering in the Northern Province of China* (London, 1847), and the same author's other works; J. D. Hooker's *Himalayan Journals* (London, 1854), his *Journal of a tour in Marocco and The Great Atlas* (London, 1878); E. H. Wilson's *A Naturalist in Western China*; J. M. Cowan's *The Journeys and Plant Introductions of George Forrest* (London, 1952).

For the student, again, there are two sources of primary importance: the files of *The Gardener's Chronicle* which cover the period from 1841 onwards. And those of the *Journal* of the Royal Horticultural Society, or rather, for the early period, that is, from 1812, the *Transactions*.

It is, of course, not possible to offer a bibliography of modern gardening. But it is worth mentioning that the standard work of reference used by both professional and amateur gardeners in Britain is the Royal Horticultural Society's *Dictionary of Gardening* in five volumes including the Supplement (Oxford, 1956). The first edition was edited by Fred J. Chittenden, O.B.E., F.L.S., V.M.H., and the second by Patrick M. Synge, M.A., F.L.S.

Indexes of People and Places

Page numbers in italic type, plate numbers in roman

People

Aberconway, Lord, *65, 207–9*
Addison, Joseph, *42, 65, 66*
Aiton, William, *116*
Aiton, William Townsend, *116, 117, 124*
Amherst, Alicia, *61*
Annesley, Richard Grove, *42*
Atchley, S. C., *169*
Aubrey, John, *59*
Augusta of Saxe-Gotha, Princess, *115–16*
Austen, Jane, *69, 113, 131*

Baker, Sir John, *163*
Balls, F.K., *169*
Banham, Reyner, *57–63, 66, 153*
Banks, Joseph, *71, 116, 117, 124*
Bardolf, William, *160*
Barry, Sir John, *122*
Barton, Dean, *60*
Bellori, *65*
Bembo, Cardinal, *61*
Blomfield, Reginald, *131*
Blunt, Colonel, *28*
Boscawen, Canon, *16, 222*
Bradley, Dr James, *115*
Bridgeman, C., *62, 66, 121*; 47
Britton, John, *59*
Brooke, Justin, *26*
Brown, Launcelot, *28, 32, 36, 57, 59, 62,*
    66, 68–9, 72, 73, 74, 117, 121, 160
Buckman, James, *169*
Burlington, 3rd Earl of, *63–4*
Burton, Decimus, *118, 122*
Bute, Lords, *68, 116, 117*

Campbell, Colin, *59*
Campbell, Sir George, *205, 216*
Cane, Percy, *243, 247*
Capel, Sir Henry, *114*
Carews of Beddington, *22*
Caroline of Anspach, *117*
Carson, Rachel, *18*
Cecil, Robert, *22*
Chambers, Sir William, *62, 116, 121–2*
Chang, Y.Z., *38*
Charles I, *26*
Charles II, *24, 250*
Chaucer, Geoffrey, *262*
Cheere, John, *61, 62*
Chester, Sir John, *63*
Chi Ch'êng, *30*
Chung-Shu, Ch'ien, *38*
Cipriani, *116*
Clarke, Mary (Mrs Repton), *70–1*
Claude, *10, 28, 58, 59, 65, 66, 113*; 23
Clifford, Derek, *121–2*
Clusius, *22*
Cobham, Lord, *68*
Coke of Holkham, *73*
Comber, Harold, *159*
Comber, John, *156*
Confucius, *36*
Cook, Captain James, *117*
Cornwallis, James, *164*

Danvers, Henry, *26*
Davidian, H.H., *217*
De Caux, Salomon, *22*

284

Places
*Colour plate numbers in
roman numerals*